9 OCT 197.   MAXWELL.    821.91

Please renew/return this item by the last date shown.

So that your telephone call is charged at local rate, please call the numbers as set out below:

	From Area codes 01923 or 0208:	From the rest of Herts:
Renewals:	01923 471373	01438 737373
Enquiries:	01923 471333	01438 737333
Minicom:	01923 471599	01438 737599

L32b

Hertfordshire
COUNTY COUNCIL
Community Information

− 4 OCT 2002

L32a

D1345299

Poets of the Thirties

Poets of
The Thirties

by

D. E. S. MAXWELL

Letchworth
Public
Library

London
Routledge & Kegan Paul

First published 1969
by Routledge & Kegan Paul Ltd
Broadway House, 68–74 Carter Lane, E.C.4

Printed in Great Britain by
Butler & Tanner Ltd, Frome and London

© D. E. S. Maxwell 1969

No part of this book may be reproduced
in any form without permission from
the publisher, except for the quotation
of brief passages in criticism

SBN 7100 6397 0

Letchworth
Public Library

808 | 821·91

20093 '18

B69·14335

Contents

Acknowledgments

Grateful acknowledgment is made to those named below for permission to quote from the works listed:

Poems (1930, 1933), *Look, Stranger!* (*On This Island*), *The Orators*, *New Year Letter* (*The Double Man*), *For the Time Being*, *Collected Shorter Poems* 1930–1944 and 1927–1957: W. H. Auden, Faber & Faber Ltd., Random House Inc.; for excerpts from occasional essays and reviews, W. H. Auden, Curtis Brown Ltd.

Poems, *Illusion and Reality*, *Studies in a Dying Culture*, *Further Studies in a Dying Culture*, *The Concept of Freedom*: Christopher Caudwell, Lawrence & Wishart Ltd., The Executors of the Estate of C. St John Sprigg; for excerpts from Christopher Caudwell's unpublished poems, T. Stanhope Sprigg, esq.

John Cornford: A Memoir (ed. Pat Sloan): The Executors of the John Cornford Estate, the Editor, Jonathan Cape Ltd.; for the excerpt from a letter by John Cornford: Peter Stansky and William Abrahams, *Journey to the Frontier*, Constable Publishers, London.

Selected Essays, *The Use of Poetry and the Use of Criticism*: T. S. Eliot, Faber & Faber Ltd., Harcourt, Brace & World Inc.; 'Dante' in *The Sacred Wood*: T. S. Eliot, Methuen & Co. Ltd., London.

A Gun for Sale (*This Gun for Hire*), *It's A Battlefield*, *The Confidential Agent*: Graham Greene, William Heinemann Ltd., The Viking Press Inc.

'Looking Within', 'What shall be the signal for departure', 'October': John Lehmann, *New Signatures*, *New Country* (both ed. Michael Roberts), *Cambridge Poetry 1929*, The Hogarth Press Ltd.

Collected Poems 1954, *Transitional Poem*, *A Time to Dance*, *Revolution in Writing*: C. Day Lewis, Jonathan Cape Ltd., The Hogarth Press Ltd., The Harold Matson Co. Inc.

Collected Poems 1925–1948 and (E. R. Dodds ed.) *Collected Poems*: Louis MacNeice, Faber & Faber Ltd., Oxford University Press.

The Disappearing Castle: Charles Madge, Faber & Faber Ltd.

'Epitaph for a Contemporary': William Plomer, *Collected Poems*, Jonathan Cape Ltd.

Introduction to *New Signatures*: Michael Roberts, Janet Adam Smith, The Hogarth Press Ltd.

Vienna, *The Burning Cactus*, *The Still Centre*, *Collected Poems*: Stephen Spender, Faber & Faber, Random House Inc., A. D. Peters & Co.

'Steel April': A. S. J. Tessimond Literary Estate, The Hogarth Press Ltd.

Poems and Contradictions: Rex Warner, The Bodley Head.

'Sunday': Edward Upward, *New Country*, The Hogarth Press Ltd.

Titles in brackets are those of the American editions.

I

Marx and the Muse

THE nineteen-thirties is a plainly demarcated period, with slump at its beginning and war at its end. In the political mythology of Europe it now recalls 'depressed areas', dole queues and hunger marches, street fighting between fascists and communists, violence steadily eroding peace in Manchuria, Abyssinia, Spain. Hysterical dictators ranted at hypnotised democracies; 'refugees' entered the common experience. Yet how common the experience was in England is debatable. The newsreels of the time, a fair indication of what interested the public, were as much taken up with sports and the exploits of aviators, with film stars and bathing-beauty competitions, as with images of political apocalypse. Middle-class life was comfortable; summers were hot, prices low, popular songs optimistic or soothingly romantic. Louis MacNeice caught the spirit perfectly in *Autumn Journal*:

> And sun shone easy, sun shone hard
>   On quickly dropping pear-tree blossom
> And pigeons courting in the cobbled yard
>   With flashing necks and notes of thunder.
> We slept in linen, we cooked with wine,
>   We paid in cash and took no notice
> Of how the train ran down the line
>   Into the sun against the signal.

So a perhaps more typical set of memories might run, oblivious of the threats to peace, of poverty, unemployment, fear of being sacked. Still, whatever the awareness of them, these were undeniably the facts of many lives. They were symptoms of a deeper insecurity. Its causes, complex in detail, are simple enough in general outline.

War, suffering, loss had been the European experience after 1914, though indeed for most people the indignities of the Industrial Revolution were slowly being removed. Materially and spiritually, the Great War had proved a ravenous adventure. Inherited modes of conduct and belief lost certainty, having failed to prevent, having perhaps brought about, the four years' destruction. At a remoter level, science and scepticism had been optimistically encouraging their decay. To replace the now fragmented traditions there was nothing, even for those who disliked them, so familiarly understood, so long a part of living experience. The European was like an animal stimulated to a conditioned response when its performance has been made impossible. Where the whole terrain has altered, the signposts gone or unintelligible, one path, however forbidding, may seem as hopeful an issue as any other. Yeats was right to ask, in a different metaphor,

> *And what rough beast, its hour come round at last,*
> *Slouches towards Bethlehem to be born?*

The nineteen-thirties was to supply an answer. Its nature was less spectacularly apparent in England than in the Continental countries. But the symptoms, even as they appeared in England, established for those fully conscious of them a comfortable assurance of where political good and evil lay. The evidence persuaded intellectuals to the left; and, as economic depression and violence persisted, further to the left. Communism offered dramatic and radical solutions to dramatic and radical defects. It had a coherent philosophy, sufficiently abstract to be worth talking about, a romantic apparatus of intrigue and a practical success in Russia. The Labour Party, in contrast, seemed dowdy, more concerned with respectability than with action.

As Maynard Keynes pointed out at the time, the traditional English liberal stock, those who 'won us our civil and religious liberties and humanised the working class last century'[1], moved

1. 'Democracy and Efficiency', Maynard Keynes interviewed by Kingsley Martin, *New Statesman and Nation*, 28 January 1939, p. 122.

its home to a new faith. Idealists found ideals, and a formula for implementing them, in marxist socialism. They felt that the marxist view of society and its ills, and of art and culture too, was at least considering real problems. It provided a vocabulary for inclinations not necessarily marxist in themselves. It diagnosed the faults that provoked discontent: poverty, oppression, industrial decay in society; in the arts torpor, stodginess, irrelevance to practical living in contemporary civilisation. The degree of sympathy varied. E. M. Forster was benevolently attentive. 'I am not a Communist,' he said, 'though perhaps I might be one if I was a younger and a braver man.' He chided Virginia Woolf for failing to do justice to 'the Auden-Isherwood generation'. A. L. Rowse saw a new vision, which he communicated to *The Criterion* in April, 1930: 'Marxism is something more than a body of theory, and Communism than a political system. It is a Renaissance of its kind: it has the vitality of a new humanism.' Among others, Day Lewis, John Cornford, Christopher Caudwell were positively committed to this.

Isherwood himself, in *Mr Norris Changes Trains* (1935), gives a sensitive analysis of the impediments to total engagement. The 'curious, restrained passion' of a working-class audience at a communist meeting arouses in Bradshaw, Isherwood's narrator, a rueful half-communion. Though he may want to help, his background and upbringing cut him off from the vitality and the communal strength of will he senses in them. The characterization of Bayer reflects this sympathy. He is an idealization of the party leader, tough, knowledgeable, dedicated, and with great personal charm. His 'extraordinary eyes', his 'mere repose . . . hypnotic in its intensity' captivate Bradshaw. The 'informal, cheerful activity' of Bayer's flat, animated, comradely, is the antithesis of the 'padded, sombre, luxurious hotel' housing his Nazi opponents. Isherwood is not erecting a moral frame of reference from the technicalities of marxist ideology; if he were the novel would be less tolerant of Mr Norris's shady manœuvrings as a comically ineffectual double agent. But it is the communists whom he credits with a realistic appraisal of society, constructive purpose, and a creative, not, like the Nazis, a merely brutalizing, discipline. More intensely than Graham Greene's London, Isherwood's Berlin is a battlefield of spying, informing, armed violence. In

3

its kaleidoscopic decay, the communists represent the alternative to fascism which both enshrines humane values and is enduring enough to be politically effective. Isherwood, like the other writers, felt the excitement of a new philosophy which appeared to leave nothing in doubt.

In fact, its formula for correcting the ills of society envisaged violence on a scale that would have appalled nineteenth-century liberal humanists. The existing order and its custodians were to be literally destroyed and a proletarian state established. Marxist vocabulary, however, made it possible to talk of hair-raising violence without having to visualise the reality. Contemporary left-wing poetry, in many ways documentary and precisely observant of facts, also disguised the messiness of actually killing people. Surgery provided a convenient image: 'The hour of the knife', 'the major operation', 'a bed, hard, surgical/And a wound hurting', the 'surgeon's idea of pain'.[1] Such figures associated bloodshed with scientific efficiency, curative purpose and a romantic sense of dedication. Images of growth and harvest (fulfilment), of flight (aspiration), of spying, intrigue, war (positive action) changed a political programme into a crusade. Power-stations and tractors, oilwells, grain-elevators, towering cities, all kinds of complex machinery, gleaming and functional, symbolised what science and socialist organisation could accomplish. The mourners in Stephen Spender's 'The Funeral'

> *. . . dream of the World State*
> *With its towns like brain centres and its pulsing arteries.*

Day Lewis in *The Magnetic Mountain* describes the energies of this new world's builders as

> *. . . tools, dynamos, bridges, towers,*
> *Your tractors and your travelling-cranes.*

Richard Goodman's squadrons 'wheel, immense, towards the sun' and cancel 'the scribbled frontiers' to create, 'like flower' (? ex-

---

1. The first two quotations are from Day Lewis, *The Magnetic Mountain*; the third from W. H. Auden, '1 January 1931', *Collected Shorter Poems*, p. 161, originally the first of 'Six Odes' in *The Orators*; the fourth from W. H. Auden, 'Prologue' in Michael Roberts, ed., *New Country*, reprinted with a few revisions as 'Perhaps' in *Collected Shorter Poems*, p. 104.

ploding bombs) the world-state. A. S. J. Tessimond's 'Steel April'
looks forward to 'the new civilisation'—

> *the plane long delayed, behind schedule some centuries,*
> *   held up by cloudbanks,*

but now inexorably advancing,

> *turning rebellion to a fanning breath and tradition to a*
> *   jet of flame.*

In 'Looking Within', by John Lehmann, a dead king symbolises
some outmoded way of life or social ideal, kept artificially in
being by the tyranny of sentries, guarded frontiers, spies in ports.
Rebirth comes

> *in countries over there*
> *With much-desired sleek buds and burst of leaves,*
> *Release of sap, new songs.*

The lone rebel, heroic, resourceful, pitted against organised
society, was the hero of the myth, the Reichstag fire trial its first
confrontation of forces:

> *Three years ago Dimitrov fought alone*
> *And we stood taller when he won.*[1]

These writers were quite a small group. Their audience, perhaps
at its height a little more numerous than poetry normally com-
mands, was limited. Nevertheless, the new sympathies they expressed, their rendering of conflict, conspiracy, revolutionary
change, were remarkably pervasive. In less esoteric forms their
attitudes got through to a wider public.

II

The thirties produced an adventure story quite different in its
assumptions and sympathies from the thrillers of the twenties.

1. The preceding quotations come from: Richard Goodman, 'The Squadrons'
(*New Country*); A. S. J. Tessimond, 'Steel April' (*New Country*); John Lehmann,
'Looking Within' (Michael Roberts, ed., *New Signatures*); John Cornford, 'Full
Moon at Tierz: Before the Storming of Huesca' (Stephen Spender and John
Lehmann, eds., *Poems for Spain*).

John Buchan and 'Sapper', if they did not give way to, were at least supplemented by Graham Greene and Eric Ambler. In the thriller, Bolsheviks ceased to be uncouth and hairy terrorists. For Greene and Ambler the world of financial cartels, political assassination and intrigue supplies the background and the narrative impulse. They employ melodrama, but it is melodrama whose origins in life were real enough. The characters are aware of, and the plots dramatise, the political struggle between left and right, with more affection for the ideals of the left than fiction designed primarily to entertain had shown in the previous decade.

With the exception of James Bond, Bulldog Drummond is the nastiest hero of popular fiction. 'Sapper', however, is so simpleminded that only the touchiest liberal could take him seriously. His hero, in the novel that introduces him, looks back affectionately to the excitements of the Great War. Bored with peace he advertises in *The Times* for any commission promising danger. The offer he accepts leads him to his first encounter with the redoubtable villain, Carl Peterson, who is his adversary over the books collected as *Bulldog Drummond's Four Rounds with Carl Peterson*. A master of disguise, Carl appears in various innocuous and (but for one mannerism spotted by Drummond) impenetrable roles—a respectable lodger in a small hotel, a wealthy financier, a clergyman. He takes cocaine but (like Sherlock Holmes) is its master. Ruthless, vindictive, he is also poised, charming, humorous. His ambition is the straightforward one of amassing vast sums of money by such outrageous schemes as torturing an inventor to make him divulge his process for manufacturing precious stones, or terrorising civilization with a liquid whose smallest drop on the flesh is lethal.

All this is more or less the old stock of sensational fiction. In these enterprises, however, Carl Peterson draws his rank and file from fashionably unappetising sources—Jews and Bolsheviks uniformly unwashed and (except in superior numbers) cowardly. Dissatisfied with Scotland Yard's failure to chasten these malcontents, Drummond organises his friends into the Black Gang to dispense private justice. Their methods range from forced washing to horsewhipping and killing. In his hearty way, Drummond shares the fascist worship of violence and private armies and has the same emotional antipathies. For Drummond and his creator the villains are the Jews: wealthy and Machiavellian or poor and vicious; and Soviet Russia: the murder of the Czar's family, social and economic chaos, brutish revolutionaries. The ideas, even allowing for 'Sapper's' not very athletic intelligence, are lumpishly formulated.

'Sapper's' heroes are brawny aristocrats. Eric Ambler replaces them by professional men—an engineer, a reporter, a schoolmaster—accidentally caught up in espionage and conspiracy. His plots, ingenious and plausible, turn on the power-groupings of Europe in the thirties and underground alliances between big business and politics. Their credibility comes partly from Ambler's tart and cool-headed style, partly from the knowledgeable (and neutral) interpolations of the details of recent European history: the shifts of Roumanian foreign policy in the twenties and thirties (*Uncommon Danger*), the unstable loyalties and gangsterish practices of the Berlin-Rome axis (*Cause for Alarm*). The imagined events merge readily with the facts (extraordinary enough) of history. In *Uncommon Danger* a petroleum combine employs a 'political saboteur'—a professional whose skill is 'the manipulation of public opinion by means of incidents, rumours or scandals'. He is to influence oil-concession reform in Roumania by arousing public opinion against Russia. In *Cause for Alarm* an English armament firm's representative in Italy augments Germany's suspicions of its ally by giving a Nazi agent secret information about Italian arms expansion. The real hero of both novels is an American-educated Soviet agent, Zaleshoff. Ambler presents him sympathetically, and while acknowledging does not insist on the evidences of Soviet despotism. For Zaleshoff spying is a business like any other. He is efficient and ruthless, his first aim to promote Russian interests. But Ambler allows him humanity, an engaging personality which resembles Bayer's and an idealism underlying his immediate objectives.

The admission into popular writing of Zaleshoff's occasional marxist pedagogy—'Isn't it commonsense to replace an old, bad system with a better one?'—betokens a new indulgence towards marxist thought. The general tone is temperately sceptical of the idealistic professions of right-wing politicians and business men: their aim is power and profits, their by-products the dole, unemployment, blacklists and intimidation. Novel sentiments: and more dispassionate than they appear in summary. They do not, for instance, persuade Marlow, the unhappy amateur spy in *Cause for Alarm*, to take their side in the dispute of ideologies. Ambler's liberal sympathies do not distort his sense of character. Instead of Sapper's cut-out heroes and villains we have credible human beings; for narrow intolerance a commerce of ideas which the thirties had optimistically extended to a new voice.

Graham Greene plots his novels less tidily than Eric Ambler. They are full of blatantly engineered coincidences and improbabilities. They also present characters of much greater psychological complexity, themes of good and evil more serious, and more intensely realised. To isolate the political matter, the contemporary detail and the thrillerish action in Greene's novels of the thirties is to give a very partial view of them. But those elements are there. Drawn immediately from the period, they express very different attitudes from Buchan's use of the same convention.

In *The Lost Childhood* Greene has written favourably of Buchan's adventure stories. They were the first to construct their drama from violence and mystery invading the lives of respectable, conventional citizens. In *The Power-House*, Leithen, 'who was afterwards Solicitor-General', when pursued across a London patrolled by the agents of a super-criminal, realises 'how thin is the protection of civilisation. An accident and a bogus ambulance—a false charge and a bogus arrest—there were a dozen ways of spiriting one out of this gay and bustling world.' In *Huntingtower* a feud between Russian Bolsheviks and a beautiful émigré Princess involves a retired Glasgow grocer and a number of ex-soldiers, one of whom says of their adventures, 'Oh, it sounds ridiculous, I know, in Britain in the twentieth century, but I learned in the war that civilisation anywhere is a very thin crust.'

Buchan's novels pierce the crust at appropriately incongruous points. Peaceful Scottish glens, solidly urban London, the world of clubmen, country gentlemen and suburbanites become the settings for kidnapping and murder. The First World War and the years following it showed how vulnerable civilised society is; Buchan's perception of this gives depth to his chronicles of romantic adventure. Yet Buchan was too sure of the values that counted and would win through to identify the ambiguous reaches of human conduct. The 'jolly party of hard, clean, decent fellows' is always there to fend off disaster: Richard (later Sir Richard) Hannay, Sandy Arbuthnot (later Lord Clanroyden), Sir Archibald Roylance. Villains and heroes, conventionally imagined, are plainly distinguished. *The Power-House* outlines the pattern of Buchan's conspiracies: a master-criminal uses the socially disaffected—anarchists, Bolsheviks, malefactors of all kinds—to carry out his nefarious schemes. Later novels elaborate the formula.

Huntingtower (1922) and *Castle Gay* (1930) both present deposed monarchies struggling against their Communist pillagers. The ultimate villain is Soviet Russia, which has become the centre of an international cabal: 'the unfettered crime in Russia is so powerful that it stretches its hand to crime across the globe and there is a great mobilising everywhere of wicked men'. *The Three Hostages* (1924) deals with a conspiracy in depth. The front line finds its recruits 'among the young Bolshevik Jews, among the young entry of the wilder Communist sects, and very notably among the sullen murderous hobbledehoys in Ireland' (who had 'shirked the war' and so become especially subject to mental disorder). Behind these 'there [are] sinister brains at work' organising profit 'on a huge scale in a sinking world'. Among these masterminds, we may assume, would be the malignant capitalist Jews of *The Thirty-Nine Steps* who are the 'unsleeping enemies' of the Russian aristocrats in *Huntingtower* and the secret manipulators of Germany's 'bloated industrials' in *The Three Hostages*. At the back of all is Medina, perverted mystic, master of strange occult powers, who 'wanted to win everything that civilisation could give him, and then wreck it'. Buchan is perceptive here too, predicting 'that the great offensives of the future would be psychological . . . that the most deadly weapon in the world was the power of mass-persuasion'. But Medina, with his faked-up Eastern philosophy and trumpery arts, is an unconvincing embodiment of the danger.

Buchan's novels express the attitudes of the class in which he had won a place. The decent chaps are public-school men, aristocrats (and *évolués* like Hannay), independent but loyal peasants. Plutocrats and Bolsheviks equally are beyond the pale. Though sometimes highly intelligent, they have a liking for 'Kaffir tricks'. For

Hannay and the others of his *totem* the code is a little more flexible. Hannay is allowed to reflect, apparently without disturbing his creator, 'If I were in Central Africa, I would get Medina by the throat, and peg him down and torture him till he disgorged.' Buchan is a great deal more perspicacious than Sapper and has a more elegant style; in the upshot his view of life is very similar. The pre-1914 world had gone. Buchan interprets his insights into its successor in the old terms.

Huntingtower appears to assume that the revolution in Russia might be reversed. Perhaps the Soviet survival encouraged the younger writers of the thirties to look at its philosophy more seriously. Certainly Graham Greene, revising the Buchan formula, does not share the same clear-cut certainties. Of the novels he wrote in the thirties four are particularly relevant to the new political emphasis: *It's a Battlefield* (1934), *England Made Me* (1935), *A Gun For Sale* (1936) and *The Confidential Agent* (1939).[1] The three latter are set in a world of reactionary financier/aristo-crats, powerful and unscrupulous: Krogh in *England Made Me*, Sir Marcus in *A Gun for Sale*, L. in *The Confidential Agent*. These men control their affairs, which affect the lives of everyone, by illegally manipulating vast sums of money, by intimidation and murder by hired thugs. Krogh, who resembles Kreuger, the Swedish match millionaire, is benevolently paternalistic to his employees as long as they make no trouble. Over the period of the novel he is supporting his international network of companies by short-term loans and fraudulent cross-borrowing. Andersen, a stolidly respectable Socialist in the Swedish factory, is organis-ing a strike which would endanger the whole precarious financial structure. Krogh has him framed and sacked. Andersen's son, who 'believed in justice. He had seen it working, the idle man dis-missed, the industrious rewarded', is beaten up. Anthony Farrant, a feckless intruder who has learnt too much of the chicanery, is murdered.

Greene's attitude to these events is, politically, detached. Reported by his various observers, they are particular manifesta-tions of a world basically unjust and imperfectly understood even by those who seem most in control of its affairs. He advocates no

1. Of these *A Gun for Sale* and *The Confidential Agent* are what Greene calls Entertainments, as distinct from novels.

doctrinal remedy. His selection of material, however, draws attention to an order in which the wealthy are more likely than the poor to get their own way. The impersonal complexity of its institutions is typified in Krogh's vast office block, from which the porter turns young Andersen away 'not quite as confident as he had been in the comradeship of other men'. As Stephen Spender remarked in the *Auden Double Number* of *New Verse* (November 1937), 'the mere statement of social realities today, if it goes far enough, both suggests a remedy and involves one in taking sides'.

Though Krogh's jobbery provokes the final crisis, the political theme is subordinate to the main interest, which is rather psychological than social. Capitalist double-dealing is more central to *A Gun for Sale*. Sir Marcus is the millionaire owner of Midland Steel. Through an intermediary, Davis, he hires a hare-lipped professional killer, Raven, to murder a Czech Socialist statesman. The ensuing international crisis reaches the verge of war, the arms market flourishes and with it Midland Steel. But Davis has paid Raven in stolen notes. A double pursuit develops, of Raven by the police for robbery, of Sir Marcus and Davis by Raven for revenge.

Again, personal relationships are at the core of the novel: between Raven and Anne, the first person he has trusted, who betrays him; between Anne and her fiancé, the policeman pursuing Raven; between Acky, the unfrocked clergyman, and his wife. Raven confesses to Anne that he killed the statesman. It is his ultimate act of trust, his release from the isolation of his disfigured face, his memories of the heartless orphanage and his mother's suicide, a whole life of bitterness and suspicion. Anne's sympathy for Raven cannot assimilate this crime. The statesman had been poor, withstood the wealthy and powerful, was one of 'us', people like her and Raven: 'suddenly his mouth which had never before struck her as particularly ugly came to mind and she could have retched at the memory . . . She felt a desperate hatred.'

The novel anatomises Raven's morbid psychology and its echoes in the urbanised, disintegrated world around him. The social scene reflects the violence and ugliness of Raven's mind; in an ironic interpretation of the phrase's meaning, Raven is a social animal. Most of the action takes place in the provincial town of

Nottwich, home of Midland Steel, mean, squalid, fog-bound, where there was no excuse 'for one half of the world being ignorant of how the other half lived'. Its guardian is Mather, Anne's fiancé, who is 'part of an organisation. He did not want to be a leader, he did not even want to give himself up to some God-sent fanatic of a leader, he liked to think he was one of thousands more or less equal working for a concrete end: not equality of opportunity, not government by the people or by the richest or by the best: but simply to do away with crime which meant un-certainty.' Above him and his tidy assumptions fly the aircraft 'guarding the Nottwich mines and the key industry of Midland Steel'. They fly again in the mock air-raid which covers Raven's final journey to Sir Marcus. A national show of force masks private vengeance. At this stage Sir Marcus reviews his achieve-ments: 'Armament shares continued to rise and with them steel . . . the future was really very rosy indeed.' Shortly, before being shot down himself, Raven is to kill both him and Davis with, as Sir Marcus says, 'A Colt No. 7. The factories turn out thousands.'

Raven is on one side; set against him for their various reasons are Davis, Sir Marcus, Mather, finally Anne. But the line between good and evil is obscure, force and betrayal as much the weapons of one party as of the other. Greene's adroit cross-cutting of scenes aligns the political and the personal actions. Against the hysteria of Europe Raven acts out his private mimetic obsessions. The two intersect and comment upon each other. Greene was not writing a propagandist work. Had he been, he would have interpreted Raven and Mather more intolerantly.[1] Yet for the reader in 1936 the novel would have readily supported the left-wing version of a society in decline. The graceless industrial town with its dingy housing estates and slatternly streets condemns the society of which it is a part. As D. reflects of a similar setting in *The Con-fidential Agent*, 'bombardment was a waste of time. You could attain your ruined world as easily by just letting go.' When Raven finds that Acky's wife has connived at Davis's attack on Anne, he

---

1. Conor Cruise O'Brien, on the other hand, sees Greene's policemen—Mather and the Assistant Commissioner in *It's A Battlefield*—as evidence of a tendency in Greene and other modern English writers to idealise 'the instru-ments and symbols of the law'. Dr O'Brien, of course, may be exhibiting the Irish tendency to suspect them. See O'Brien: *Maria Cross*, p. 62.

thinks, 'this was evil: that people of the same class should prey on each other'. The slogans of the time lie behind these scenes: Social Betterment, Equality of Opportunity, Class Solidarity.

It's a Battlefield, the most directly political of these novels, deals ironically with the champions of these slogans. It satirises the follies and weaknesses which can find refuge in the Communist Party: phoney intellectualism, selfishness, the longing to reduce facts to abstractions. The odious Mr Surrogate does not really want a reprieve for Drover, a Communist bus driver sentenced to death for killing a policeman at a public meeting. He prefers to see Drover as a martyr to the Communist cause. Orating to an apathetic Party gathering, Surrogate 'saw Caesar fall and heard Brutus speak (and) called again through the streets of imperial Rome', happy 'among his glamorous abstractions'. He and his fellow-misfits are unlikely makers of a revolution. It is made clear, however, that there are reasons outside their own inadequacies for the beliefs they profess.

The central figure in the novel is the Assistant Commissioner. His very refusal to be committed testifies to the wrongness of the conditions which make some sense of Communist protest. Like Mather, but with more sensitivity, he tries to see himself simply as a paid official doing a job. Justice is not his business, which is to catch offenders against laws decided by others. Yet he resents the inequities of what his job makes him do: 'He knew quite well the cause of the discrepancy; the laws were made by property owners in defence of property; that was why a Fascist could talk treason without prosecution; that was why a man who defrauded the State in defence of his private wealth did not even lose the money he had gained: that was why the burglar went to gaol for five years; that was why Drover could not so easily be reprieved—he was a Communist.' He confesses that he does not believe 'in the way the country is organised . . . that wages should run from thirty shillings a week to fifteen thousand a year, that a manual labourer should be paid less than a man who works with his brains'. A metaphor used by D. describes the social dislocation which has led this conventional, inarticulate man, of the same background as Buchan's MacGillivray, to such uncharacteristic speculations: 'It was as if some code of faith and morality had been lost for centuries, and the world was trying to reconstruct it from the unreliable evidence of folk memories and subconscious desires—and perhaps some hieroglyphics upon stone.'

The action, the setting, and what might be called the latent ideology of D.'s adventures in *The Confidential Agent* are of the same kind as those already discussed. D. has come to England to buy coal for a left-wing government in a country where civil war has broken out. Mistrust and suspicion within his own party obstruct his purpose as much as the efforts of the rival agent. This total disrepair of confidence is one outcome of the deterioration in traditional codes of faith and morality. The new ideology is complex, sophisticated and unfamiliar. D. doubts even his own orthodoxy: 'there were aspects of economic materialism which, if he searched his heart, he did not accept. . . . He was haunted for a moment by the vision of an endless distrust. In an inner pocket, a bulge over the breast, he carried what were called credentials, but credence no longer meant belief.'

In the development of the action—all of it seen from D.'s point of view—his marxism emerges as humane and undogmatic, a compassionate response to suffering and poverty. He is a pragmatist who, accepting a worthy ideal, keeps in mind the difficulties of choosing a means at once expedient and just, tainted motives, the temptation to betray the ultimate end for an irrelevant personal triumph. In the story of Roland and Oliver he identifies two sorts of behaviour still active in the world. When a university lecturer before the war D. had discovered the 'Berne MS' of *The Song of Roland*. In this text Roncevaux is a defeat with neither point nor grandeur, Roland a romantic braggart 'more concerned with his own glory than with the victory of his faith'. He is the type of the egotist whose self-centred vision misrepresents the reality around him. Oliver is the true hero of the tale, the realist who when he saw the Saracens urged Roland to summon back Charlemagne and his armies. D. recognises in Oliver the sober-minded vision called for in his own affairs.

It's a Battlefield glances at a similar contrast between Antony and Brutus, with whom Mr Surrogate identifies himself. Brutus's reasoning is always logical, his conclusions invariably wrong. He miscalculates after Caesar's death in allowing Antony to speak, in his own disastrous speech, at Philippi. His inclination to simplify, to generalise, to transform things into abstractions deceives him.

After the assassination Caesar's blood ceases to be a physical object. It becomes an emblem—of 'Peace, Freedom, and Liberty'. Antony, the practised politician, keeps the mutilated corpse before the eyes of the mob. Obsessed with principles and abstractions, Brutus, for other causes than Roland but to the same effect, misapprehends the circumstances which Antony can so resourcefully manipulate. Mr Surrogate is no Brutus, but he dissociates himself from the world of fact with the same facility.

The double antithesis, Roland-Oliver, Brutus-Antony, provides one set of references in Greene's polity of shifting faiths and confused belligerents. He is more interested in failure and its causes (and therefore in Rolands and Brutuses) than in success; more concerned with the psychology of his characters than with passing judgment on the politics they profess: with their souls than with their votes. Nonetheless the characters are firmly set in a political world, whose assumptions reverse those of the Buchan ethos. It is not only that Greene picks up the resonances of the period's marxism. He also formulates the peculiar indeterminacy in its mapping of new courses in thought and action. Against this background, of which Greene is so sensitive and discriminating an annalist, we must read the various recensions, by poets and critics, of marxist argument, social and aesthetic.

III

As Greene's 'mere statement of social realities' goes far towards implying a choice of sides, so does that of the thirties poets. For them as well, the background of sleazy towns, abandoned mines and factories is a décor which documents a belief. It is the converse of the buoyant images of powered flight, complex and efficient machines, gleaming cities of the future. Day Lewis's *The Buried Day* testifies to the imaginative thrust of seeing in the Oxfordshire countryside 'the weedy fields, the roof-rent barns', and in the Gareloch the rusting, idle steamers, 'reminders of the times we lived in'. In the poems he wrote in those times 'cursed towns and devastated areas', 'derelict mills and barns roof-rent' activate the lyric core of feeling and idea.

Examples could be multiplied from the work of Stephen Spender, John Lehmann, Louis MacNeice, of all the poets moved by its dreary heraldry to protest against a society in decline. Apart from the evidence of their senses they had as example the technical virtuosity of W. H. Auden, whose poetry, as most of them have acknowledged,[1] first turned their eyes to the imaginative potential of these symptomatic townscapes. In that setting Auden put in motion (the world of the thriller again) miniature dramas of spying and conspiracy, guerilla attacks in frontier areas and on the centres of established power. A composite picture of life derived from these poems would be sensational indeed. Stephen Spender's 'Perhaps' opens with a

> *chancellor clutching his shot arm (and that was*
> *Perhaps*
> *a put-up job for their own photographers)*
> *the parliament their own side set afire*
> *and then our party forbidden*
> *and the mine flooded, an accident I hope.*

'The Uncreating Chaos' presents another statesman attacked—

> *The pigeons scatter*
> *Above the pavement at the fatal shot.*

Two verses of Day Lewis's Poem 20 in *The Magnetic Mountain*, setting out the corruption of England, build up a swiftly changing montage of episodes of betrayal: the weak committing suicide, inventors cheated by industrialists and driven to death, servile collaborators who (metaphorically) poison reservoirs and release germs on whole cities. Poem 27 attacks the firms 'Who sell an armament to any cause.' For such as these was intended 'the necessary murder' in the original version of Auden's *Spain*.

The imaginative writing of the thirties created an unusual *milieu* of urban squalor and political intrigue. This kind of statement—a suggestion of decay producing violence and leading to change—as much as any absolute and unanimous political partisanship gave this poetry its marxist reputation. Communism and 'the communist' (a poster-type stock figure) were frequently invoked. In Richard Goodman's 'Sorrow' the young communist 'standing alone once more', heroic in defeat, sees his dreamt-of towns and grain towers 'go down, like châlets, before the attack'.

1. See, for example, Stephen Spender, *World Within World* and C. Day Lewis, *The Buried Day*.

In Auden's 'Poem' in *New Country*, 'Like a sea-god the communist orator lands at the pier'. There was a common use of such tableaux to proclaim a common dissent from the existing order. On the precise details of how it was to be altered and what would be the nature of its communist successor there was less general agreement. Like most dogmatic faiths, communism has been fertile in schism and niceties of interpretation. The English intellectuals found in it not one canon but a variety of doctrines. Their rhetoric and their invented situations were leftist; politically, each poet devised his own orthodoxy.

In consequence there was frequent bitterness at supposed lapses from purity. Commitment had to be total. Day Lewis's 'The Conflict' said, 'only ghosts can live/Between two fires'. William Plomer's 'Epitaph for a Contemporary' dismissed the neutral liberal—'a saunterer on battlefields/Cannot expect his peregrinations to last'. But to what courses should this total commitment lead? The Christmas 1936 issue of *New Verse* carried a reply from Geoffrey Grigson to D. S. Mirski, who had accused *New Verse* of 'systematically hounding Day Lewis for what it regarded as an excess of communist loyalty'. In May 1937 Grigson contributed a sardonic attack on Day Lewis for having joined the selection panel of The Book Club ('pimping to the mass bourgeois mind'). In Autumn 1938 Stephen Spender was still uneasy about this, and also about Auden's acceptance of the King's Medal for poetry. Spender himself fared no better. Louis MacNeice's *Modern Poetry* notes 'the disapproval among official communists aroused by Spender's *Trial of a Judge*', a play whose intent was pro-communist and anti-fascist. Auden now considers his *Spain* 'to be trash which he is ashamed to have written'; on its publication orthodox marxist critics did not think much better of it, though for different reasons. Its reference to 'hours of friendship' blossoming into 'a people's army' (words excised from the *Collected Shorter Poems*) failed to placate Edgell Rickword in the *Auden Double Number* of *New Verse*. According to Rickword the lines,

> *To-day the expending of powers*
> *On the flat ephemeral pamphlet and the boring meeting,*

are heretical and demonstrate 'the aloofness of the intellectual', the poet's 'continuing isolation, falsifying the perspective of social development and delaying the re-integration of the poet into the body of society'. Christopher Caudwell in *Illusion and Reality* argued that Auden's art, like that of Day Lewis and Spender, displayed 'extraordinary and quite unnecessary outbursts of bourgeois independence and indiscipline or quite apparent bourgeois distortions of the party's revolutionary theory'. He also believed (with some justice) that the poets were more enthusiastic in prescribing the marxist regimen for others than for themselves. T. S. Eliot was controversial. Francis Scarfe's 'Beauty, Boloney' included him in its pantheon of heroes; W. T. Nettlefold's 'Fan Mail for a Poet' satirised his retreat (so it appeared) to Christianity.

Many of these quarrels simply cultivated iconoclasm for its own sake. But as their existence suggests, there was no uniformity of belief. The reason for this wrangling—apart from the factionalist nature of communism—was the novelty in English politics of the marxist theses, and the assumption that they must simplify a set of problems that was in fact irreducibly complicated. This power of synthesis was one strong attraction of marxist theory. According to the caustic summary in Mirski's *The Intelligentsia of Great Britain*,[1] 'What became important in their eyes was not the materialistic dialectical method, but the resultant fact that marxism provides a well-built system of criteria. System, system, system— that was what the British intellectuals run crying after as soon as they lose faith in aforementioned Nanny empiricism.'

Marxism combined these scientific and logical criteria with the immediate appeal of a call for change and, above all, for action. Romance tricked out reason. So, turning from the view they had glimpsed from what Virginia Woolf was to call their 'leaning tower',[2] the young poets described what they had seen, analysed the 'well-built system' with varying degrees of acceptance, pro-

1. Edmund Wilson tells us that when Mirski 'had returned to Russia to pursue a Soviet literary career, he had been forced to publish this book, unmasking, as it was then called, the English writers among whom he had been living in exile'. See 'The Classics on the Soviet Stage' in *The Shores of Light*.

2. In John Lehmann ed. *Folios of New Writing* Autumn 1940. Her contention was that the writers of the thirties, like all writers, sat 'upon a tower raised above the rest of us' but that their tower had slanted to give them a view of nothing but decay and social injustice. In pique and self-pity they blamed the tower—'middle-class birth and expensive education'— for their sense of guilt and intensified its deviation to the left.

claimed the obligation to act. Their action, on the whole, con-
sisted of lecturing, writing books and pamphlets, organising aid
for Spain, arranging meetings, demonstrations; many visited,
some served in, Spain, Auden briefly as an ambulance driver. On
the other hand, it is true that their extensive travel and residence
abroad, particularly in Germany (Auden, Isherwood, Spender,
Lehmann), gave them an uncommon awareness of the evil taking
shape and growing in power in Europe.

For the most part their activity was very different from the
explosive confrontations they imagined, the political theory
behind it covering the whole left-wing-liberal spectrum of the
multiplying periodicals: *Left Review*, Claud Cockburn's *The
Week*, Middleton Murry's *The Wanderer*, *Cambridge Left*, *Plan*,
Fact, the publications of The Left Book Club. Literary magazines
dedicated themselves to encouraging workers to write and pro-
moting a 'proletarian literature'. The Introduction to *New
Signatures* explained that Stephen Spender's 'The Funeral' 'suggests
new possibilities for English poetry . . . poetry is here turned to
propaganda, but it is propaganda for a theory of life which may
release the poet's energies for the writing of pure poetry as well as
provide him with standards which may make simple and direct
satire possible again'. In *The Whispering Gallery* John Lehmann
recalls his excitement on receiving Edward Upward's short stories
for *New Writing*: in them, a communist viewpoint found expression of considerable literary power. That communism
attracted them is beyond question; but few of them were communists in any sense doctrinally acceptable to official marxists (i.e.
Stalinists). They were—the comment is not meant uncharitably—
Rolands and Brutuses, some of whom were to die for their beliefs,
in Spain, shamelessly exploited by Stalinist bureaucrats.

Auden clearly illustrated the real indeterminateness of their
position. His fairly scanty prose writings of the period have their
marxist flourishes. Reviewing Baden Powell's autobiography he
describes the Scout movement as 'a class weapon'. E. M. Forster's
biography of Goldsworthy Lowes Dickinson leads him to specu-
late that to arrest the decay of civilisation 'physical violence,
loathsome as it is', may be necessary.[1] A few years later, speculation

---

1. The quotations are from, respectively, 'Life's Old Boy', *Scrutiny*, March
1934 and 'Goldsworthy Lowes Dickinson', *Scrutiny*, December 1934.

became fact. In Spain, Loyalist good and Rebel evil aligned themselves, it appeared, according to marxist prophecy. Writing from Valencia in 1937, Auden observes that because of the Spanish Loyalists' 'wish to live', which could find no other expression than violence, 'General Franco has already lost two professional armies and is in the process of losing a third.'[1] He approves the vigour and colour of life in the Loyalist sector and sees 'the bloodthirsty and unshaven Anarchy of the bourgeois cartoon . . . doing all those things that the gentry cannot believe will be properly done unless they are there to keep an eye on them'.

Though at the time their virtue seemed patent, the politics of the various pro-Government groups were in fact highly equivocal. George Orwell was later severe with idealists who had failed to recognise what his own experiences on the Loyalist side had taught him of communist duplicity. Still, it is difficult to see how anyone of the mildest liberal sympathies could at that time have denied the Loyalist cause. Auden's profession of faith is to his credit, the more so as he did not exempt marxism from the obligations he thought right for democracy. His rather pompous rebuke to the Scout movement holds also that such organisations are a conservative force in any society. Teaching loyalty, they discourage reform, which 'is always disloyalty to King, President, or Commissar'. Similarly, in entertaining the possibility of violence he keeps his first attachment for the cast of mind represented by E. M. Forster and Lowes Dickinson. 'People and civilisations,' he says, 'are saved by a change of heart . . . whether, if we are concerned enough, it can be brought about by "mental fight" alone, we cannot answer, but . . . it is particularly important that those capable of waging the latter should not lose patience: to such Lowes Dickinson and also, I think, E. M. Forster, are examples permanent and alert.'

Auden has since said that he and his friends were interested in 'unmasking middle-class ideologies, not with the intention of repudiating our class, but with the hope of becoming better bourgeois'.[2] This disclaimer may seem whimsical, in view of the above quotations and, for example, of the zeal with which *The*

1. 'Impressions of Valencia', *New Statesman and Nation*, 30 January 1937.
2. 'Authority in America', *The Griffin*, March 1955.

Dance of Death presents 'the decline of a class' of whose members the Announcer says, 'there is death inside them'. There and elsewhere Auden's poetry expresses a thoroughgoing antagonism to the middle class. His *Poems* (1930) displays the poet apparently engaged in the political struggle for a new society. The antagonists are not at all precisely defined, but some of the poems do explicitly identify them. The financier is warned, 'The game is up for you and for the others.' (XXIX) Number XVI urges that love

> *Needs more than the admiring excitement of union, ...*
> *Needs death, death of the grain, our death,*
> *Death of the old gang.*

Poem XXII ('Get there if you can and see the land you once were proud to own') tells us who the old gang are: big business men, suburbanites, parents, and a strange rogues gallery including Bowdler, Baudelaire, Freud, and Flaubert. Other poems borrow from Freudian psychology to analyse the individual and national distress. Number XVI describes the growth from pre-natal security to adult death-wish:

> *Perfunctorily affectionate in hired room*
> *But takes no part and is unloving*
> *But loving death.*

The financier and his friends of number **XXIX** are manic-depressive and 'prey to fugues'. Poem III, drawing on the marxist dialectic of history, puts the poet on the side of destiny:

> *Think—Romans had a language in their day*
> *And ordered roads with it, but it had to die:*
> *Your culture can but leave—forgot as sure*
> *As place-name origins in favourite shire—*
> *Jottings for stories, some oft-mentioned Jack,*
> *And references in letters to a private joke,*
> *Equipment rusting in unweeded lanes.*

Auden is grasping whatever weapons come to hand to express, in an arrestingly cryptic manner, youth's habitual protest. The grounds of attack shift bewilderingly. In 1937 Edmund Wilson complained that Auden, having taken his stand, was 'at a loss what to do next'. But Auden had never taken 'a stand'. He had rather

NB

gestured towards a number of possible positions than occupied any one of them. Wilson was nearer the mark, though hardly doing justice to Auden, when he wrote that his paraphernalia of spies, adversaries and warfare 'sounds less like anything connected with the psychology of an underground revolutionary movement than like the dissimulated resentment and snootiness of the schoolboy with advanced ideas going back to his family for the holidays'.[1] Auden was labelled a marxist because this was a convenient and fashionable term for social dissent. Though he demonstrably had a deep and sympathetic understanding of marxian philosophy, he raided a variety of intellectual systems, not to be snooty, but for the metaphors to create an extravagant poetic pantomime. It is instructive to recall Day Lewis's account of him in his *Transitional Poem:*

> *never done*
> *With cutting and planing some new gnomic prop*
> *To jack his all too stable universe up:-*
> *Conduct's Old Dobbin, thought's chameleon.*

Auden's '1 September 1939' characterised the thirties as 'a low dishonest decade'. The highly individualistic patrons of marxism were, no doubt, both self-deceived and the dupes of the Party hierarchy. But their practical accomplishment was negligible, whether in securing a dominant position for English communism or (beneath the jargoning the real object of the Party professionals) in advancing Soviet foreign policy. Strangely, it was *bourgeois* art, so extensively disparaged, that benefited most from the interest in marxism. 'Social realism' is a dreary cliché, but with the other marxist axioms it brought under fresh scrutiny the relationship between art and its subject-matter and between art and society. By setting up new categories of value the thirties poets reassessed and perpetuated the more exclusively aesthetic 'modern' movement of Eliot, Pound, Joyce. Their criticism explains, indirectly, what they were about in their poetry. As Eliot has said, 'The poetic critic is criticising poetry in order to create poetry.'

1. 'The Oxford Boys Becalmed', *The Shores of Light*, pp. 669–70.

IV

The progress of the artist is a continual self-
sacrifice, a continual extinction of personality
T. S. Eliot (1917)[1]

Further, he [the critic] will conceive of art, like
life, as being a self-discipline rather than a self-
expression *W. H. Auden* (1941)[2]

As the quotations above indicate, there are unexpected resem-
blances between the pronouncements of T. S. Eliot and those of
W. H. Auden. Auden is thinking of the formal limitations which
art imposes. To render his creative impulse the writer must
regulate and give design to it. He must, therefore, in the words of
Auden's essay, possess 'a consciousness of the whole of the past in
the present', if he is to produce anything more than 'a slight
personal modification of [his] immediate predecessors', which
would not be true 'originality'. These views clearly resemble
Eliot's on the fertilisation of genuine novelty by a deep awareness
of the writings of the past. Eliot censures 'exaggerated novelty,
a novelty usually of a trifling kind, which conceals from the un-
critical reader a fundamental commonplaceness'. He commends
'the historical sense . . . a perception not only of the pastness of the
past but of its presence'. Thus for Eliot, as for Auden, 'not only
the best, but the most individual parts of [the poet's] work may be
those in which the dead poets, his ancestors, assert their immortality
most vigorously'.

Auden's essay considers also the question of poetry and beliefs.
It affirms the moral influence which works of art exert and, at the
other end of the process, the influence of moral values on works of
art. Belief and the form in which poetry expresses belief are inter-
dependent: 'False beliefs lead in fact to bad poetry, and bad poetry
leads to a falsification of belief.' In Western society as it is, the
faith which Auden thinks works of art should serve is Christian,
orthodox, conservative. It is a democratic faith recognising the
rights as well as the obligations of the individual, but suspicious

1. 'Tradition and the Individual Talent', *Selected Essays*, p. 17.
2. 'Criticism in a Mass Society', in G. Grigson ed. *The Mint*, No. 2, p. 13.
The essay by Auden was first published by Princeton in 1941.

of reformist zeal. 'Man,' says Auden, 'is a fallen creature with a natural bias to do evil.' The premiss of the faith is original sin not automatic progress, with the consequences for religious and political belief which assent to this proposition necessarily implies. One consequence is that, being naturally depraved and fallible, the individual cannot be the sole mentor of his actions in any sphere. Hence, for example, in artistic innovation, the need to be aware of the cultural past. The tenor of the essay is that while a monolithic orthodoxy is repugnant, some authoritative community of faith is desirable. Its tone is sceptical of liberal notions of progress. Such were the beliefs which in 1941 coloured Auden's advocacy of self-discipline rather than self-expression in art. He was in fact affirming briefly and categorically, and for much the same reasons, the philosophy of art, tradition and belief more delicately elaborated by Eliot over the twenties and thirties.

In the thirties, the younger poets too, Auden among them, were advocating self-discipline in the arts. Their understanding of it, however, was quite different from Eliot's, or from Auden's in 1941. This divergence of meaning was part of a larger re-orientation. In its broadest terms, it re-appraised Eliot's version of the relationship between poetry and reality, between the imaginative structure of words, feelings, ideas, and immediate, concrete actuality. That is a shorthand which, while it is convenient, gives only the barest idea of the many intricate paths of communication between the two.

Eliot's criticism minimised the importance to writing or appreciating a literary work of anything outside the work itself: religion, politics, its audience, even, in the most empirical sense, the 'experience' which supplies its matter. According to his essay on Massinger, poetry is a medium which stretches language to the furthest compass of expression, 'through words perpetually juxtaposed in new and sudden combinations, meanings perpetually *eingeschachtelt* into meanings'. The meaning is not the paraphrasable content; it is inseparable from the particular words which express it; the quality of the poetry depends on the use of language. So Eliot considered Massinger an inferior poet to Tourneur or Middleton because his language lacked the synthesising power of Tourneur's or Middleton's, not because of any deficiency in Massinger's 'view of life', or elevation of thought, or perceptiveness of vision. Even the celebrated 'objective correlative', in 'Hamlet and his Problems', is not a point of reference outside the work of art. It is the imagined circumstances exterior to a character in a play, which must account adequately for the character's feelings. Factual knowledge of, for example, the older Hamlet stories on which Shakespeare worked, or of changes in the meanings of words, will help the critic's or reader's understanding. But apart from information of that sort, guidance from outside a particular work of art can come only from other works of art, whether for the critic seeking to appraise or for the writer in his 'intolerable wrestle with words and meanings'.

'Tradition and the Individual Talent' presents the literary or aesthetic community made up of all these separate works as a self-contained organism. For the writer, Europe is the artistic tradition of Europe, 'which does not superannuate either Shakespeare, or Homer, or the rock drawing of the Magdalenian draughtsmen'. Paradoxically, familiar intercourse with this living past is indispensable for 'the important critic . . . who is absorbed in the present problems of art, and who wishes to bring the forces of the past to bear upon the solution of these problems'.[1] What applies to the critic applies with equal force to the writer, a great part of whose labour, Eliot contends in 'The Function of Criticism', is 'critical labour: the labour of sifting, combining, constructing, expunging, correcting, testing'. The writer works in this universe of symbols, creating a structure, detached from reality, of words and combinations of words. Tradition, the evolutionary record of such designs, is the testing-ground of his own experiments.

This is a much more serious doctrine of art for art's sake than the dandyish posturings of the nineties, though a line of descent is traceable. Eliot made heavier and more systematic demands of the poet and critic than the aesthetes did. While his earliest poems reveal a smack of the dandy in his make-up, he had the temperament of the scholar as well. His reviews of Georgian poetry in 'The Egoist' in 1918 deplore the modish indifference to professional standards. He speaks of the 'serious writer of verse' who 'must be prepared to cross himself with the best verse of other languages and the best prose of all languages'. He disparages 'the British worship of inspiration, which in literature is merely an avoidance

---

1. 'Imperfect Critics', *The Sacred Wood*, pp. 37–8.

of comparison with foreign literature, a dodging of standards'. Again the emphasis is on cross-movement between different areas of literary achievement, between the contemporary literatures of different nations as between the past and the present. Eliot is requiring not a dilettante pottering among fashionable imports but an arduous discipline of learning the craft.

Eliot's writings do state opinions which appear to contradict this purely aesthetic interpretation of the nature of poetry. 'Tradition and the Individual Talent' says that the business of the poet is to use 'ordinary emotions'; ' "Rhetoric" and Poetic Drama' that he must take 'genuine and substantial human emotions, such emotions as observation can confirm, typical emotions'; 'Philip Massinger' that the absence of 'all the personal and real emotions' is one cause of Massinger's poetic debility. Such statements return poetry to some kind of contact with reality. It is an association, however, which Eliot prefers to leave undefined. His comments on it dwell upon the distance between the 'real emotion', the experience, and the poem to which it leads. The starting-point will be no more recognisable in the poem than its constituent elements in a diamond; nor, to press the analogy, is the diamond created in order to display its elements. *The Use of Poetry and the Use of Criticism* denies that the object of a poem is to 'communicate experience', for 'what is there to be communicated was not in existence before the poem was completed'. Similarly, in the words of 'Tradition and the Individual Talent' again, 'the difference between art and the event is always absolute'. In any case, the quality or intensity of the original experience has no bearing on the quality of the poem. To suppose that it has is to replace literary judgment by semi-ethical criteria of sublimity. What really counts is 'the intensity of the artistic process, the pressure, so to speak, under which the fusion takes place'.[1]

As with the relationship between poetry and the phenomenal world, so with that between poetry and systems of ideas 'explaining' life. Eliot's instinct was to segregate the two. But the problems are not identical. In Eliot's discussion, experience is morally neutral: he is not considering the quite different matter of the artistic propriety of this or that kind of experience; a philosophy, on the other hand, provokes acceptance or rejection. Eliot had

1. 'Tradition and the Individual Talent', *Selected Essays*, p. 19.

therefore to ask, to what extent does our appreciation of a literary work depend on our attitude to the beliefs it embodies? The long essay on Dante, *The Use of Poetry and the Use of Criticism*, and parts of *The Sacred Wood* take up the question. Ideally, the answer is that both belief and disbelief are equally irrelevant to aesthetic enjoyment and that the quality of the philosophy is irrelevant to the quality of the poem as artistic creation. That is, a system of beliefs to which one cannot assent will not impede our appreciation of a great poem, like the *Divine Comedy*, to which that system is in some way central; and it is not the agnosticism subsumed in Prospero's 'Our revels now are ended' which gives the speech its power. Eliot distinguishes between the '*belief attitude*' of a man reading a theological treatise and that of the same man entering the imaginative world of a great poem structured around the same theology. The second situation, to over-simplify the distinction, arouses intellectual curiosity, not partisanship.

In practice, however, the reader cannot dissociate art from belief. Eliot confesses to finding more pleasure in the poetry when he shares the beliefs of the poet. But again he is anxious to detach the two aspects. He shifts the issue, so that it becomes rather a question of the intellectual respectability of the metaphysic, and— a consequence—its readiness to be absorbed into artistic form. Some ideas offend us not precisely because we disagree with them, but because they seem too puerile and incoherent to be worth the least consideration. Others, while we may not accept them, we recognise as 'coherent, mature, and founded on the facts of experience'.[1] In the former category, for Eliot, come Shelley— 'so puerile that I cannot enjoy the poems in which they occur';[2] and to a lesser extent Blake—whose genius lacked 'a framework of accepted and traditional ideas'[3]—and Lucretius, whose philosophy 'applied itself to life too uniformly, to supply the material for a wholly successful poem'.[4] Conversely Wordsworth, though his social ideas were not to Eliot's taste, escapes this criticism. So does Dante, not because Eliot found his philosophy sympathetic,

1. *The Use of Poetry and the Use of Criticism*, p. 96.
2. ibid, p. 91.
3. 'Blake', *Selected Essays*, p. 322.
4. 'Dante', *The Sacred Wood*, p. 162. This is the short essay on Dante, written before the one which appears in *Selected Essays*.

but because it 'had undergone a more complete absorption into life than [that] of Lucretius'.[1] And into poetry, for Dante's achievement was 'to find the concrete poetic equivalent' for his system of ideas. In short, the aesthetic greatness—which is what really matters—resides in something outside the ideas; but some ideas are incompatible with such greatness. George Orwell appears to have taken a rather similar view in 'Politics *vs* Literature', where he remarked that he could imagine a good book being written by a Catholic, a communist, a fascist, an old-style liberal or an ordinary conservative, but not by a spiritualist, a Buchmanite or a member of the Ku-Klux-Klan, who represent views not compatible with sanity.

Eliot's is a nicely articulated theory, though the difference is a fine one between simply disagreeing with a philosophy and saying that it has not the body even to give it an intellectual presence. There is a temptation to identify the two, to account for disbelief by denying reality to the ideas one repudiates. Indeed, as Edwin Muir has pointed out in *Essays on Literature and Society*, that is the approach of David Daiches to the content of Eliot's own later poetry. Certainly the intention of Eliot's theory is to isolate 'philosophy in literature' from 'philosophy in life', where ideas excite belief and disbelief and the response produces action: going to this or that church, voting for a political party, reading certain books; and in the extreme, physical aggression and defence.

The ideas which will engage the present-day writer's imagination are likely to be social and political, either general political convictions or an attitude to specific issues. Such ideas may prompt him to devote his art to advocating them. Here, in Eliot's view, if the work is to be more than simple propaganda the political theory must fulfil the same conditions that admit any philosophy into literature. *The Use of Poetry and the Use of Criticism* has an interesting passage which argues that the communist writer, if he is to use his beliefs as the material of his art, must use them not as *held* but as *felt*; not as doctrine but as informing his emotional responses. So, just as Christian poetry does not consist entirely of hymns, communist poetry need not consist entirely of panegyrics upon the Soviet State, though Eliot held that its development would produce a literature totally meaningless in Western Europe.

1. 'Dante', *The Sacred Wood*, p. 163.

As for literature which takes up an attitude to transient political issues, Eliot's position is that the work, like Dryden's *The Hind and the Panther*, can survive its association with disputes that have ceased to be of any interest or concern: the poetry gives life to the attitude, not the attitude to the poetry. A corollary is that the original effectiveness of the work as propaganda is not necessarily an index to its literary merit.

Despite this apparent effort to disengage literature from a narrow 'social consciousness', Eliot was well aware that society acts upon literature, not only bringing new ideas and new subjects within its ambit, but also affecting the sensibility of the writer and through him the forms of his art. The effects which society produces upon literature are, in the end, literary effects. In 'The Metaphysical Poets' Eliot saw the difficulty of modern poetry as a consequence of the interplay between a complex and varied civilisation and the 'refined sensibility' of the poet. Although its causes may be social the difficulty, according to 'Swinburne as Poet', is essentially a linguistic and formal one: the modern writer, like Conrad or Joyce, is dealing with a language struggling 'to digest and express new objects, new groups of objects, new feelings, new aspects'. In the same way, the radical changes in poetic form in Wordsworth's time were a symptom of profound changes in society and the individual.[1] To evolve forms congenial to such changes, rather than merely to reproduce the forms of the immediate past, the writer must be alive to the mutable world of objects. That is its only interest for him as a writer. Here too, Eliot is taking issue with 'the error of the poet's trying to do other people's work'[2]— the work, it might be, of the social reformer, the politician, the anthropologist—in a medium which has its own totally different purposes.

Yet the process by which society acts upon literature is not a one-way transaction. In 'The Social Function of Poetry' Eliot's thesis is that the only direct duty of the poet is to his language: by enriching and developing it as a medium of expression, he preserves it from deterioration. Indirectly, he benefits society: by maintaining the continuity between the culture of the past and that of the present; by invigorating 'the speech and sensibility of

1. *The Use of Poetry and the Use of Criticism*, p. 75.
2. ibid, p. 152.

the whole nation'. For the poet 'in expressing what other people feel' is also 'changing the feeling by making it more conscious', that is, making people more aware of their own deepest feelings, which have in them something communal, not personal and isolated. And if the capacity to express a wide and subtle range of feeling degenerates, so, in the long run, may the general capacity to feel any but the crudest emotions. The poet draws, certainly, on the living idiom of the spoken tongue; its vitality is essential to him; but he gives interest on his borrowings by extending and refining the power of verbal expression. Literature responds to the changing character of social life; society absorbs a sense of its own identity from literature. The size of the poet's audience is irrelevant. Ideally, the poet in a healthy civilisation will have a wide appeal to all social levels, though not the same kind of appeal at each of them. But this in fact no longer happens. What matters now is that the poet should be assured of a small audience. Through this audience and through the assimilation of 'genuine novelty' of form and expression into the work of more popular writers, the language generally develops, keeping pace with and clarifying the developments of life itself.

This has been a somewhat partial account of Eliot's ideas on the relationship between literature and life. One might construct a different one from some of the quotations already given, and from such opinions as in the one in 'Charles Whibley', that 'permanently interesting content' is as important as 'good style'. Eliot's theory is in fact balanced and comprehensive, remarkably free of self-contradictions and designed to do more than simply rationalise prejudices, though personal antipathy (which Eliot generally admits) colours some of his judgments on individual writers. Yet the summary of it here, though incomplete, gives a fair impression of its general emphasis on segregating art from 'experience', and on the importance of the European tradition. The writers associated with the twenties, like Ezra Pound, Aldous Huxley, Richard Aldington, Rebecca West, directed their criticism towards aesthetic analysis and the writers of the past, of France especially; in the thirties, poets and critics sought to integrate themselves and their work with society and its immediate problems.

Eliot has the reputation of being pontifical. The thirties writers, who tended to declare their views more ingenuously, often outdid him. Geoffrey Grigson complains that Eliot, despite his ability to see 'objects as themselves and as symbols, all at once', set about 'the pedantic establishment of a culture universe in which a quotation is as much an object as a chair'.[1] So ran the general burden of reproach. Tribute, unanimous in what it found to praise, preceded similarly uniform disparagement. The Preface to the *New Verse* anthology, *The Crest on the Silver* (Grigson), *Critique of Poetry* (Michael Roberts), *A Hope for Poetry* (Day Lewis), *Modern Poetry* (Louis MacNeice), *The Destructive Element* (Stephen Spender) admire the early Eliot of 'The burnt-out ends of smoky days' and the True Church 'Wrapt in the old miasmal mist', both for his non-conformist social attitudes and for the concreteness of his poetic manner. His poems, says Grigson, 'almost alone in such new poetry as I had read, were *applicable*'. But after 'The Hollow Men' Eliot's Anglicanism, his conservative politics, the retirement of his poetry into a private drama of the spirit seemed to impair that applicability.

The change, according to Michael Roberts, was the result not of a poetic development but of a philosophical about-face which left Eliot without any sense of a need for action or 'an understanding of our relation to the world of transient things'. Even in *The Waste Land* it was now possible, knowing how Eliot had developed, to see foreshadowings of this dissociation from actual life. Stephen Spender held that the pub scene in *The Waste Land*, naturalistic in intention, gave no sense of an origin in experience. In the later poetry, 'the outer world of reality is viewed either as digested experience, or else as "impressions": impressions that only seem important for what they impress on the mind, without regard for the reality which is doing the impressing'.[2] MacNeice's *Modern Poetry* makes the same point. Words are essentially social, both in origin and in function. Their connotations develop from their social use, their purpose is communication. They are 'community products', and the poet's business is to use them in a way

1. Geoffrey Grigson: '*New Verse*' *Anthology*, p. 20.
2. Stephen Spender: *The Destructive Element*, p. 160. In the same breath Spender undermines his own authority as an observer of life. By way of contrast he instances James's Mrs Verver and the prince, whom, he says, 'any pub-crawling prostitute could understand very well'.

that will make the 'things' mentioned in his poem its primary feature, a theory which exactly reverses Eliot's emphasis.

The argument, then, is that the failure of Eliot's poetry is a linguistic one. It uses language improperly, not to re-create and convey reality but to set up a barrier between the aesthetic experience and the experience of common life. This supposed vacuity of language was attributed not to literary but to philosophical causes. It originated in a false attitude to life. At best, Eliot was negative, engaged in passive 'contemplation of a world in fragments [while] his successors are more interested in tidying it up' by voicing 'practical ideals'.[1] At worst, he was condoning the structure of a society whose national resources were 'exploited for private profit' and whose church was 'willingly subservient to the temporal power [which] enforces the distribution of goods and services by an antiquated and inadequate system'.[2] The argument, of course, catches up with itself: to detach poetry from reality enfeebles its language and turns it from progressive to reactionary ideas which produce an enfeeblement of language.

Roberts gives as one reason for his admiring Eliot's early poetry its independence of any exterior system of ideas; he really means its apparent independence of any system of which he would disapprove. What the argument comes down to is the simple claim that a left-wing faith, as well as being the only morally reputable choice, would enliven the poet's vision, give his work relevance and vitalise its style. Louis MacNeice, asserting that 'literature is not, in spite of Plato, essentially second hand' goes on to say that in his own time major literature required 'a sympathy . . . in the writer with those forces which at the moment make for progress'.[3] Comparing Stephen Spender with Rupert Brooke, whose talents he considers more or less equal, Grigson claims that Spender's superiority comes from his sympathy with the spirit of an age uncongenial to Brooke's particular kind of insipidity (though on these grounds Brooke might be taken as an awful warning against too full a sympathy with an age).[4] That spirit was taken to be leftist, and left-wing opinions were associated with documentary

1. Louis MacNeice: *Modern Poetry*, p. 12.
2. Michael Roberts: *Critique of Poetry*, pp. 216, 220.
3. *Modern Poetry*, pp. 198, 204.
4. Grigson, *'New Verse' Anthology*, pp. 16–18.

realism: to report accurately was in fact to condemn. Mass Observation (founded by Charles Madge, a communist poet, and Tom Harrisson, the anthropologist) and the 'Labour Research Department', an appendage of the Communist Party of Great Britain, were two manifestations of the belief in the value to progressive movements of accumulating facts. The poets, in their own way, were to pursue the same objective. They were to be 'good reporters' and so subject themselves 'to a discipline of objects and events'.[1]

Eliot's poetic theory and his later practice obstructed that discipline. He undervalued the importance to poetry of experience, actuality and belief, and compounded the error by celebrating the wrong sort of experience and the wrong sort of belief. Eliot's problem was the same as that of all his contemporaries, to find a form which would contain their vision of the chaotic present.[2] To solve his technical problems Eliot turned to tradition, which in time disabled his powers of response to the present. The impersonality which the 'historical sense' was to develop turned out to be really a one-man retreat into a private world of abstractions. The community of tradition was just another bolt-hole from reality.

What the poets of the thirties wanted was some kind of artistic solidarity which would correct the individual vision, an impersonal or collective wisdom to direct and shape the personal witness. One of the dilemmas they most earnestly investigated was 'the individualist predicament'. The editors (Montagu Slater and T. H. Wintringham) of the periodical *Viewpoint* (afterwards *Left Review*) represented it—with some confusion of thought—as standing 'for militant communism and against individualism and metaphysics in art. It declares that the work of art is an organic individual creation and that it can only exist in its integrity in a classless society, in a completely communistic state; that art must become the production and the property of all.' The problem was to achieve that synthesis—or anything like it—in a society manifestly far from classless and communistic. Eliot's example seemed, in the ways shown, not merely irrelevant to but

1. ibid, p. 15.
2. Stephen Spender's *The Destructive Element* discusses this question. See pp. 11–17.

obstructive of that synthesis. Marxism, which had the political answers, might prove to have the solution here too.

Stephen Spender examines the predicament in 'Poetry and Revolution' (*New Country*), *The Destructive Element* (1935) and *Forward from Liberalism* (1937). By 1933 Spender and Isherwood had seen the forces of left and right deploy in Germany; at home the right, whether it called itself Conservative, Labour or National, was indolently entrenched, at the same time, it appeared, monumentally apathetic and astute in doing down the proletariat. Russia was building 'towns that are planned as towns, in a country of electric power and air transport'; the most the English government could do was 'to help a private company build an Atlantic liner, for the use of the rich'.[1] In England, too, since 1933 with the repeal of the 1920 Agriculture Act, the countryside had fallen increasingly into neglect, uncultivated fields, dilapidated farms. In 1930 two and a half millions were unemployed. In 1931 the Means Test further reduced an inadequate dole; the town of Jarrow, with the liquidation of its shipyard, became an unsavoury emblem of industrial collapse. By 1935 Sir Oswald Mosley's Blackshirts had perfected their technique of public violence and Jew-baiting; and in 1936 proposed to put up one hundred candidates at the next election. Abroad, in 1934, Dollfuss wiped out the Austrian socialist movement; in July of the same year the Austrian Nazis murdered Dollfuss. The next year Italy bombed and gassed Abyssinia. 'One group of horsemen,' wrote Mussolini's son, 'gave me the impression of a budding rose unfolding as the bomb fell in their midst and blew them up. It was most entertaining.'

When *Forward from Liberalism* appeared the civil war in Spain had just begun. This was an occasion as much of hope as of despair. Here, perhaps, was the opportunity for a final confrontation between international socialism and the fascist alliance. Indeed, all the odious portents here recounted had their obverse. If Mosley's support grew, so did that of the Left Book Club (12,000 members in 1936); if the Labour Party in Britain was numbly passive, the *Front Populaire* government in France was an exhilarating model of effective socialist unity; if Germany was the power-house of fascism, the Soviet Union, as the Webbs put it, was *A New Civilisation*? The query was lightly stressed. *Forward*

1. *Forward from Liberalism*, pp. 190, 180.

from Liberalism excused Soviet excesses (the Trotskyist trials, forced collectivisation) as unavoidable, and drew admiring attention to Stalin's protest against the treatment of the kulaks. The provisions of the draft Soviet Constitution (published in full in the *Left Book Club News*) were taken to indicate that while Germany was intensifying its barbarity Russia was proposing to contain democracy within a communist system. It was true that higher groups could reverse popular decisions ('a privilege rarely exercised', according to Spender); but the movement was towards 'greater freedoms'.

It was difficult then to foresee the acquiescence of Leon Blum and his Popular Front government in non-intervention in Spain, which turned the scales in Franco's favour; impossible to predict the Nazi-Soviet pact of 1939 or the remote future of Khrushchev's 1956 anti-Stalinist speech. Every age has its illusions, even the illusion of being disillusioned; these of the nineteen-thirties were at least generous. Within their framework Spender addressed himself to finding ways in which *bourgeois* art could best serve right ends and the *bourgeois* writer play his part in realising the 'greater freedoms'. He considered the same questions as Eliot, but was less concerned with 'significant form', technique and pure aesthetics than with taking up into art the social realities of the moment. Central to his enquiry, as to Eliot's, was the adequacy of the individual talent.

Spender's encounter with marxist thinking on these topics leads him into some uneasy intellectual manœuvring. To begin with, in 'Poetry and Revolution', his complaint is not against any indecorum in the communist position. The problem is to make the communism of a writer inheriting a *bourgeois* tradition in a *bourgeois* society more than a purely academic exercise. It is economically impossible for him, in society as it is, to be anything but a *rentier* or a capitalist hireling. Only a cultivated minority of his own privileged class can appreciate his art, which is essentially an imaginative escape intercepting action. The future of society and of art lies with communism, but the *bourgeois* artist can do little either to bring that future into being or to anticipate the forms of art it will evolve. As a communist, however, he has certain advantages. He is not an isolated rebel casting about to build up a systematic philosophy of protest. Within the marxist frame-

35

work the *bourgeois* work of art may, without violating its own tradition, reflect the disruptive elements present in society and making for its overthrow and reconstruction. In this way the writer can identify the social issues for the 'practical revolutionary' and so may speed the coming of the new society. It is for the poet, as best he can, to let his communism determine his field of vision and draw his individual perceptions into a pattern.

But will the writer, sacrificing his individualism, become propagandist, not artist? 'Poetry and Revolution' is content, on the whole, to argue that aesthetically satisfying *bourgeois* art may (though with difficulty) be good communist propaganda. Both *The Destructive Element* and *Forward from Liberalism* try to justify a special dispensation from strict Party control for the communist writer in a *bourgeois* society. Again, they take the view that marxism provides such writers with 'objective and social symbols' for their attitudes. These symbols range from 'the industrial towns and distressed areas' to the   philosophical counters of marxist thought, which make it possible to write about 'the moral life of one's time'. Right or wrong, the marxist premisses deal with the world of fact. They interpret and judge political and social realities; take the writer a step beyond mere 'literary realism'; and enable him to derive from the present the achieved social system of the future.

All this would retrieve the situation produced by such doctrines as Eliot's. But communism needs two kinds of supporter; the professional who will not jib at subordinating ends to means to maintain Party unity; and the 'clerk'; the critic within, who will measure the 'party line' against the ends of justice which communism itself purposes. The repressive and obscurantist policies of the 'Russian Association of Proletarian Writers' (though by 1937 comparatively liberalised) suggest to Spender that communism is liable to fixation in dogma. Adopting its general tenets, the writer can take an objective view of its specific policies. As a corrective to marxist obduracy Spender recommends 'the other great modern analytic system', Freudian psychoanalysis.

Freud's theories were in fact another powerful non-literary influence on the period's writers. His discoveries revealed the queer submerged motivations of human behaviour. He had destroyed the whole basis of Victorian morality and its concept, now happily found to be naive, of 'normal' mentality. Another, rather inconsistent, reason for admiration was that he had restored the individual to a properly important status. The real marxian theorists, like Caudwell, considered him to be misled by the usual 'assumptions of a bourgeois idealist'. But in Spender's view, by synthesising marxism and psychoanalysis the writer will be able 'to write about society as a whole, and not about the individual severed from his background'. Meanwhile, presumably, the 'professional revolutionaries' were to be getting on with the job without troublesome crises of conscience.

Finally, Spender distinguishes between the functions of prose and poetry. Prose may fittingly be direct propaganda, stating facts, urging action. Poetry conveys truths emotionally apprehended from the interaction between an individual sensibility and a particular situation. It does not advocate action; but it may so irradiate the situation that the need to act becomes imperative. Spender does not formulate the precise distinction very clearly. Its purpose was to sanction the appearance in poetry of individualist deviations.

Generally, the literary marxists of the thirties found it easier to go along with marxism in the field of politics. In art they made reservations of which Spender's are typical. Day Lewis's *A Hope for Poetry* (1934, 1936) questions the value of the marxist dialectic as, for example, a basis for satire: a merely postulated future is too insubstantial a ground. Marxism will preserve the poet from the illusion of 'pure poetry', keeping before him the realities of the world he lives in; but of equal importance is his 'artistic integrity', which may resist the cruder political expedients. Naturally, the real Party men despised these *bourgeois* conditionings. Edgell Rickword's comments on *Spain* are a case in point. Edward Upward—the 'Chalmers' of Isherwood's *Lions and Shadows*, the near-mythical undergraduate of Spender's Oxford[1]—went over totally to official communism, passing beyond the territory of nervous self-questioning. In *World within World* Stephen Spender tells how he asked Upward what he thought of the Moscow trials in which Yagoda had been sentenced to death. Upward answered, ' "What trials? I've given up thinking about such things ages ago" . . . he now admitted no point of view which

1. *World within World*, p. 102.

was inconvenient to the Party.'[1] Spender's autobiography, one should add, gives a rather partial account of his own activities. As Julian Symons has pointed out in *The Thirties*, it is instructive to compare Spender's contemporary report in *New Writing* on the 1937 Madrid Writers' Congress with the account in *World within World*. The latter plays up a cynicism which Spender must clearly have been at pains to exclude from the earlier version.

Of all the writers who took a rigidly marxist view the most incisive intelligence was that of Christopher Caudwell. His main literary studies are *Illusion and Reality, Studies in a Dying Culture* and *Further Studies in a Dying Culture*.[2] Their interest is that they display a sensitive and independent mind working from a total, not an eclectic, acceptance of marxism.

Caudwell regards art and science as complementary activities of the human intelligence. Science explores, categorises, interprets the workings of the physical world. Taking selected pieces of external reality, it has the purpose of demonstrating their relationship to each other and to material nature generally. Its object is truth. *Further Studies* distinguishes it from poetry and defines the relationship between the two: 'Science and art represent the profit on social capital. They are pushed out into the deserts of the unknown by the very workings of society. They lead, but they were instructed; they find new worlds of life, but they were supported by the old. Always we find terms drawn from the labour process to be adequate in describing their function, and only this can describe the nature of Beauty and Truth.' The province of poetry is the inner human world of feelings. Its medium is language, which 'was created to signify otherness, to indicate portions of objective reality shared socially'. Its material is isolated fragments of external reality which in a poem acquire an emotional content not part of their objective existence but now, through the poem, 'made to live in the common world of

1. Upward left the Party in 1948, having persuaded himself that it 'was becoming un-Marxist'. See the conversation in Iain Hamilton ed. *the Review* No. 11-12; and for his literary views, 'Sketch for a Marxist Interpretation of Literature' in C. Day Lewis ed. *The Mind in Chains*.
2. The following account is based on Caudwell's writings generally. See in particular *Illusion and Reality*, pp. x-xi, 171-5, 214-19, 293-301; *Further Studies in a Dying Culture*, pp. 110-13; 'D. H. Lawrence' in *The Concept of Freedom*, pp. 11-17, reprinted from *Studies in a Dying Culture*.

perceptual reality'. Emotion, that is, is created and given a social value, as with the product of any labour process. This distinguishes art from dream or phantasy. Dream is uncontrolled, its elements associated without conscious direction. It remains private to the dreamer. It satisfies desires and impulses in a world of unreality; it is an evasion of action. Poetry 'externalises emotion' and 'produces social commodities'. It links the inner to the outer world, the individual to his community.

Art, then, has essentially a social function. Dream is 'self-expression'. Art is not. It satisfies the artist by synthesising the individual experience and objects socially shared; the audience by generating new emotions from pieces of external reality and so modifying its audience's perception of those pieces. It creates new attitudes. Up to this point the marxist quality of Caudwell's theory lies mainly in its terminology, its emphasis on poetry as an instrument producing change, on its communal nature and on the primacy of its relationship with the objects of the phenomenal world. He also considers the question raised by *bourgeois* sceptics, is marxist art merely propaganda? To ask the question, according to Caudwell, implies a simplification of a complex matter. His argument has established the social function of art. In *bourgeois* society the artist has generally only two choices, either to produce commercialised trash or to stress the individual experience to the point where its expression becomes wholly personal and formless—Dadaism, surrealism. The first panders to debased tastes; in the latter the 'thing experienced' entirely disappears and communication ceases. The only significant modern artists—Caudwell instances Lawrence, Gide, Dos Passos, Eliot—realise that 'pure art' is unsatisfactory. Recognising the revolutionary situation around them they use their art to influence its outcome. The choice for them, finally, is between communism and fascism. The artist must align himself with one or the other.

In that sense, art is propaganda; but this does not mean that communist poetry must consist of strident revolutionary slogans, any more, to use Eliot's analogy again, than it means that Christian poetry must consist entirely of hymns. Neither does it mean that communist art will superannuate the art of the past—just as, for Eliot, novelty did not invalidate tradition. It is another stage in the continuous evolutionary sequence. In the new dispensation the old will still seem beautiful, seen now 'through a kind of mist or aerial perspective of intervening time, changing and toning its hues. The old beauty has been gathered up in the new.'[1]

In *New Verse* for May 1937 Auden reviewed *Illusion and Reality*. 'I agree with it,' he says, remarking that its discussion 'of the essentially social relation of words, art and science . . . provides a more satisfactory answer to the problems which poetry raises' than the theories of I. A. Richards. The approval is understandable. In earlier essays[2] Auden arrives independently at similar conclusions. Like Caudwell he contrasts phantasy and art. There is common ground between the two activities. But uncontrolled phantasy, day-dream, wish-fulfilment, is basically an attempt to compensate for failure to meet the demands of reality. The poet introduces control. He takes 'data from the outside world' and consciously disposes them into artistic form, reconciling 'the unwilling subject and object'. His medium is words, which are a social product common to him and his audience. He uses them to develop undisciplined phantasy into deliberate phantasy 'directed towards understanding', not escape. Phantasy and poetry diverge in their form and in their purpose. Phantasy is chaotic, isolated, barren; poetry well-made, public, socially functional. But the function of poetry, Auden concludes in the introduction to *The Poet's Tongue*, 'is not concerned with telling people what to do, but with extending our knowledge of good and evil, perhaps making the necessity for action more urgent and its nature more clear'.

Auden borrowed the last phrase from his poem, 'August for the people . . .', dedicated to Christopher Isherwood:

> *So in this hour of crisis and dismay,*
> *What better than your strict and adult pen*
> *Can warn us from the colours and the consolations,*
> *The showy arid works, reveal*
> *The squalid shadow of academy and garden,*

1. *Further Studies in a Dying Culture*, p. 78.
2. See the introduction to *The Poet's Tongue*, ed. W. H. Auden and John Garrett; 'Psychology and Art Today' by W. H. Auden in G. Grigson ed. *The Arts Today*.

Make action urgent and its nature clear?
Who give us nearer insight to resist
The expanding fear, the savaging disaster?

The 'savaging disaster' is the destruction of the virtues which might create a better society. Foremost among them is love, for Auden at this stage of his career a word of protean significance.[1] Certainly among its evil manifestations is self-love, which Auden consistently anathematises. It is the origin of aimless phantasy and withdrawal from the world, a product of individualism in a fragmented society. Part II of 'A Happy New Year' (a poem variously cannibalised after its first appearance in *New Country*) speaks with evident disapproval of 'the isolated personal life' which can be disciplined only by surrender to the mysterious 'lords of limit'. A later revision (in 1945) to 'the isolated dishonest life' removed from 'personal' the opprobrium of 'isolated', for Auden in the thirties a necessary part of its connotation. 'A Communist to Others', also in *New Country*, rejects 'personal regeneration' as the 'one salvation'; and in a favourite image depicts the 'unhappy poet' fleeing reality

To islands in your private seas
Where thoughts like castaways find ease
In endless petting

as some kind of masturbatory release. Even love between two individuals is not enough. The poem ends with a call for trust in a catholic love 'outside our own election' which will hold 'in unseen connection' the individual members of society. But for all its mystical overtones this is a love with the practical object of setting society to rights. Widely-rooted, unifying men of good will, it will secure the necessary collective action. Poetry may help to awaken it. 'You,' Auden says to the poet, 'could help us if you chose.'

There is of course some conflict between these ideas and the marxist thesis that 'we must change the world in order to change ourselves'.[2] But there must be a group either to bring about the

1. See Joseph Warren Beach: *The Making of the Auden Canon*, pp. 18–21.
2. Christopher Caudwell: 'A Study in Bourgeois Psychology: (i) Freud' in *The Concept of Freedom*, p. 132 (reprinted from *Studies in a Dying Culture*).

changes; or, the historical dialectic having mechanically produced them, to exploit the new situation. It is to such a group that the individual must relinquish his individuality, such a group whose collective purpose poetry may strengthen; and which, in turn, will enable the poet to transcend his personal isolation. As Monroe K. Spears argues, Auden's ideas have always had a markedly religious strain. Hindsight does not want for clues to account for his later development. Even as late as 1940, however, his ideas are politically, not theologically, oriented.[1] Society is the natural condition of man, the individual 'the product of social life'. There is nothing beyond society to encompass and give meaning to the personal life. Auden accepts Marx's 'view that physical conditions and the forms of economic production have dictated the forms of communities'. Evil is preventable and a socialist society will release the individual's full potential. A year later, Auden has undergone his great conversion. The social millenium is an illusion, man naturally depraved and bidden now to subdue his erring self within the Christian discipline. Auden's 'marxist phase' is over.

But no corresponding change took place in his poetic manner. He continued to meet Grigson's criterion for *New Verse* that a poem should take notice, 'for ends not purely individual, of the universe of objects and events'. Only the ends had changed; the poems of the new dispensation still created from their 'objects and events' a dramatic myth which extends their bearings beyond a simply local and immediate relevancy. It was Caudwell's achievement, in his few poems, to have distilled poetically allusive statements from an uncompromising marxism; it was Auden's to have converted his marxist borrowings into a series of coherently generalising images. From his exploration of marxist thought he took what he could accept politically and use poetically. Unlike Spender, he did not dissipate his creative energies in fretting over narrowly political controversies. Of all the thirties poets he is most at home in the poetic fable he constructed from marxism.

1. See W. H. Auden: 'I Believe' in C. Fadiman ed. *I Believe*, pp. 17–31.

II

Christopher Caudwell and John Cornford:
Poets in the Party

ZRA POUND said that he and Eliot used the Gautier stanzas of *H. S. Mauberly* and *Poems* (1920) because they believed 'that the dilution of *vers libre* . . . had gone too far, and that some counter-current must be set going'. But Michael Roberts's introduction to *New Signatures* gives no credit to Pound and Eliot for their practice of a stricter form. In his picture of events, the poems of *New Signatures* burst unprecedented upon a scene dominated by esoteric poetry and free verse. They restore an eighteenth-century discipline to newly discovered 'rhythms not alien to the normal movement of English speech'; and with this 'respect for eighteenth-century ideals' combine 'a revolutionary attitude' hostile to any culture dependent on 'a depressed and miserable lower class'. According to *New Signatures*, 'Mr Auden's *Poems* and Mr Day Lewis's *From Feathers to Iron* were . . . the first books in which imagery taken from contemporary life consistently appeared as the natural and spontaneous expression of the poet's thought and feeling.'

Looking back on the period, Julian Symons says: 'The technical problem that faced these poets was that of expressing revolutionary sentiments, which was something "new" in English poetry, in some appropriately "new" language. A great deal was said at the time about the way in which images were drawn from pylons and pitworks, from the operation of machinery, from psychology and science, but really the break with the twenties was sharper than

43

that. The first lines of Auden's poem ["We made all possible preparations"] are deliberately "unpoetical", they set out to shock over-refined sensibilities.'[1] Yet there is nothing of the sort in Auden's poems which could not be paralleled in Eliot's early poetry, in the 'patient etherised upon a table' and Prufrock's lobster; and nowhere in the thirties poets any more effective equivalence between new style and new experience than in

> *The muttering retreats*
> *Of restless nights in one-night cheap hotels.*

How strange that the remarkable and varied achievements of the twenties should be so suddenly wished away, at the wave of an introduction; and by the New Presbyters of the *avant-garde*. It was a dethroning of idols whom few had ever really venerated.

Yet Michael Roberts had good reason, as in *New Signatures*, to be polemical. Auden, Day Lewis and the rest were not merely rehashing Eliot: they made much more, for example, of social ephemera, often to excellent purpose. Nor were their courses any easier than Eliot's had been. If Eliot is now seen in command of the inter-war years, in the thirties the view was different. In the twenties the General Staff (Squire, Shanks, MacCarthy) of the Old Guard still patrolled the literary columns of the weeklies, relishing the Georgians and rebuking dissenters. Their warrant held good into the thirties. Geoffrey Grigson has recounted his skirmishes with St John Ervine, Ivor Brown, 'the hacks of Fleet Street' and 'the bloodless followers of the *London Mercury*'. Division also weakened the rebels. 'Experimentalism' had its vapourings, well exemplified in *Wheels* and the pretentious whimsies of Edith Sitwell, consistently one of Grigson's *New Verse* butts. At the time, however, she was for many a key figure in the revolt, lumped in with her betters because she claimed the same enemies.

The confusion is understandable. In such a welter of innovation (real and supposed) even Bloomsbury was uncertain. Along with Eliot ('The Hollow Men' and 'Journey of the Magi') the Hogarth Press *Broadcast Anthology of Modern Verse* (1930) included poems by Rupert Brooke, John Drinkwater, Edith Sitwell, J. C. Squire and the trashy 'war-poet', Robert Nichols. In the *Cambridge Poetry* anthologies of 1929 and 1930, which also had the Hogarth

1. Julian Symons: *The Thirties*, pp. 11-12.

Press *imprimatur*, many of the poems would have been reassuringly familiar, in form and content, to Edwardian readers. Julian Bell contributes two impressionistic landscapes to the 1929 volume; John Lehmann's 'October' reaches a vaguely symbolic conclusion:

> *Somewhere the voices that I cannot hear,*
> *Beyond the din*
> *Of blatant day's devices, fountain-clear*
> *Their chant begin.*

His 'Travel Bureau' in the 1930 collection laments (though perhaps intended to welcome new outlooks?) the unattainable lands of romance, 'Where twigs begin to cloud with whorls of green/ And purple flags are bursting from their case.' John Davenport's 'Dying Gladiator', more adventurous, is a poem by an undergraduate who knows the right places to visit, picking up the addresses from 'Gerontion' and *The Waste Land*: 'an empty house, no tenants', 'a squalid alley', 'a rat-infested mews'. It is a very literary piece, affecting a style as a substitute for real experience of the urban ugliness and modern despair to which it pretends a response. The poems where Eliot's influence is apparent show, like this one, the susceptibility of his manner to bad parody.

The lesson of the anthologies is that the inheritors of the literary revolution of the twenties had still to sort out its real gains. By chance, for many poets it was politics which began to supply a subject, an experience about which they found they had something to say. With that, the heterogeneous technical experiments acquired definition and proportion. They had a content to attach themselves to, instead of operating in a vacuum of feeling (the fallacy that aping a style creates a content and an attitude). Not that the perplexities altogether vanished. As we have seen, Eliot's stock fluctuated. Was he the betrayer of his revolution—or what his successors took to be his revolution? Might not poetry relapse into the timidity and irrelevance from which he had rescued it? There was now, however, a sense of direction. Poets set to specific problems of expression: to make poems from the exotic ideas and language of dialectical materialism and the society which was giving it relevance.

Clearly the influences and the motives at work were confused. The confusion, understandably, carried over into the poetry and into the theory that accompanied it. A new style was wanted, some recension of the modernist techniques which would adapt them to the social mission of poetry; or entirely supersede them. But at the time, a concern for style was suspect: *bourgeois*, subjective, individualist. The critical viewpoint of R. D. Charques was common: 'What part does literature play in the making of history and the urge towards social revolution?' Answering his question he is 'not concerned in the first place with aesthetic values'.[1] Where he does consider them they are represented as distractions from the proper job of the artist, to make his work effective in the class struggle. Eliot (formalist aestheticism), Joyce (isolated self-expression), Aldous Huxley (aristocratic disgust) all misconceive their purpose. They are out of touch with their fellow citizens and the revolutionary movement of the period.

The thirties poets thus faced a conflict between their inherited concern (*bourgeois*) for aesthetic standards and their acquired knowledge (marxist) that this was vain self-indulgence. At times, faith resolved the dilemma, taking novel ideas for originality of expression. Much of what was praised as formal innovation was in fact unusual mainly in its sentiments. Where Michael Roberts praises the poets he might normally disparage he is revealing: Blunden's 'I have been young, and now am not too old' because it asserts 'virtue in humanity'; Eliot's 'Marina' because it expresses a 'clear vision of action' and may be read 'as an actual Christian or Communist poem'.[2] But poetry with a leftist slant, whether intended or as in 'Marina' accidental, though a qualification for critical favour, did not ensure it. Louis MacNeice and Geoffrey Grigson are less Young Turkish with the major figures than Charques. Nevertheless they compile a comprehensive black-list. For Grigson, in a post-war essay, George Barker, Stephen Spender, Edith Sitwell and Dylan Thomas are reinstating an inept and insipid romanticism; for MacNeice, Pound, Cummings, Graves and the Sitwells are 'so many blind alleys'.[3] Deviate from an-

1. R. D. Charques: *Contemporary Literature and the Social Revolution*, pp. 9 and 59.

2. Michael Roberts: *Critique of Poetry*.

3. Louis MacNeice: 'Poetry Today' in G. Grigson (ed.) *The Arts Today*, p. 39. Grigson's essay is 'How Much Me Now Your Acrobatics Amaze' in his *The Harp of Aeolus*, pp. 151–60.

other's orthodoxy and, 'Handy-dandy, which is the justice, which is the thief?'

While the convergence of poetry and politics gave a sense of direction it did not, then, produce conformity. The poetry of Day Lewis, Spender and Auden benefited both from their attempts to conciliate the ethical and aesthetic dissensions which communism provoked and the assertive, proselytising enthusiasm it generated. In some ways the most interesting verse, as an historical specimen, was in the categorically propagandist poems. Day Lewis, Spender and Auden all wrote a number of poems of this kind, in which emotional fervour eliminated any intellectual misgivings. One might compile a sizeable anthology of these 'occasional' pieces by many different poets, where Party zeal well outruns aesthetic decorum. Such poems were, indeed, much more the normal expression of anyone with poetic pretensions and left-wing sympathies than poems of doubt or the divided mind, a remarkable tribute to the hold which communism established over the intellectuals.

The record of left-wing intellectuals in the thirties is now quite completely documented.[1] The thoroughpaced true believers among them kept up with every twist of the Party line and swallowed—or helped concoct—every doctoring of Soviet enormities by the Party theoreticians. They took on a variety of parts: some officially in the Stalinist oligarchy, consolidated in England in the twenties, which transmitted Soviet policy to the CPGB; some openly displaying their Party membership to be touted around as bait for highbrows; some 'crypto-communists' instructed to keep their membership secret; some 'fellow-travellers', not Party members but communists in all but name. The authority of the law, of science, of the arts could be advertised in support of whatever extravagances Stalin might devise. The writers and poets did not, generally, belong to the inner ruling coterie. Some, however, occupied influential positions in communist circles: Claud Cockburn ('Frank Pitcairn' of the *Daily Worker*); Edgell Rickword (of an older generation, having served in the First World War), an adviser to the publishing firm of Lawrence and

---

1. In Henry Pelling: *The British Communist Party: A Historical Profile* and Neal Wood: *Communism and the British Intellectuals*, from both of which the following account takes its information.

Wishart and with Montagu Slater a member of the International Association for the Defence of Culture. The poets were rather among the dupes, the self-deceived, than the systematic manipulators of fact. Their propaganda value was none the less for that.

Even poems which were not explicitly communist were assumed to be condemning the capitalist system and heralding its communist successor. All they need do was to speak at all of revolution, even of new life, of future perfection, struggle, war, defiance; or draw attention to idle factories, slums, tumbledown farms. They absorbed this particular colour from their readers' prejudices, shared by the poets though not necessarily made evident in a particular poem. *Left Review* considered the First Chorus of *The Dog Beneath the Skin* proper to its pages, though the poem's only conceivable left-wing element is its brief characterisation of rather a dilapidated countryside. This might attest *Left Review's* broadmindedness, but its sponsorship makes that unlikely. It appeared under the auspices of the British Section of the International Union of Revolutionary Writers, a communist-controlled body with its Headquarters in Moscow. No doubt *Left Review* published the poem in the perfectly justified expectation that its readers would take it as marxist protest; and with this, at the time, its author would hardly have quarrelled. What is a little strange is the very slender internal evidence for the attribution. That it should have been so read is not, however, surprising at a time when Michael Roberts admired 'Marina' because its symbols ('the awakened, lips parted, the hope, the new ships') were so neutral that they might prompt a communist inference, remote though that was from T. S. Eliot's intention. The same suppositions would have been at work, with more reason, to advise the readers of Ruthven Todd's 'It Was Easier' not just that the scene it depicts is Civil War Spain; that as well, the boy killed by a bullet is a Loyalist, the 'black planes' Fascist, and the 'gun aimed at me' at the end of the poem the menace of the dictators— German and Italian, not Russian.

There were innumerable poems of this sort. Their interpretation depended upon an agreed but unstated attitude to objects and events. Many of them are accomplished enough to give pleasure still. At their best they accurately fix a scene, a mood in which personal tensions found public symbols, releasing individual lyrical statements from a body of shared attitudes. In Rex Warner's 'Sonnet', 'The brightness, the peculiar splendour', the perceptive vision which observes beauty of form in random objects—'sun on bark, or an old piece of tin/ are always in the mind like points for lighting'—is a defence against the alert guardians 'of the dying order'. The poem is kept alive by its precision of sensuous detail and the association of this with a general moral commitment (not a particular political attitude) to a world whose fluctuating variety demands a corresponding flexibility of mind. Vernon Watkins's 'The Collier' implicitly arraigns this 'dying order' in the autobiographical history of a dead miner. In 'This Excellent Machine' John Lehmann takes the instruments of modern technology as a symbol of the world of nation states—'some fool will press the button'—and wonders why so 'few are asking Why not scrap it?' They are all poems of a revolutionary philosophy which could often as well be fascist as communist. Michael Roberts's 'In Our Time' calls for a 'leader' who will satisfy 'People asking for a home, a plot of earth'; and W. H. Auden now sees *The Orators* as the work of someone 'who might well, in a year or two, become a Nazi'. The immediate and limited political relevance ascribed to these poems was a passing aspect of the period. Almost as spontaneously as hygroscopic substances absorb moisture from the air, poets and poetry readers were absorbing marxist assumptions.

Other poems made these assumptions more explicit. This is not to say that they illustrate every nice refinement of official policy, such as the novel conciliatory doctrines, established by the mid-thirties, of 'collective security' and 'the United Front', which exempted the Party from its earlier obligation to somewhat promiscuous abuse of 'pacifists', 'warmongers' and social democrats. It was not the policy dickerings but the broad abstract principles, the millenial phantasies, of communism, that animated the poems. In John Lehmann's 'What shall be the signal for departure?', a boy leaves a railway station, his undecided fate resumed in lines of considerable beauty:

> *whether to drift*
> *Down swollen waters, to be drowned in fact*
> *Washed out one evening in the April floods,*

> *Or after the firing through the streets be killed*
> *In a last stampede, or fortunate reserved*
> *To cheer the morning generations dreamed.*

In the pre-millennial armageddon which the poem envisages, heroic strikers and the victims of hunger make up the army of good. A. S. J. Tessimond's 'Steel April' comprehensively attributes to capitalism the sufferings of colonised races, workers and artists:

> *pearl-divers diving their lungs out; tin workers*
> *breathing in tin . . .*
> *Yeats grown bitter; Baudelaire with syphilis;*
> *Van Gogh mad.*

The poems contributed by Richard Goodman to *New Country* eulogise communist solidarity, quickening action and the inevitable final solution of history.

Rex Warner's 'Hymn' is a call to 'lovers of life, to workers' to rally round the symbols of the hammer and sickle. With a good deal of prep-school abuse—'You there, who are so patriotic, you liar, you beast.'—and incendiary prediction—'No broker is left alive'—it transfers to the programme of the militant left the animation and gusto of the scenes in Warner's more typical nature poems.[1] 'Mallard', 'Lapwing', 'Longtailed Tit', 'Curlew at Sunset', 'Chough' all discover a nature full of jubilant noise and movement. The birds 'bucket through the sky', 'squawking', 'clipping the misty air', 'fingering the blowy air', 'swing and hustle in the bunchy trees'; leaves are 'spinning, dipping, slipping'; a wind 'whistling a wintry air'. The settings glow with primary colours, blue, red, amber as in 'Curlew at Sunset'. Into this turbulence and brightness some of the poems insinuate, discreetly enough, a 'political' object lesson. 'Spring Song' urges the observer to see the invigorating, cleansing forces of nature, not its scummy backwaters. 'Light and Air' pleads for the refreshment of a stuffy world,

> *that we may make way for ruin and rebuild*
> *houses to welcome air, ready for the light of spring.*

---

1. Rex Warner: *Poems and Contradictions*, from which the quotations from his poetry are taken.

The 'Egyptian Kites' are the

> *wheeling symbol of an old world*
> *in the reeling blue serene, looking for something*
>   *dead.*

The poet's intuitive response is to certain qualities in nature; the period encouraged an identification of these qualities with the liberation promised by communism.

Charles Madge's 'Letter to the Intelligentsia' resembles 'Hymn'. It is an account of conversion to communism by intellectual persuasion and the impact of social wrongs; and an artless summons to others to join the poet:

> *. . . If anyone will come along to-night*
> *To the local with me, honestly he'll know I'm right.*

By the early nineteen-forties the intriguingly exotic (and in English society misleading) 'local' would have been inaccurate. The CPGB had then set out to 'naturalise' Party terminology. The 'Politburo' had become the Political Committee, factory 'cells' had become groups and 'locals' branches. But Charles Madge's poems[1] do not normally deal in such practical detail. Indeed, they do not normally distract the reader with an easily discernible prose sense and would be unlikely to find much of an audience at any local.

In 'On Awakening' the title explains the capricious abruptions of scene and the word sequences determined by sound associations, not meaning. 'On One Condition' seems to imagine another possible universe in which 'an open way', 'A door half open to surprise', 'writing in the road', might if recognised have secured the passage from one world to another, unifying the two in a new creation: 'If it had been.' 'Bourgeois News' is typical of a number of prose fables. It reports, flatly, a world ravaged by natural disasters, interpolating accounts of bizarre public and commercial enterprises. After a brief description of an attempt to salvage a wreck, it ends quite at random 'when three quarters of those present made for the door'. This intellectual slapstick was no doubt a diversion for a young poet wanting to shock orthodox expectations with a little futuristic tomfoolery.

1. Charles Madge: *The Disappearing Castle*, from which the quotations from his poetry are taken.

The background of the poems, never localised, is bare rocks and stones, deserts, cold spaces, toppling planets, dying civilisations. The 'statements', riddling in themselves, follow an enigmatic logic; the images read like arbitrary conjunctions of abstract and physical, portending but not clarifying some profound significance. In 'Solar Creation' the sun 'Is the director of all human love' and 'we are the commotion born of love', moving through 'dimensional earth'. By the riverside, creation endlessly continues,

> *And over all, like death, or sloping hill,*
> *Is nature, which is larger and more still.*

Individually the poems are teasing, suggesting a meaning never quite articulated. Collectively, the surrealist techniques express a disintegrating *bourgeois*-capitalist world and sensibility. It is a poetry of flux, confusion, its apprehensions dislocated like (or consciously to reflect) a foundering social system.

One sequence, like most of the poems in formally strict quatrains, has perhaps a specific basis in marxist thought. 'Delusions' I–VIII ('Landscapes' I–IV intervene between IV and V) makes an interesting attempt at a poetic statement of the communist analysis of modern history: the initial development and triumphs of capitalism, its phase of waning energies and final confrontation with the working class, and the emergence of the proletarian state. 'Delusions' I remarks the consolations of sex and drink which assure the *bourgeois* that his insubstantial world is inviolable. The second, in images of a syren island and the myth of Tantalus, expresses the now illusory prospect that *bourgeois* civilisation, 'Driven along by life's impulsive tide', can achieve any fresh advance in art or science. But the *bourgeois* still deceive themselves that the 'paradisal image' is realisable—

> *Till, one fine day, still hoping against hope*
> *In spite of all this once to be exempt*
> *From nature's warrant and the hangman's rope,*
> *The bourgeois perishes in his attempt.*

The third moves to the final phase, the proletarian revolution. In this poem 'the great unruly crowd' is taking 'the bourgeois palaces by storm' until 'some little Lenin of the mob' invokes

'The bayonet of proletarian law' and disciplines the pillagers. In time the capitalist luxuries will become

> *Symbols of love, relating then no more*
> *To the exploited, suffering, human mass,*
> *Incentive to no vast imperial war*
> *But innocent and valueless as glass.*

The allegory of the remaining 'Delusions' is less obviously marxist. Without drawing at all on marxist terminology these poems create a succession of brief fables embodying the frustrations of the second phase of *bourgeois* society. In IV the oases of a desert scene lure on travellers who cannot interpret the hieroglyphs explaining 'The secret of the desert'. 'Delusions' V concerns exile from a lost paradise whose 'broken relics' have lost their meaning:

> *A panting savage hurries to the woods,*
> *And in ecstatic ruin dumbly stands*
> *Glad to behold the murder of his gods.*

Number VI similarly, but through a different parable, warns a pilgrim against the bewitchment of an enchanted fastness in a woodland clearing. It is a projection of his own deluded ambitions. He

> *strains his eyes*
> *On to the polar image of his heart.*

A feudal castle, in 'Delusions' VII, represents the withdrawn soul of the modern world, isolated in the dead ends of traditional philosophy:

> *Abstract Will,*
> *Brennpunkt, inverted Sex, or racial dream,*
> *The old collective phantom lingering still*
> *To fascinate, to murder and to seem.*

The anti-climax of 'to seem' is intentional. The first, dynamic phase of capitalism appears throughout the poems only as half-forgotten, misunderstood or distorted impulses of a once vital energy.

These accounts certainly oversimplify and probably in detail misinterpret the poems. One wonders, for instance, what 'Delusions' VI intends by:

> *A retina matured with other skies*
> *Receives the impressions that the woods impart.*

Is this an insight into truth (and if so whence derived?) which may safeguard the pilgrim? Is it like the 'broken relics from the past of man' in number V which, presumably for an elect only, 'Exert their splendid force against the laws?' But there is no need to worry after detail. Many of these poems do successfully intimate, in a language surely consciously recondite, their cryptic drama of the creative flux of time. Only the laws of the historical dialectic can discipline it, perhaps as the poems impose their neat formal rigour on their visions of a crumbling world.

II

Though not rigidly set apart from one another, distinct categories of 'communist' poetry are recognisable: poems whose marxist sympathies, though not explicitly stated, were to be inferred; designedly 'popular' poems in which familiar communist symbols and vocabulary made their political allegiance specific; and poems that created an esoteric personal iconography for marxist thought. Within the two latter categories two men of very different backgrounds, John Cornford and Christopher Caudwell, wrote poems of considerable literary as well as historical interest, Caudwell particularly.

John Cornford was born on 27 December 1915. His family was of a distinctively English social class: upper middle class, liberal, intellectual, well-to-do. His mother Frances Cornford, the poet, was a grand-daughter of Charles Darwin. Francis Cornford, his father, was a notable classical scholar, a Fellow of Trinity College, Cambridge and Laurence Professor of Ancient Philosophy. In 1929 John went to Stowe, where he began to interest himself in and to write poetry. He thought little of his mother's poems and his letters home criticise them ruthlessly. He was equally severe with his own efforts to arrive at what he called a 'live' and 'individual use of language', though W. H. Auden commented favourably on the promise of a poem sent to him by John's

English master. By 1932 he had abandoned poetry for politics. A seemingly instinctive leaning to socialism—the heir to his family's liberalism—led him to study *Das Kapital* and *The Communist Manifesto*. Like so many of his contemporaries he saw in the society around him a wasting sickness which validated the marxist analysis.

When he left Stowe in 1933 he spent a few months at the London School of Economics before taking up his scholarship at Trinity College, Cambridge. In London he joined the Young Communist League, took an energetic part in left-wing student affairs and began to live with a Welsh girl, also a communist, whom his biographers call Ray.[1] Around the same time he broke off an intense emotional relationship with his cousin Elisabeth. Of this he wrote, with some self-conscious dramatisation, 'I am very sorry in one way, though I am always glad of any break with the past that reflects my own position from a new angle. If one's ready to kill and be killed for the revolution, this kind of break doesn't make too much difference.' The 'Sad Poem' which he wrote at Cambridge may originate in this rupture, though it is closer in time to his separation from Ray, in his second year at Cambridge and after the birth of their child, when he fell in love with Margot Heinemann. His family accepted all these excursions with resigned tolerance.

At University Cornford pursued his political activities with enormous vigour. He brought the undergraduate communist group to flourishing life, played a major part in Armistice Day demonstrations, was secretary and eventually vice-president of the Federation of Student Societies and contributed polemical essays on art and politics to *The Student Vanguard* and *Cambridge Left*. The former carried his controversy with Julian Bell, who took issue with Cornford's thesis that contemporary writing should be judged by its contribution to the class struggle. As in his argument with C. Day Lewis, Julian Bell's clearly valid point was that the intellectual communists were 'simply writing romantic subjective poetry about their revolutionary feelings'. Their work

1. Peter Stansky and William Abrahams: *Journey to the Frontier Julian Bell and John Cornford: their lives and the 1930s*. The brief account of Cornford's life given here is indebted to this fascinating biography for its facts. I am similarly indebted to the poet's brother, Christopher Cornford.

established no communication with the working class and would foment no revolutions. Cornford could find few English poems to cite in refutal of this viewpoint. But he remained persuaded that such poetry could be written, and in his own writing attempted it. He was also putting his theories into practice outside as well as within the university. He picketed, agitated in support of a bus strike, helped the Cambridge Labour Party candidate in the 1935 election, and in 1936 was arrested in Birmingham for handing out Trade Union recruitment pamphlets. Academically, his career was outstanding. After a starred First in Part II of the History Tripos he was awarded the Earl of Derby Research Scholarship. All these remarkable abilities he unquestioningly dedicated to the Communist Party, which he joined in 1935.

There is some arrogance, egotism, smugness in the writings which explain his loyalties; perhaps to some extent also in his personal relationships. But he redeemed this by toughly realistic self-appraisal and the idealism which made him put theory to the test of rough and tumble political action. His friends recall his gaiety and vitality, his exuberant sociability, a facet of his nature quite absent from the rather humourless essays. His brother, Christopher, remembers him as essentially a gentle and compassionate man, physically a little timid, his luminous good nature irresistible. Those who were close to him loved him. With the outbreak of the Spanish Civil War he demonstrated the earnestness of his public commitment by immediately joining the Loyalist forces.

Officially accredited to the *News Chronicle* as a correspondent, Cornford joined the P.O.U.M. militia around 11 August 1936. It was a strange and apparently random choice. The P.O.U.M. was a Trotskyite group frowned at by the Party, which in time set about its destruction. But in the heady days of 1936 these internal disputes had not yet hardened into policy. Sent to the Saragossa front Cornford took part in the capture of Perdiguera and the attack on Huesca and was wounded. He wrote 'Full Moon at Tierz' on the eve of battle and 'Letter from Aragon' probably just before going on a brief leave to England, where he criticised both the ideology and the military ineptitude of P.O.U.M. After about three weeks he returned to Spain on 5 October *via* Paris. The *Comité d'Entr'Aide au Peuple Espagnol* assigned him and the group of volunteers he had assembled to the International

Brigade. He was in the heavy fighting in and around Madrid which frustrated the Nationalist attack on the city. In September the British section was sent to the Cordoba front to support a campaign designed to relieve pressure on Madrid. In an attack on the village of Lopera on 27/28 December Cornford was killed. His body was never found; how he died is uncertain. The reports of his fellow soldiers leave no doubt of his endurance, his courage and his rapidly acquired skill as a soldier.

In the Loyalist army of Spain multi-national recruits, inadequate training and obsolete equipment aggravated the frustrations inseparable from army life. Promised equipment never arrived. The half-trained instructed novices. Billets were mostly squalid and the winter was bitterly cold. Cornford's letters do not blink these facts. But beyond the physical distresses, Spain for Cornford was communism in action. The proletarian unity of Barcelona during his first visit inspired him. As Orwell also felt, this was true revolution, not just war. He took strength too from the mixed fear and exhilaration of close combat, given meaning for him by its revolutionary purpose. The ironies of all this need no underlining now. The period's idealisms, blindly or cynically fostered, shaped his life and appointed the form of his death. His poetry remains as his own account of what gave meaning to the squandered life.

Cornford's poetry is inspired, partly, by embracing as a virtue the old-fashioned *bourgeois* association of communism with the bogey of 'free love'. As part of its liberating mission, communism would ease sex from its *bourgeois* repressions. In a number of poems, Cornford takes from his own experience of love metaphors which link the redemptive power of communism with the healthy enjoyment of normal sex, fascist destructiveness with perversion and psychopathic lusts. Generally, his purpose was to connect this personal content with communist 'orthodoxy, to express in poetry the unity of thought and action, to translate necessity into terms of the poetic imagination'.[1] 'Necessity' here is the impersonal government of history which ensures the realisation of the marxist prediction; aware of this, the individual will subdue to it the irregular impulses of self. In 'All this half-felt

1. Stephen Spender and John Lehmann (eds.): *Poems for Spain*, Introduction p. 12.

sorrow' a rocky coast—'my purpose, heavy as rock'—repels 'the vague sea' which 'wanders in the blind, cold, useless dark'. The land/sea antithesis appears to carry a traditional significance. The land is order, stability, the sea confusion and flux; and here the outcome of their dialectic is to subdue the waters—the seemingly directionless turmoil of events—to land—the individual vision whose prospect reveals the hidden design. The poet has thus a more than subjective claim to assert, 'I am the answer'. The development of the metaphor does not bear very close inspection and may conceal a simpler and more personal origin—the parting of lovers—not wholly compatible with the wider conflict it has been extended to represent. The poem ends,

> *How much must we hurt each other before you let*
> > *yourself know*
> *What my strength and your misfortune decided long ago?*

'Sad Poem' declares this origin and makes similar use of it. The first three verses are a reluctant leave-taking of the loved one after an affair whose responses have begun to cool. The recognition of past delights and their present atrophy marks out the necessary moment of departure, 'cruel as the surgeon's knife', but 'better than the ingrown canker'. The mood is resigned, quite successfully caught in the laconic coda:

> *No words to say, no tears to weep.*
> *Don't think any more, dear, rest your dark head*
> > *on my shoulder,*
> *And try to sleep, now, try to sleep.*

Following this in the Cornford memorial volume[1] nine verses turn abruptly to the theme of social revolution, a 'break for good with the old way of living', the transition inexplicitly proposed in the second verse with the poet's feeling of 'new life fighting in me to get at the air'. The 'you' which in the first three verses is the girl has become an audience of the hostile or unconverted, interpolating its objections, and towards the end changes yet again to a

1. Pat Sloan (ed.): *John Cornford: A Memoir.* 'Poems Written at Cambridge' appear in pp. 170-9, from which the quotations are taken.

supporter. These verses envision scenes of riot and sabotage bursting out 'at the closed works, or fallen bridge':

> The sky is darkening with great clouds,
> And from the cold north the sullen crowds'
> Songs startle the streets of the derelict town.

The 'hammer', the 'sickle' sharpened 'to a cutting edge', 'the light of our five-point star' nerve the masses to endure the struggle and rally 'Students and Workers' to the 'RED FRONT!'

Despite the poem's denial of romanticism—

> Not the dreamed-of battle on the windy plain,
> But light slitting the eyelids in the cold dawn—

there is a disproportion between the pledge to 'Throw pepper in the eyes of the policeman's horses' and the expectation, 'the crazy structure of the old world's reeling'. The poem blows up the reality of hunger marches, street scuffles, baton charges into the final Homeric engagement. It comes alive in its brief glimpses of fact—the mass protests in the north, the dawn vigil—where language and rhythms lock mood and scene together. In a sense its predictions came true, but by way of the unglamorous post-was legislation which reconstructed English society.

The mythopoeic fancy is also at work in 'As Our Might Lessens' (title and epigraph derived from Ode V of Auden's *The Orators*), on a more tenable basis. Its background is the genuinely nightmare Europe of fascist 'interrogation' and torture—'camphor and pincers fouled urine and blood', girls 'raped by madmen', 'our men, castrated'. The viewpoint tracks into history for analogues of the modern decadence:

> For those whose tortured, torturing flesh
> Stirred at the body under the lash,
> The painted boy in the praetorian's bed;

and withdraws from the accumulation of grisly detail to give a panorama of a new dark age:

> Black over Europe falls the night,
> The darkness of our long retreat,
> And winter closes with a silent grip.

The release of these psychotic energies underlines the primacy of action over abstract thought unrealised in deeds:

> *Action intervenes, revealing*
> *New ways of love, new ways of feeling.*

'Love's wanton buttocks' and 'A naked girl, the future at our side' symbolise the counterforce of the communist ideal. *Bourgeois* philosophy and art—'poets conjuring lotus words'—are ineffectual evasions. Only total commitment to the life-directed acts of love, 'Stronger than the force by which its life was crushed' and stored in the proletarian masses, can survive.

It is an ambitious poem, handling its themes and transitions resourcefully. Cornford here disciplines his feelings and ideas more strictly than in most of his longer poems and largely subdues his stridency. The four parts have a logic of ideas: the atavistic brutality of the 'carrion men'; the counterworking ideal of love in action; the exhortation to collaborate in strength; the future reward. And they have intense unity of passion. The diction captures the strain and pressure of mental and physical struggle; the Audenesque *sententiae*—'Not by any introspection/Can we regain the name of action'—generalize forcefully upon the bleak detail of the poem's modernised Norse saga world; the stanza form and rhythms are moulded to the feeling, as in the firmly conclusive ending:

> *And love brings comfort to the bed,*
> *Of the outcast disinherited,*
> *Warming the frozen limbs till zero-hour.*

In this poem Cornford found adequate symbols for the violence of his personal identification with marxism.

Two other poems written at Cambridge, 'Keep Culture out of Cambridge' and 'Sergei Mironovitch Kirov' are separate treatments of two themes that have a place in 'As Our Might Lessens'. The first castigates what it sees as the attitudinisings of *bourgeois* art—'Webster's skull and Eliot's pen', 'The donkeys shitting on Dali's food'—and proclaims, 'All we've brought are our party cards/Which are no bloody good for your bloody charades'. Cornford's knack of phrasing is briefly evident—'The important words that come between/The unhappy eye and the difficult scene'—but the poem comes through as a piece of undergraduate bravado. Kirov, assassinated in Leningrad in 1934, is one of the activists whose fortitude is celebrated in 'As Our Might Lessens'. Built round Cornford's favourite images of death, wounds and blood, and the vocabulary of strain and effort, it presents Kirov as one of the saints of communist hagiography, destined to 'throw a longer shadow as time recedes'.

Though Cornford's Spanish War poems do not greatly extend his strictly poetic achievement, they are memorable as human documents. They read as if the presence of death and disaster had urgently demanded this outletting. The conditions in which he wrote them, tedium and active physical danger alternating, gave no opportunity of constructive revision. 'Full Moon at Tierz: Before the Storming of Huesca' is an agonised meditation on his own adequacy to the threat of violent death, the self-questioning forced under control by the unpersuasive sloganising at the end:

> Raise the red flag triumphantly
> For Communism and for liberty.

'Letter from Aragon' is loosely versified reportage of the horrors of death in battle. These were the earliest days of the war, and Cornford gives to an Anarchist the poem's closing message to 'the workers of England'. One wonders what would have been his reaction to the later Stalinist campaign of vilification against Trotskyists, Anarchists and other maverick groups, when internal political rivalries took precedence over the conduct of the war.

Some passages in both poems stick in the mind. 'Full Moon at Tierz' evokes movingly the shock of displacement from the familiar supports of home, and the complex European integrity which binds together the Spanish War, the concentration camps of Germany and the England of idle industries:

> Now the same night falls over Germany
> And the impartial beauty of the stars
> Lights from the unfeeling sky
> Oranienburg and freedom's crooked scars.
> We can do nothing to ease that pain
> But prove the agony was not in vain.

> *England is silent under the same moon,*
> *From the Clydesdale to the gutted pits of Wales.*
> *The innocent mask conceals that soon*
> *Here, too, our freedom's swaying in the scales.*

But neither these war poems nor 'Culture' and 'Kirov' have the finished quality of 'Unaware', printed in *The Listener* in 1934 over the pseudonym Dai Barton.

'Unaware' is an intriguingly cryptic statement of crisis precariously overcome by strength of nerve and muscle, 'climbing granite wall' or 'Homing at evening tired after sailing'. The image of the evening return from the sea to the threat of storm is immaculately visualised:

> *Beyond boats' foamwide wake*
> *Eyes unsurprised*
> *See over dunes first sign of rains*
> *And skyline blacken.*

But the last stanza reverses the expected conclusion of triumph or achievement. The effort of will is misdirected. The strivers have set themselves to feats of survival that can merely defer ultimate disaster:

> *And compromised with fate*
> *They'll hear in fear*
> *The clock's strict time tick out their doom*
> *Who had fallen better.*

Though the reader can infer one, the poem draws no political moral. Its monosyllabic periods, concrete details and rhythms delicately appropriated to the various actions are physical emblems. They render Cornford's strangely compounded universe of deterministic laws and stoic individual dedication, fittingly set in a reminiscence of the austere terrains of Anglo-Saxon epic. No doubt this came partly from Auden, but it is much more than a cultivated literary response. The Norse-saga world appealed to the same imaginative depths in him as the sad cadences of Sibelius, whose music he loved.

Cornford's handful of poems is a side-product of his political activism. His personal tensions and an occasional submissively elegiac note modify the over-confident propagandist intent.

Private experiences supply symbols for his vision of communism as a universal social and individual liberation; the reiterated images of struggle mitigate the insistence on marxist historiography. Perhaps in his Spanish experience he sensed a confirmation of the Romantic faith that defeat might bear as strong a witness to the human spirit as victory. Though not under total control, the poems establish a world of progress desperately maintained by clutching and grappling to avert the threatened fall. Cornford was genuinely committed to his revolutionary philosophy. His poetry is a fascinating effort to give his commitment aesthetic form.

III

Christopher St John Sprigg was born in London on 20 October 1907, the second son of a family with a tradition in professional journalism. It was not active in politics, impartially content with the alternatives of nineteenth-century liberalism and conservatism. Its interests were literary and artistic: Christopher's mother, Jessie Mary Caudwell, from whom he took his pen name, was a talented professional artist and miniaturist. She died in 1916 when she was forty-four. His father, Stanhope William Sprigg, born in Dublin in 1866, was the eldest son of Captain Stanhope Sprigg, who edited the *Nottingham Guardian* and later *Berrows Worcester Journal*. Educated at King's School, Worcester, he went on to edit papers in Sheffield, Nottingham and Southampton. In London he founded and edited Ward, Lock and Co.'s *Windsor Magazine* and later edited *Cassell's Magazine*. At the turn of the century he was for a time literary editor of the *Daily Express* and then represented the old morning *Standard* in New York. During the Great War he was Assistant Director of the American Section of the Ministry of Food and in 1918 became advisory editor to C. Arthur Pearson Ltd. He subsequently founded his own literary agency, wrote a number of novels and several books about the war, including a biography of William Morris Hughes, the wartime Prime Minister of Australia. He died in 1932.

For Christopher's family, the arts as well as being a private pleasure had, so to speak, a technical interest. The business of journalism and editing kept them closer to general society than the coterie world of the intellectuals. Ideological fashions blow strongest in the rarefied Oxbridge air. John Cornford's communism was the more predictable, Christopher Caudwell's perhaps fundamentally the more understandable. He was born into, in a sense, a nomad tradition, ready to pursue unfamiliar tracks: a family with a wide circle of friends gathered from many places; a profession familiar with the medium of words serving a variety of intellectual purposes. He inherited and extended this tradition, and not only in politics; also, for example, into science and technology, all the more remarkably because he was in everything his own instructor.

After his childhood at East Hendred in the Berkshire Downs the pattern of his early years resembled that of his father's. He went to Ealing Priory School (now St Benet's), a Roman Catholic college, where his interest in poetry and science both soon became evident. At this stage of his career he intrigued his school-fellows, though he did not always please them, by his capacity to grasp and argue in support of any belief, whatever might be his private opinion. In 1922 he joined the *Yorkshire Observer*, of which his father was literary editor, training as a reporter and also reviewing novels. After a couple of years he went to London to take up the editorship of *British Malaya*, and in 1926 joined his elder brother in founding a specialist aeronautical publishing company. He edited one of its technical journals and outside his full-time work for the firm began his astonishing proliferation of activities.[1] He studied mechanical engineering, aerodynamics and physics. His comprehensive understanding of theoretical concepts is attested by *The Crisis in Physics*, written in 1936 and consistently esteemed by academic physicists. He experimented as well in the practical applications of science; his design for an infinitely variable motor-car gear (a form of automatic transmission), aroused great interest, notably from Ricardo, when published in the *Automobile Engineer*. At the same time he was writing verse, fascinated by poetic techniques and modestly reticent, as he was with all his enterprises, about his accomplishment. In his lifetime he approved the publication of only one poem, which appeared in *The Dial* in 1927.

From about 1928 Christopher Caudwell and C. St John Sprigg began to establish themselves in free-lance writing. He wrote

1. Apart from the writings mentioned here he also wrote a number of short stories and two plays.

popular books on aviation, and between 1933 and (posthumously) 1937 had eight detective novels published, both fact and fiction under his own name. For his serious work he used his pseudonym because, by his own self-deprecating account, he wanted to protect his reputation as a writer of thrillers. These he could write in any circumstances, quite undisturbed by a background of wireless and conversation in his brother's home, where he lived happily as a bachelor both before and after his brother's marriage.

The titles of his thrillers are very much in the convention: *Fatality in Fleet Street* (1933); *The Perfect Alibi* (1934); *Crime in Kensington* (1933); *The Corpse with the Sunburnt Face* (1935); *Death of a Queen* (1935); *The Six Queer Things* (1937); *Death of an Airman* (1934). Though he wrote them tongue in cheek, he gave them carefully professional treatment. The last named typifies his rapid absorption of accurate background detail; so does *The Corpse*, part of which is set in an imaginary West African Kingdom whose customs he based on accounts of Ashanti culture. His detective, Charles Venables, rarely encounters the world of politics, remote from the 'classic' detective story which turns upon manipulating timetables and devious lethal mechanisms. *Fatality in Fleet Street*, however, opens with a riot reported from the Brezka oilwells 'in an obscure Soviet'. A mob has sacked the installations and murdered British staff. Lord Carpenter, governing director of *The Affiliated Publications* ('the thinkers of England's thoughts') plans, against the Prime Minister's wishes, to exploit the incident as a *casus belli* with the Soviet Union; and is murdered. But the politics is secondary to the required ingenuities of detection.

This light fiction was journeywork, lightly regarded, executed competently and at speed, distinct from Caudwell's search to apply marxist principles to all the pursuits of human intelligence. In fiction he moved from the thriller, whose point is contrived mystification, to his one straight novel (under his pseudonym), *This My Hand* (1936). Its subject is the psychology of the criminal, a normal, conventional person who commits murder. It is undoubtedly in part social commentary, and to that extent has political implications. The novel ends as the hangman leaves the prison after the execution: 'It looked almost as if there had been a substitution and the real murderer was escaping.' The novel, however, is not enacting an analysis of collective social guilt; its centre is the queer outlands of the individual consciousness, a fictional psychopathology of everyday life. Caudwell was circumspect about what he allowed to be published. This novel, though imperfect, promised fuller achievement. It has narrative shape; the bare, concrete prose sets up resonances of meaning; there is a disturbing sense of the fluid depths under the controlled surface 'character'. But it was his poetry that most closely occupied him and there that his marxism found imaginative inlets.

Most of his published poems were written around 1935 in the period, which began in late 1934, when he was reading extensively in marxist literature. He joined the Party late in 1935, having gone to live in the East end of London: again, theory led to practice. He devoted himself to the duties of speaking at street corners, fly-sticking and selling *The Daily Worker*. Though he disliked them, they were more to his taste than either Headquarters officialdom or the Party intellectuals; more at an effective point of struggle. He undertook them, too, because he must do himself what he asked of others. The same reasons sent him to Spain in December 1936.

A member of the International Brigade, he drove one of a convoy of lorries across France. In Spain he was made a machine-gun instructor before he had finished his own training. His letters[1] which were censored and written in that knowledge, are a mixture of generous-spirited response to intensified political experience and discreet recognition of shortcomings. Barcelona was in the turmoil, so it seemed, of reshaping its society by revolution. Writing from there on 30 December, Caudwell found it 'a wonderfully heartening sight to see the strength and rapid growth of the proletarian organisations in spite of all attempts at disruption. England seems miles and miles and years and years away already.' Army life he thought 'extraordinarily interesting; the International Brigade in its composition is so entirely different to any ordinary army; and I am beginning to understand how it has been able in quite a short time to build up a big reputation and a

1. I am much indebted to the kindness of Mr T. Stanhope Sprigg for the details from his brother's letters and for other information about his life and background. My account also draws upon the biographical sketch written by Paul Beard for the first edition of the poems and now republished in the Lawrence and Wishart edition.

special tradition'. He was in an English battalion, 'commanded by an Englishman who came out with the first English company and showed himself a first-rate commander'. It was no doubt more cohesive than Cornford's heterogeneous P.O.U.M. group, but hardly any more experienced or better equipped than the British section Cornford joined later.

On 24 January he wrote from Albacete where he was in training and anxious to reach the Front: 'but new drafts arrive each day and we *must* go to the Front as a compact, 100 per cent trained batallion. We expect to draw better arms than No. 1 Company which went straight up with old rifles and suffered fairly heavily. I am No. 1 on a machine-gun, or strictly speaking a "fusil mitrailleuse"; quite a handy little weapon but out-of-date and none too reliable.' He goes on to describe his political assignments: 'I thought when I came out here that I should throw off the responsibility of Party member and writer too but, as usual, the Party never sleeps. I'm a group political delegate—strictly speaking, a non-party job—instructor to the Labour Party faction and joint-editor of the Wall newspaper.' Political watchfulness, hasty instruction, suspect weapons. Within a week, finally, a letter reported the completion of 'training' and was anticipating action: 'Things look like being more interesting in two or three days— which means you may not hear from me for some little time.'

In London his brother worked tirelessly to persuade Party leaders to prevent just that. Communist bureaucracy is like any other. They remained obtusely unconvinced that Christopher would, in the narrowest view, be of more use to them alive. At last his brother was able to show advance proofs of *Illusion and Reality* to an influential Party official. Christopher's recall was recommended. He was already dead. He had fallen in battle at the Jarama River on 12 February 1937, one of the greatest losses, as artist and as human being, of the Spanish War. Unconsciously, he had written his own epitaph in one of his translations from Latin. It prefaced the posthumous selection of poems made at his request by Paul Beard, a personal friend:

> *Unhappy men, who roam, on hope deferred*
> *Relying, thinking not of painful death!*
> *Here was Seleucos, great in mind and word,*

> *Who his young prime enjoyed but for a breath.*
> *In world-edge Spain, so far from Lesbian lands*
> *He lies, a stranger on uncharted strands.*

Caudwell's published poems are certainly his best. But the considerable body of manuscript and typescript[1] from which they were selected contains a number of very fine poems. It is an absorbing record of intensively sustained experiment in style and technique. Caudwell seems to have composed fluently, unless he destroyed his earlier drafts. The 'Voyage to Arabia' and the 'Translations' (from the *Greek Anthology* and the *Odes* of Horace), written in two exercise books, have few verbal emendations though extensive stanza erasures. This is true also of the poems in typescript—the great majority. Some, including certain of the published poems, are tentatively assembled as collections, one called *Point of Departure*, another, dated 1926, *Smoke and Diamond*. What generally strikes the reader, though, is not so much an accumulating design as a great variety of subject and manner. 'Sales Pastoral', for instance, is light verse which jargons entertainingly of Spring in the jargon of advertisements. A series of epigrams neatly formulates 'A Tory M.P.', 'A Wicked Man', 'Colonel X'. They have an epigrammatic bite more extensively deployed in Caudwell's only poem on a specific political event, 'Heil Baldwin', written after the Anglo-German Naval Agreement of 1935. It recounts the early history of the Nazi state and characterises its principals:
Hitler—

> *In person meagre and in accent shrill;*
> *The law obeying—now the law's his will;*

Goering—

> *Who had but one idea his life long—*
> *That he was of importance—and that wrong.*

The climax is the Reichstag fire trial, the ignominious failure to break down Dimitroff, the vindictive sentence on Torgler:

> *For in the Nazi state those who to crime*
> *Add an acquittal have the harder time.*

1. Again, I am in debt to Mr Sprigg for allowing me access to these papers.

'Heil Baldwin' is an openly propagandist piece, lively and technically well managed. However, one cannot imagine Caudwell persevering in a style that so exactly appropriates a traditional model.

'Kensington Rime' turns the wit to more esoteric purpose. It is a modern imitation of 'The Ancient Mariner', rather like Auden's ballads but preceding both 'Miss Gee' and 'Victor'. Its protagonist, Miss Miffin, stops the narrator outside his boarding house:

> She lays her skinny hand on mine
> I drop my folded Times
> I cannot move no eye so glares
> Except with nameless crimes.

Miss Miffin tells how she killed a brightly coloured bird in Kensington and wore it in her hat. She goes on a voyage of penance; when she is shipwrecked,

> God in his mercy saw my plight
> And sent a paddle boat.

It takes her to Margate, where Rosie gives her absolution:

> She spoke me words of comfort sooth
> Out of a megaphone
> And backwards would she creep and croon
> In childish tone . . .
>
> I leapt up straight as light as air
> Then knelt down in the dust
> I closed her eyes with banknotes five
> God will provide I trust.

Each day Miss Miffin has to tell her tale to the first young man she meets and recite Rosie's 'childish prayer':

> If to do good were to do good
> Then to do good were meet.

The poem is a surrealistic, sinister-jocose parable of neurotic guilt satisfied by an inane formula of atonement, a mordant burlesque of the Ancient Mariner's Christian morality.

Many of Caudwell's unpublished poems do in fact express a

deep distaste for Christian apologetics. The point of 'The Consolations of Religion' is that it is always man, exercising 'God's ill-advised concession of free-will', who masochistically sets about the impossible task of justifying God's ways to man. In 'The Kingdom of Heaven', with a narrative contrivance rather like Herbert's in 'Redemption', an office block unexpectedly gives access to Paradise. Notices line its walls:

WHITE TIES PLEASE. NO NIGGERS. PLAY THE GAME.
DO NOT SPIT.
THIS WAY TO THE KINGDOM OF HEAVEN.

The narrator asks for God in one of the offices and is told he is out. He continues his search—'The commissionaires/Are civil, and put their harps aside'—until he comes upon the manager 'muttering in his sleep':

> *If they find God the place will have to close.*
> *That is why I tell them God is only Out.*
> *Don't tell the boys God'll never be in.*

The most ambitious of the unpublished poems is a long elegiac sequence on the dead of the Great War. Its title is *The Requiem Nov. 11—1921*. Inside the title page it is called *The Requiem Mass*, from whose parts the individual poems take their names: 'Introibo ad Altare'; 'Confiteor'; 'The Absolution'; 'The Collect'; 'The Epistle'; 'The Tract'; 'The Gospel'; 'Credo'; 'Deus Qui Humanae'; 'Lavabo'; 'The Secret Prayers'; 'Preface'. *The Canon*, a series of five poems which follows, was evidently conceived as part of *The Requiem*. The last four of its poems are named: 'The Consecration'; 'The Communion'; 'Requiescat in Pace'; 'The Last Gospel'. 'The Assignation 1916', a separate poem, could also find a place in the scheme.

The Requiem is not pacifist protest, though its focus is the war's vast squandering of life. Some of its poems are spoken by the living celebrants, some by the dead soldiers they commemorate. From the crosscutting of the two the motives and compulsions of war, declared and unrecognised, take clearer shape. Where 'Introibo' presents the service as a tribute honestly paid in order to 'remember for our sakes/And theirs as well', 'Confiteor' reveals less admirable motives, not admitted, for entertaining images of war: their phantasy-escape from 'the petty cares' of life. The mind visualising scenes of destruction in battle now confesses, 'Whence by so much am I blood-guilty now.' Phantasies culminate in deeds,

> *Therefore a hundred thousand young and bright*
> *Who learned from us a likewise dream of flight*
> *Have looked their last upon the honest light.*

The dead soldiers, asking the living to forget and 'war no more' speak 'The Absolution'. In war the hope of honour through heroic death had sustained them. Now 'The Collect', implying their error but respecting their courage, solicits for them

> *The honour that they thought they won,*
> *The pardon they desired.*

The disaster of the war was so enormous, its suffering watched by an indifferent God ('The Gospel'), that it drives the intellect to seek some meaning or purpose in it: this is the direction of the sequence. Innumerable dead seem to cancel out any 'medicine of belief': a lesson 'clear, and cold, and clipped' from 'an unannotated script'. 'Credo' returns to the soldiers' heroism, admirable even though inspired by the discredited tag, ' "Dulce et decorum est . . ." ' It is

> *The help of man, a bulwark built of flesh,*
> *And justified in wars.*

Despite the disparagement, 'Deus Qui Humanae' (which in the Mass praises man's redemption through Christ), describes the soldiers, without irony, as 'Strong bulwarks of our pastured land'. 'Requiescat in Pace' bids them farewell—'We to our life. They to still sleep.'—and affirms the virtue of heroism. Orwell had roasted the pacifism of the left because it sneered at heroism, which its own cause might stand in need of. 'Requiescat in Pace' has such an occasion in prospect:

> *We (it may be) to greater wars,*
> *To murders done for purer stars*
> *Making more wives and mothers weep.*

Like Auden's now jettisoned 'necessary murder', Caudwell's

'murders done for purer stars' takes heart from an end that would
ennoble the bravery profaned by the Great War. But despite this
conclusion, the sequence hardly reduces to order the perplexities
it often so finely expresses. Its poems stand separately as troubled
commentaries on a disaster that struck deep into Caudwell's
imagination.

Though the Great War may have begun a questioning of
orthodox judgments that led Caudwell to marxism, that can be
only a partial explanation of his politics. The same distress led
others in their own different directions. Caudwell's humani-
tarianism took him along paths we can now only conjecture to the
philosophy that then seemed likeliest to satisfy it, and to satisfy as
well the demands of his intelligence, seeking logic and pattern.
In the published poems as in the unpublished, there is a constant
search for intellectual control of feeling, calling upon a marxism
that in the poetry remains submerged.

Caudwell's poems are wholly unlike those of any poet, whatever his political persuasion, writing in the thirties. He draws here
and there on the concepts of technology, science and psychology,
often the basis of witty glosses on traditional themes. In his short
play, *Orestes*, Apollo and the hero encounter each other in the
Harley Street consulting room of Dr Tape, a psychiatrist; and the
Furies authenticate their office with a catalogue of properly
scientific achievement:

> *We can report remarkable behaviour*
> *Of every sainted race in every age.*
> *We have observed in detail Christ's psychosis*
> *And the neurotic fits of Socrates . . .*
>
> *We have published a monograph on trophallaxis*
> *Exhibiting the human parasite:*
> *Its sexual habits and autophagy,*
> *Its aberrance, self-mutilation, fits.*

In one of the 'Twenty Sonnets of Wm Smith' the speaker lays
claim to inventory 'The sense-receptors love is moulded on'. But
the emblematic pylons, aircraft and other machinery, the drab
townscapes and shuttered factories are absent; and the verbal
setting for the occasional modernisms cultivates an almost archaic

formality of tone and diction. A passage from 'The Art of Dying' seeks into Seneca's tolerance of death:

> Old Seneca has much rehearsed his death
> And finding to expel his quiet breath
> Is no more pain to him than to inspire it,
> Reasons to breathe life out when death require it
> No worse than breathing in life with a cry,
> The harsh experience of our infancy:
> Suspects he was enamoured of the womb
> As now of life (then feared as now the tomb)
> Proposing logically once dead to hate
> As much the prospect of a further state.

The concluding simile, like most of Caudwell's imagery, clarifies an idea, not an impression of the senses:

> So revellers will outwatch the starry skies
> And once recumbent are as loth to rise.

The elided structures and the diction recall the 'polite' colloquialism of Pope, neither the more fashionable thirties vernacular nor its revamped 'Anglo-Saxon'. And though concerned with ideas, the passage is far from agitprop homiletics in either vocabulary or 'notional content'.

Caudwell's poems conduct a complex and individual quizzing of various metaphysical enquiries into life. Caudwell enjoys embedding a meaning in imagined situations ('The Hair', 'Twenty Sonnets of Wm Smith'), semi-historical fictions ('Tierra del Fuego', 'Classic Encounter') and biographical facts ('Donne's Reverie', 'The Stones of Ruskin'). Other poems ('Hymn to Philosophy', 'Essay on Freewill') comment directly upon philosophic theory. Caudwell scrutinises human endeavour in its diverse forms, all aimed at securing some psychological defence against the intimidating distances of historical time. Man acts, because he must, as though he controlled his destiny, though aware that the energies of mind and will conflict with those of the flesh, which limit them; and that all his designs, public and private, are vulnerable to the ironic reversals of history. Personal relationships, especially love, and the efforts of art and philosophy to discover truth, are all, in part, defensive operations against human fallibility and transience. Caudwell's poems bring to mind T. E. Hulme's observation of 'the bitter contrast between what you think you ought to be able to do and what man really can'. But Caudwell displays the contrast more with stoicism than bitterness, often with wit and, noticeably in a number of the unpublished poems, compassion.

Of the published poems, 'Hymn to Philosophy' and 'Essay on Freewill' give most concisely the dryly reflective flavour of his stoicism. 'Hymn to Philosophy' invokes philosophy in its heyday as a Grecian youth combining juvenile grace and strength with wisdom and maturity, solacing human cares. But it is a human creation, its days numbered by newly glimpsed allurements. 'The scientific sportsman' picks off the 'winged Idea down the rainbow sliding'. Preserved like a stuffed bird, it still attracts the poet's interest, though he deplores its simulated life:

> *I see your stuffed breast and boot-button eyes*
> *Preserved in cases for posterity*
> *And lean on my umbrella thoughtfully.*

> *I have caressed your sort, I must confess,*
> *But give me beauty beauty that must end*
> *And rots upon the taxidermist's hands.*

The suggestion of the 'beauty that must end' seems to be that we cannot artificially perpetuate the relevance of superseded forms. Their displacement recognised, they must renew their life in man's imagination, if at all.

'Essay on Freewill' is a chilling digest of the impotence of our deeds—'broken horns of glass/Cast on the cold Atlantic shore'— to preserve what we most prize, our personal being. Abruptly juxtaposed in the second verse, Newton's ascetic dedication and the empty rituals of City men suffer the common oblivion of self. With a man's death, his private identity is lost to knowledge. Two finely conceived metaphors identify the collective fate:

> *Our vain regrets are dinosaurs*
> *Infesting coalseams of the hours*
> *Our hopes as fast as time can spin*
> *Pressed up in calf-bound books like flowers.*

The deadpan final couplet exemplifies the basic human longing:

> *Remember me when I am dead*
> *The last thing that Napoleon said.*

The poem speaks obliquely through its images and examples, not by direct statement. We cannot tell just how Caudwell found place for the strange injunction, after he has characterised the futility of deeds in the first verse—

> *Write your revenge on the white doors*
> *The white huts of the leisured class.*

The *rentier* is as subject as any to the processes which the poem remarks. But so, presumably, would be any successor to him. The poem's intention is not to draw a political moral. Its half-uttered professions leave a strong impression of the pathos of human endeavour.

'The Hair' also has to do with death, but in an entirely different context. It is a love poem, a Donne-like interrogation into the portents of a hair fallen from the mistress's head. A part of her beauty, the hair, perhaps destined to outlast them,

> *. . . is not nearly you. I'd take in lieu*
> *Of you perhaps your letter, promise, heart*
> *(You owe a heart). But I'll reject a part*
> *For not a million parts can make the you*
> *That my desires phantastically pursue.*

It is a reminder of death and the slow decline of beauty to whose relics the poet imagines himself clinging, literally beyond death:

> *They will find*
> *No hairy bracelet round your wristbone tied*
> *For not until all moveables have gone*
> *Shall I give up to death your skeleton;*
> *Not even then, for round your ribs will be*
> *The bare arms of my own anatomy.*

The treatment of this traditional theme gives no hint of Donne's images of a mystical union within the union of the flesh. The two lovers are purely flesh and blood and in those alone their love exists.

The 'Twenty Sonnets of Wm Smith' pursues further the nature of love. All but three follow the orthodox sonnet form, though neither a Petrarchan nor the Shakespearean rhyme scheme. The sequence mocks the assumptions and the conventional diction and properties of romantic love poetry. Wm Smith and his unnamed mistress—no better than she should be ('I lease your bed from many able wights')—prove 'love's bourgeois pleasures' in boarding houses, while the landlady 'Glides through the aspidistran brake'; in a cheap hotel—'The sheets are clean; and now they know us well'; uncomfortably forced 'Through lonely streets to sneak up draughty stairs'. The sonnets have thus a framework of incident, but there is no 'plot' and no final consummation of the affair.

Wm Smith records his lusts and satisfactions, provoked at times, like Shakespeare in 'The expense of spirit', by a love which is merely the physical act—'A matter for that charlatan, the spine'. But with knowing self-confidence he couples any glorifying of love with the claptrap of roses, the nightingale, the moon, 'Insultingly betraying love's hot spell'. Sonnet IX disposes of Philomel:

> *The nightingale! it only needed that—*
> *For this ex-reptile of an old-wives' tale*
> *With her lost only asset maidenhead*
> *To caterwaul into the sweaty night;*

and her window-dressing—

> *Lonely headlands, scraped by whispering clouds*
> *And those great bumpers, filled with heady wine!*

Sonnet XII preludes the arrival at the cheap hotel with a sardonically compounded 'classical' décor:

> *Tritons lift shells, the grapy bubbles pulp*
> *Against the silver blades which, music-smitten,*
> *Woo on the goddess's barge, and she, pearl-sphered,*
> *Leans forward, gold hair on curds bosom dripping*
> *And snuffs the crinkled incense. Doves descend*
> *And nymphs elaborately girt with swags*
> *Draw back the pleated clouds from a blue sea*
> *Where a plump brig pursues a spouting whale.*

'Much skilled in derogation's art', the poet devises new euphemisms for his pleasure. Sonnet XIV presents it, ingeniously, as an analogue of the dialectic:

> *nor indeed are you unskilled*
> *In body's older dialectice*
> *Where thesis and antithesis achieve*
> *By friction a diviner synthesis.*
> *How oft have we disputed! Till the skies*
> *Paling, have bid us cease philosophize.*

Like a number of the other poems, this praises the lady for her skill in the practices of love, their love for its matter-of-fact abandonment of otherworldliness. Sonnet VI is an irreverent dismissal of religious consecration. The lovers obey a set of nursery-rhyme injunctions—'Lift the church and find the altar/Lift the altar; find the stone';

> *We found the occupation childish,*
> *And while the organ, solemn, godlike,*
> *Pealed out of the stained-glass windows*
> *We fornicated to its tune.*
> *Jones, more mystic, with a groan*
> *Bashed his brains out on the stone.*

The last poem goes directly on from the final self-congratulatory lines of No. XIX:

> *We have been honest and song's naked sight*
> *Now promises unpalated delight.*

No. XX begins,

> *In which we shall have earned the rose—the rose*
> *Whose petals crumpled by a thousand sighs*
> *Were virgin and unfingered once God knows.*

It seems to envisage the stale symbols—rose, nightingale, moon—restored to the meaning and freshness they once had, 'two thousand years ago'.

Wm Smith is hardly Caudwell's prolocutor, at any rate not directly. He appears rather as the *homme moyen sensuel*, assuming a hardboiled front but obscurely sensitive to a lost depth of experience debauched by a world of cheapened values; and briefly imagining how 'the time must come' that will repair the corruption. Formally, his poetic cycle modulates to his fallen condition the traditional manner of the lover's complaint: as with its subject, so its form. Sonnet XIX confesses,

> *The body of my song is too corrupt,*
> *Foul with the staleness of great athletes' beds.*

'The Stones of Ruskin' similarly laments the artist's present estate. Its example is the old age of Ruskin, when his congenital inability to focus his thoughts became outright lunacy. Ruskin's intemperate hostility to Michelangelo's voluptuous paintings and his own infatuations over nymphets account for Caudwell's treatment of his fate. The poem imagines him 'Forsaking the decorous slim-waisted Misses/Of a Greek-Oxfordised mythology' and borne to the Land of Women. They fall on him, 'libidinous and strong', and by their caresses drive him mad. Nowadays, 'Such foul enchantments wait for all us bards.' The lucky few die in their youthful frenzy, 'in garrets starved or blue gulfs drowned';

> *Some in dress suits, protective mimicry,*
> *Succeed in imitating business men*
> *And the hawk Furies baffled pass them over;*

others enter an insane private universe of destructive phantasy: pretty much obedient, in fact, to the marxist prognosis for the modern artist, though the poem makes not the slightest directly ideological confession.

Nor do 'Tierra del Fuego' and 'Classic Encounter'. The first describes a Spanish landfall on the bleak southern tip of South America. Seen through the seamen's superstitious eyes, the crossing of the Straits is a journey of signs and portents. Strange fires ('in rank seraphic ranged/An orderly regression of bright eyes') light up 'the hoarse bird-bearing night'; according to the captain, attendant angels 'Ingeminating some creative hymn'; to an arquebusier, the 'touch-flares' of a devil 'Gorged with the larded flesh of heretics'. On shore they find a rabble of cave dwellers:

> *Mere brutes they knelt, revering Christian giants.*
> *A few we spitted on our swords; the rest*

> *Our priests whipped till they owned the Christ; one girl*
> *Ape-faced, but breasted well, our captain took*

Technical superiority and the strength and ruthlessness of superstitious faith easily subdue a weaker group. The incident drama-
tizes an early phase of the aggressive union of Christianity and
capitalism. Any moralising is left to the reader to infer from the
historical cycles of ascendancy and decline. The moral may be that
morality is irrelevant: cultures pursue their own interests to the
extent of the power they command. The clipped syllables of the
last two verses, where the conquerors get down to business, mark
the split from the euphonious phrasing of the captain's edifying
visions, which conclude: 'Look that you keep your hearts and
speeches clean.'

In 'Classic Encounter' the ghosts of Greek soldiers recall to the
poet their 'too-much-memoried end' at Syracuse in 'an older
bungle' than Gallipoli. The verses 'Of our Euripides' persuaded
their captors to return them to Athens but were of no avail against
death when that time came. Neither genuine military survivors
nor honourably fallen, they wander friendless through the after-
world. They leave the poet,

> *and as the rank mists took them in*
> *They chanted of the God to Whom men pray,*
> *Whether He be Compulsion, or All-Fathering,*
> *Or Fate and blind.*

The alternative deities include the figures of classical mythology
to whom the Athenian spokesman refers—Charon, Cerberus,
Rhadamanthos; and the god of 'The sunburnt ghosts of allied
soldiers/killed on the Chersonese.' Whatever God man conceives,
none judges or ordains a rational world. The poem is an intellectu-
ally detached narrative. Its purpose is to animate competing
speculations on human destiny, unarbitrated by the poet.

Death, art, love: these are the main objects of enquiry in
Caudwell's poems. It is by enquiry, a delicate balance of meanings
and possibilities, that his poems attach an attitude, what he called
an 'emotional content' to their 'manifest content', which 'is
symbolic of a certain *piece* of external reality—be it scene, problem,
thought, event'.[1] This is the method of his longest published poem

1. *Illusion and Reality*, p. 124.

'The Art of Dying', frequently revised between 1926 and 1934. It is in heroic couplets whose sentence structures, as in 'The Hair' disrupt the Augustan symmetry of the form. Unlike 'Wm Smith' and 'Classic Encounter' it does not relay its commentary through an interposed narrator. Its 'manifest content' is a set of ideas and feelings about death.

Because it is the inevitable end, death has provoked man to either some variety of fatalistic resignation, like Seneca's, or intimations of immortality. Donne, identified as 'wit's saint', 'to passion vowed/Then God', found in both obsessions a miraculous triumph over death. Others commend death as a release from the burdens of life; or in youth an escape from the enfeeblement of age. Sleep, which images death, nourishes illusions of a super-sensual reality:

> *you have in dreams*
> *Seen a strange blossom which no earth's gross streams*
> *Could diet.*

The romantic emblems of 'Wm Smith' characterise the dream-world:

> *the moon was queen*
> *And told Rapunzel from her tower to lean*
> *And loose her hair into the garden close:*
> *The nightingale would chatter to the rose*
> *Of desperate fables, hopes as old as death*
> *Which, as their age imports, exchange for breath,*
> *Your breath, and gladly given, but sleep fled.*

Death—endless sleep—may perpetuate these phantasies; or finally confound them. A long passage enlarges on the resemblance between death and sleep (natural or induced by opium—'This flower is sacred to death's anchorite'). But only death can bring 'Soul's last eternal equilibrium'. This is the final condition, the end of the individual's journey, the world of the dead, tranquil, static, when the flux of life is put behind. In the poem's beautifully cadenced conclusion the hosts of the dead occupy an eternal stillness, not any extension of life:

> *But do not fear, since millions have passed*
> *This way (which everyone must tread at last)*

> *Without complaint, and like the punctual host*
> *Of heaven gleams each cold and distant ghost*
> *Alone in the vast ether; in our sight*
> *Some trepidations foreign to pure light*
> *May make them shudder, but in truth all are*
> *Content and constant as the Polar Star*
> *There, where the sea from useless labour rests*
> *And hangs unmoving at the heaven's breasts.*

The imagery of these closing lines makes a strangely mystical conclusion to the cool and intricately mounted ironies which inspect the other disputes with the meaning of death. What does the change of tone signify? The exact dating of Caudwell's poems is conjectural. He began 'The Art of Dying' before he turned to politics, but the final version probably belongs to the period of his first interest in marxism, which is in essence as apocalyptic as any religious faith. The vision of a revolutionary transformation of society, not the theory of surplus value, sends people to the barricades. Marxism renounces the prospect of a reward beyond life for a millenium attained in the world of slums and factories. 'The Art of Dying' appears to end with a serene acceptance of this renouncement, given poetic form. 'In life,' Caudwell said in *Illusion and Reality*, the 'piece of external reality is devoid of emotional tone'; in poetry, 'described in those particular words and no others, it suddenly and magically shimmers with affective colouring'.[1]

The 'external reality' of 'The Art of Dying', at some distance behind the poem, is an aspect of marxist theory, or Caudwell's apprehension of and response to it. So it is in most of the published poems. Only one seems to turn to the daily realities of Party life as Caudwell knew it. The central symbol of 'The Coal' is the human energy, 'This red-hot coal we bear between our thighs', wastefully consumed by *bourgeois* society, mean-spirited in its loves and commerce alike. The poet calls for a revitalising of this exhausted vigour:

> *Blow into flame O Holy Ghost*
> *The secret womb by thought made dull*

---

1. *Illusion and Reality*, p. 124.

> *To the toad's guarded brow entrust*
> *The jewelled organ, fruitfulness;*

and declares his own resolve:

> *I choose to spend it on my comrades; choose*
> *To lavish it on ignorant citizens.*
> *I choose to warm with this hard-wrested gem*
> *The conversations of the draughty streets . . .*

> *Let us haul hearty, knee to knee,*
> *And pull the whey-faced ship-wrecked in,*
> *To piece among their nakedness our clothes*
> *And in our bosoms warm their bitterness.*

So the poem professes; and so Caudwell prodigally gave his talents. Perhaps we may not call it wasteful, for he left much behind. What more he might have given the poetry suggests. Its themes are quite traditional: sensual pleasure and its poignant brevity, the progress of man through successively confident epochs. Without wilful striving after novelty, its language refreshes ideas and feelings informed by the excitement of growing perception. Marxism, as it impinged on Caudwell's consciousness, did not obstruct his poetry with idealised comrades, ranting calls to solidarity and action, diatribes against the horrors of capitalism. Gradually a point of view emerges, compatible with marxism but not overtly announced. The poems seem, indeed, the work of a man for whom marxism had become a habit of thought, not a system of ideas to be applied to experience with finicking circumspection.

III

C. Day Lewis: Between Two Worlds

THE forewords to C. Day Lewis's *Country Comets* (1928) and the first edition of *Transitional Poem* (1929) have a charming air of assurance and rather questionable modesty. With the exception of three or four 'outside the very definite unity of the present volume', *Country Comets* includes all ('deserving of preservation') of the poems which Lewis wrote between 1925 and 1928. The poems printed, 'being all direct products of a single conflict whose recurrence I should neither expect nor desire, may compensate as a human document for what they lack in maturity and restraint'. *Transitional Poem* 'is divided into four parts, which essentially represent four phases of personal experience in the pursuit of single-mindedness ... Formally, the parts fall with fair accuracy into the divisions of a theorem in geometry, *i.e.*, general enunciation, particular enunciation, proof, corollaries.' The poems pursue the qualities described in these brief prefaces. Their subjects are personal: the poet's experience of love, the feelings aroused by scenes and situations, speculations on life and man's place and responsibilities in it.

Formally, the aim is to assemble the elements of this subjective world in an integrated structure. The metaphor is to the point. The imagery of the prefaces suggests that to design the poetic sequence the poet employs scientific logic and organisation, a mathematical precision of development. As scientific method controls the objective data of science, so can it the metaphysical and linguistic substance of poetry. And without such control the 'personal experience', the 'human document', is meaningless. The language of the poems, too, acknowledges the intellectual prestige of science. Its 'new metaphysical' style combines figures drawing on the vocabulary and the concepts of modern science with more traditional conceits. From *Transitional Poem*:

(1) *Who would be satisfied his mind   and then life's pistons*
                    is no   Pounding into their secret
     Continent but an archipelago?   cylinder
                              Begin to tickle the most
                                   anchorite ear
                              With hints of mechanisms that
                                             include
                              The man

(2)   *she's   Twin poles energic, they*
     My real Antipodes,   Stand fast and generate
     And our ingrowing loves   This spark
     Shall meet below earth's spine

(3)   *although   It can unstitch*
     You poured Atlantic   The decent hem
     In this one and Pacific   Where space tacks on to time:
     In the other, I know
     They would not overflow.

(4) *Himalayas of the mind   love's terminals*
                              Are fixed in fire and wind.

The effects, if narrow in range, do refresh their themes. The poems have got past the youthful notion that because they are new to oneself one's own quite commonplace experiences will have the same intrinsic fascination for everyone else. Having something to say, Day Lewis rightly develops from these new resources of language an idiosyncratic variation on a traditional style. In the promised logic of design, though, execution falls short of intent.

Transitional Poem is certainly much more of a piece than *Country Comets* both in style and organisation. But one would hardly read from its four sections the parts which the foreword assigns to them. As well as resembling 'the divisions of a theorem in geometry', they also 'may be termed (1) metaphysical (2) ethical (3) psychological; while (4) is an attempt to relate the poetic impulse with the experience as a whole.' Two of the best known poems in the sequence are 'When nature plays hedge-schoolmaster' (17, Section 2) and 'The hawk comes down from the air' (34, Section 4). Both express the poet's instinctive recognition of an underlying unity in the disordered, various life around him. He will (17)

> *be the sponge of natural laws*
> *And learn no more of that cosmography*
> *Than passes through the pores;*

or (34) be

> *content*
> *With contemplation till*
> *The truth of valley and hill*
> *Should be self-evident.*

Nothing in either poem locates it peculiarly in the two categories it occupies nor is either poem thus distinguishable from 'That afternoon we lay on Lillington Common' (3, Section I), which is supposedly 'metaphysical' and part of the 'general enunciation'.

Transitional Poem is in fact a shifting meditation on a number of related themes. It includes love poems addressed to the poet's wife. The headmaster of the Junior School at Cheltenham, where Day Lewis had gone to teach, found them 'extremely, excessively, er, sexual'. Looking back at the poems in some wonder, Lewis himself asks how he produced 'such a relentlessly and unexpectedly *highbrow* poem . . . formidably cerebral and ascetic'.[1] He is the better critic. Perhaps half a dozen poems directly concern this particular love, what it is like, how manifested, and what it signifies. Not only are they among the best poems in the collection; in them the immediate subject leads into the wider feelings and ideas which the sequence intends to explore.

Love's moments of desire or of union, though brief, supply a point of reference in a world of flux and discord. Equally, love

1. *The Buried Day*, pp. 185, 197.

and the experience of love are part of the flux and discord:

Time, we allow, destroys	*Desire clicks back*
All aërial toys:	*Like cuckoo into clock;*
But to assail love's heart	*Leaves me to explain*
He has no strategy,	*Eyes that a tear will drown*
Unless he suck up the sea	*And a body where youth*
And pull the earth apart. (5)	*Nor age will long remain*
	To implicate the truth. (15)

Other experiences bring a similar paradoxical awareness both of the amorphous turmoil of life and of an integrity within it. Landscapes which display the aimless activities of nature also evoke the inner symmetry:

> *seeing the fall of a burnt-out faggot*
> *Make all the night sag down, I became lord of*
> *Life's interplay.* (3)

> *the pure and granite hills*
> *Where first I caught an ideal tone that stills,*
> *Like the beloved's breath asleep, all din*
> *Of earth at traffic.* (14)

> *the excellence of the serious down*
> *That shakes the seasons from its back.* (21)

Such intuitions—'a Messiah sprig of certitude', 'one slip from paradise'—are the gift of 'the single mind'. They, not abstract philosophical systems, make sense of life.

They also make the best sense in *Transitional Poem*. While Day Lewis keeps in touch with scenes, facts, events, feelings, he is lucid and direct and in control of varied rhythms and diction. But in the more transcendental passages the struggle with the Absolute enfeebles the language; the obscure is further obscured; the phrasing takes on the rather desperate ingenuity of crossword-puzzle clues:

> *They are preposterous paladins and prance*
> *From myth to myth, who take an Agag stance*
> *Upon the needle points of here and now,*
> *Where only angels ought to tread.* (14)

86

> You've trafficked with no beast but unicorn
> Who dare hold me in scorn
> For my dilemmas. (23)

Passages like these needlessly interrupt the poet's record of his experiences and feelings in the material world. But such a record was too purely subjective for the taste of the period: hence the deference to quasi-scientific techniques and their corollary of strict logic, the interpolated fragments of 'objective' philosophy.[1]

Auden was at home with abstractions. He moved easily between them and his urban and rural landscapes or his personal friendships. The result—a mood, an atmosphere, a poetic myth—was too full of incompatibles, as the marxists observed, to be really an extension of any one intellectual system. But it had sufficiently that appearance; and artistically it was perfectly coherent. For T. S. Eliot, equally an 'intellectual' poet, 'experiences [hearing a typewriter, falling in love, reading Spinoza] are always forming new wholes':[2] not being dropped in among generalising snatches of philosophy. Day Lewis does not have that response to ideas and systems of ideas which makes them a part of the world of objects and events. He is a poet, so to speak, of hearing a typewriter and falling in love, not of reading Spinoza. In *Transitional Poem* he is trying to be both; but the philosophy is unintegrated; the promised design miscarries.

Eliot had prescribed a regimen of scholarship to govern the poet's 'undisciplined squads of emotion'. The counsel of the thirties put marxist thought at the centre of the regimen. Day Lewis wrote *Transitional Poem* before his introduction to marxism. When he did turn to it, it offered him, because it appeared to grow from obvious facts, a system of ideas that he could use. In it, idea and fact seemed to be identified. On the one hand, deserted factories, slums, unemployed workers, low prices; on the other, the Materialist Dialectic, the Revolutionary Proletariat, Surplus Value. Far from distracting one from sensuous observation, the doctrine positively demanded it; and it had a place for anything that, in the light of the doctrine, one saw. Having made him

1. The poem, Day Lewis has said in his autobiography, bears the scars of his bewildered undergraduate encounter with the idealist philosophers.
2. 'The Metaphysical Poets', *Selected Essays*, p. 287.

suspicious of 'self-expression', the period also made him aware of, and gave its sanction to, a philosophy which in the England of the thirties precisely suited his cast of mind.

II

From 1918 to 1937 Day Lewis's father held a living in Edwinstowe, a Nottinghamshire colliery village. Among its slag heaps, its industrial ugliness, the daily perils of its miners, Lewis's social conscience was born. This was in the early and mid-twenties. *From Feathers to Iron*, he tells us, was the first poetry in which he found personal experience—the birth of his first child—extending itself into a metaphor for political rebirth. His conversion to communism happened gradually between 1930 and 1935 while he was teaching at Cheltenham. He was not then a member of the CPGB, though increasingly sympathetic to its ideas and active in its public affairs. It was the purely intellectual structure of marxism that engaged Edward Upward. Lewis saw it as a practical solution to an epidemic social misery. Its dogma was certainly attractive, because so positive; but the idealistic ends it proposed and its air of romantic conspiracy were the compelling force.

It gave depth even to his ludicrous skirmishes with the Cheltenham school authorities. Summoned before the Chairman of the Board of Governors, Lord Lee of Fareham, to be scolded for his association with the Friends of the Soviet Union, the young schoomaster could find some kinship with the martyrdoms of Europe: 'the context of a period, when in Germany and Italy physical violence had become a commonplace of official policy, made it seem positively sinister'.[1] At the time, the incident seemed intimately a part of the class war and the inevitable 'coming struggle for power'. Lord Lee was the fascist-minded tyrant, Lewis the hostile agent within the system. Lewis's novel, *Starting Point*, published two years after he had left Cheltenham to support himself by writing, gives the rather heightened picture of how he then saw England and his own situation in it. Its autobiographical content is unmistakable.

The novel has two dislocated plots, one explaining English decadence in Freudian, the other in marxist, terms. Incest, the

1. *The Buried Day*, p. 205.

Oedipus complex, homosexuality, corrupt self-indulgence in art combine to produce the climax of the former. Theodore Follett, an absurdly 'aesthetic' novelist, subconsciously jealous of his mother and her lover, murders both of them. The central characters in the main plot are Anthony, the socialist son of a well-to-do family impoverished by the slump; his sister, Brenda; and John Henderson, an Oxbridge friend who marries Brenda. John becomes a commercial research scientist, throwing over his socialist principles to make sure of his job. His firm suppresses his invention—Alpha Product, a cheap food—because its distribution would upset the market. Day Lewis's interview with Lord Lee evidently supplied the model for John's with the head of his firm, Lord Lewin, where again monopoly capitalism defeats the wage-slave.

Anthony has become a schoolteacher, made working-class friends, got into the same kind of trouble at his school as Day Lewis had at Cheltenham, and joined the Communist Party. He sees himself as a kind of undercover agent, but the epilogue gives a different picture. It covers a few more years in which, having given up schoolteaching, he addresses leftist meetings and finally decides to fight in Spain. Though he is now apparently in the open, the mood is still of a clandestine mission. The climax, its mood recalling Edward Upward's 'Sunday', describes his going to a Party meeting, a lyrical account of its meaning for him:

Still, he had his own, Appleton, Grove, Sinclair, Morris: all the comrades: in the streets, in the country, in prison, in factories, in the little room above the tobacconist's shop and the May-Day demonstration—they were with him and would be with him as long as he lived. He was bound to them by the steel cables of action, the filaments of belief. These men and women —the oppressed, the anonymous, the workers—history had called them out of the ranks and given them her secret orders: they were the spies she sent forward into a hostile country, a land whose promise perhaps they alone could fully realise . . . Whether their hands were grained with coaldust, marked with occupational scars, or pallid from the stagnant air of offices—it was these hands, Anthony believed, which would guide a new world struggling out of the womb. They would live and die and be forgotten: but their lives would be built into the deep foundations of the future. Of these he was one. With these he was one.[1]

Devoted to this topic, the grandiloquent, Churchillian periods pick up accurately the mood of the times.

The theme of the 'new world struggling out of the womb' appears in the poetry in *From Feathers to Iron*. It does not, however, supplant an older love for the English heritage. As Nicholas Blake, Day Lewis wrote an entertaining thriller, *The Smiler with the Knife*, which adroitly sets the traditional English pleasures— cricket, country life—against the conspiracy of a Mosley-like organisation to seize power in Britain. The opening choruses of *Noah and the Waters* contrast the thirties gimcrack civilisation with the beauty of the countryside. Day Lewis's anthology, *Anatomy of Oxford*, which displays his relish in the university's history of eccentrics, makes *Alma Mater* say, 'I shall never believe that I am properly fulfilling my task, until every young man and woman who can profit by me has the opportunity to do so.' *The Ungrateful Son* retorts, 'You believe, in fact, that only after a social revolution can you come into your own.' Revolution must come, yet Oxford be essentially unchanged. Communism has often successfully identified itself with both internationalism and the feelings and aspirations of particular national groups. So it did for the intellectuals of England in the thirties. Somehow it was to combine the best of the English inheritance with modern efficiency

1. *Starting Point*, pp. 317–18. Upward's 'Sunday' tells the story of a young man who on a dreary Sunday decides to commit himself to communism. It ends:

> But history will not always be living here. It will not always wear these sordid and trashy clothes. History abandoned the brutal fatherliness of the castle, and it will abandon Sunday and the oppression of the office too. It will go to live elsewhere. It is going already to live with the enemies of suffering, of suffering beside which yours shows like silly hysteria, with people who are not content to suppress misery in their minds but are going to destroy the more obvious material causes of misery in the world . . .

> He will go to the small club behind the Geisha Café. He will ask whether there is a meeting tonight. At first he will be regarded with suspicion, even taken for a police spy. And quite rightly. He will have to prove himself, to prove that he isn't a mere neurotic, an untrustworthy freak. It will take time. But it is the only hope. He will at least have made a start.

and social justice in a technological 'Merrie England'. As *The Magnetic Mountain* proclaimed, 'Village or factory shall form the unit'; in the poem's promised land, the products of applied science—'cantilever bridge', 'ascetic pylons'—integrate harmoniously with 'old grey towers', 'daffodils/Wind-shaken'.

All that was yet to be. In the pre-communist present Day Lewis recognised his equivocal status. His heredity and background were ineffaceably part of him; he enjoyed the pleasures of *bourgeois* art, the comforts of *bourgeois* society. But he shared too the left-wing insurrectionary hopes; he relished the isolated comradeship, the sensation of purposeful intrigue, the oncoming

> *rebel hour,*
> *Charging of barricades, bloodshed in city:*
> *The watcher in the window looking out*
> *At the eleventh hour on sun and shadow,*
> *On fixed abodes and the bright air between,*
> *Knows for the first time what he stands to lose.*[1]

'Bloodshed in city' was no more than a metaphor for ideological dissent. But it was a literal reality in parts of Europe and so had dramatically satisfying associations. Metaphorically, the poet of *From Feathers to Iron* was with the rebels at the barricades. He was also 'the watcher in the window' knowing what he stood to lose.

The poems generally evade the logic of this knowledge—understandably enough. Since the post-revolutionary society was a nebulous concept it was difficult to describe. Day Lewis resolved his dilemma, in part, by presenting the new world as the issue of a salvage programme rather than of spontaneous generation. Purged of shoddy capitalism and its class barriers, England would still be recognisably itself. Poem 29 of *From Feathers to Iron*, on his son's birthday, whimsically envisages a national renaissance and a Dickensian conversion of the evil-doers. The poet imagines

---

1. *From Feathers to Iron*, 27, *Collected Poems*, p. 74. *The Magnetic Mountain*, 30. (*Collected Poems*, p. 112) annotates 'what he stands to lose':

> *You who would come with us,*
> *Think what you stand to lose—*
> *An assured income, the will*
> *In your favour and the feel*
> *Of firmness underfoot.*

'Larwood and Voce in the Notts eleven', rusting tramp steamers getting up steam, a 'crusty landlord' renewing a lease. The blissful citizens of *The Magnetic Mountain's* new society, 'Bright of eye, champions for speed', are

> *Happy at night talking*
> *Of the demon bowler cracked over the elm trees,*
> *The reverse pass that won the match.*[1]

(Rugby football, not Association which, although it was the mass entertainment, never acquired the poetic cachet of cricket and rugby.) These unpretending images fuse into the periodic lyrical statements of old virtues restored within the new dispensation:

> *Now our research is done, measured the shadow,*
> *The plains mapped out, the hills a natural boundary.*
> *Such and such is our country. There remains to*
> *Plough up the meadowland, reclaim the marshes.*[2]

Strictly, this was subjective colouring of the dialectic, which even at the level of propaganda favoured peasants and tractors, not idealised village greens. Marxist theory, however, did have its own account of the *bourgeois* recusant's standing, in Day Lewis's phrase, 'between two worlds'. Construed as it was, this too provided for poetry in transition between the moribund and the awakening society.

The stock quotation came from the *Communist Manifesto*. 'Finally, when the class war is about to be fought to a finish, disintegration of the ruling class and the old order of society becomes so active, so acute, that a small part of the ruling class breaks away to make common cause with the revolutionary class, the class which holds the future in its hands.' It was the epigraph to John Cornford's 'Left?' and to *Noah and the Waters*, where it pointed the modern application of the fable. Day Lewis had already used it in his 'Writers and Morals', one of three papers with the collective title *Revolution in Writing*.[3] It was not a certain clearance to communist approval. Cornford looked hard at those who

1. *The Magnetic Mountain*, 34, op. cit., p. 119.
2. *From Feathers to Iron*, 1, op. cit., p. 54.
3. *Day to Day Pamphlets* No. 29, Hogarth Press, 1935. The following quotations from all three essays come from this pamphlet.

pleaded it in their behalf. He suspected some of the politically conscious poetry of prinking up the old *bourgeois* aestheticism with fashionable trappings. To Auden's 'A Communist to Others' he allowed 'virile and direct revolutionary form'; but Spender's 'The Funeral' was 'the poetry of revolution as literary fashion, not as an historic reality . . . an idealist romantic affair!'[1] Day Lewis had not quite this youthsome assurance in his own infallibility. He was quite clear, however, that the writer had to justify his work within the *Communist Manifesto's* formula.

'Writers and Morals' deals with 'the moral make-up of the average serious young writer'. This turns out to be a patchwork of Christian and liberal-humanist ethics (in decay), corrected—or perplexed—by more or less assimilated marxist politics and Freudian psychology. The young writer must establish a real sense of community with the workers and resist the temptations of capitalist society: Virginia Woolf's £500 a year and a room of one's own was now a betrayal of the class struggle. He must decide how far he can accept the more dogmatic and limiting demands of marxist theory. He may have to compromise—or appear to compromise—his revolutionary beliefs in order to remain politically effective—one of Anthony's problems in *Starting Point*. That this should have appeared a problem at all was of course a vestigial prompting of *bourgeois* morality. For the writer, marxist penetration of *bourgeois* aesthetics compounded the puzzlings of intellectuals generally. In 'The Revolution in Literature' and 'Revolutionaries and Poetry', the other two papers, Day Lewis inspects its consequences.

'Revolutionaries and Poetry' sets out the objectives of the 'worker poet', that is, the working-class poet. He was to bring into poetry: 'Indignation at the conditions under which he is compelled to live; the feeling of solidarity with his own class and the conviction that he must be a spokesman of that class; the whole range of material data, altered values and changed emotional stresses which his environment offers him.' Much sought in the thirties, the worker poet remained an abstraction, though a few left-over pieces of documentary reportage by plasterers and

1. John Cornford: 'Left?', *Cambridge Left*, Winter 1933-4. Reprinted in Pat Sloan (ed.): *John Cornford: A Memoir* (Cape 1938), from which the quotation is taken, p. 131.

seamen were still appearing in the early numbers of *Penguin New Writing*. His *bourgeois* counterparts therefore undertook his task, though 'such efforts on the part of individual poets cannot get very far without a revolutionary change in society'. By breaking their allegiance to the dying class, poets could deliver themselves from their shrunken audience and the virtually private language in which they addressed it, 'trying to simplify their way of saying things, in the hope that this will bring poetry back into popular favour'. Poetry would thus acquire an extended audience to enjoin to sympathy with the attitudes and opinions of the left. It would become really pertinent to the social struggle and the practical revolutionary. What the essay does not surrender is the absolute validity of inherited aesthetic standards. A bad poem is a bad poem, however correctly revolutionary its sentiments. Equally, a good poem may have no bearing whatsoever on the class struggle.

'The Revolution in Literature' takes *bourgeois* unregeneracy further. It predicts two acceptable lines of development for literature. One—eloquently denounced by marxists—will be an outgrowth of Freudian discoveries about the unconscious mind, 'a form of writing somewhat akin to music, depending on highly elaborated sounds, intense verbal subtlety and complex patterns of association'. The other sophisticates the programme of stating progressive ideas in simple language. As a guide to action, as 'morality writing', literature will resort to parable, much as recommended by Auden. This line of development too assumes that literature can sacrifice superficial 'realism' without abandoning its claim to deal with reality; and without confining itself to plain speech achieve a new breadth of appeal. 'Parables and fairy tales' can instruct obliquely because they 'talk to deep unconscious levels within us . . . But both poetry and parable will have to learn how to increase their surface subtlety while retaining their heart of simplicity; for the highly complex mind of modern man demands subtlety in a work of art before it will allow the essentially simple meaning to appeal to the emotions.' The prospectus for a doctrinaire popular literature is trying here to accommodate T. S. Eliot's judgment that modern art must be complex because modern civilisation is complex.[1] Eliot's view of the matter was

1. 'The Metaphysical Poets', op. cit., p. 289.

patrician. It calls for a 'refined sensibility' to apprehend the complexity; and the art it sustains can appeal only to the élite which is likewise endowed. Day Lewis credits the endowment to 'modern man' generally: the prospective audience for the simplified 'way of saying things' is both large and responsive to complex forms of rhetoric.

This ingenious attempt to carry yesterday's sacred relics to 'the class which holds the future in its hands' did not go down with the marxist critics. Montagu Slater slated 'Writers and Morals' in *Left Review*, where it first appeared. From the diminished liberal ranks too Julian Bell jeered both at the critical theory and the poetic practice. Literature grows 'in a region of dubious imagination and masked ethical intuitions', not in any kind of dogma: *Noah and the Waters* lacks tension because it trumps up a fraudulent conflict between its purifying waters and mere figures of fun. Day Lewis was refusing to admit that his literature was a creation of the *bourgeois* liberal class, which also constituted his audience. 'What', Bell asks, 'are the proletariat to make of your patchety-hoppity following of Eliot, of Hopkins, of Yeats?'[1]

Revolution in Writing is vulnerable to this polemic: it does, despite its cavillings, straiten the range of attitudes; it does make a logical mess of specifying the desirable forms and diction of the new poetry. On the other hand, it keeps a consequential social class and the urban setting within the ambit of poetry; it rightly insists on the poetic value of concrete reality, the details of actual life which give substance to the ideology. They are there to be reported as facts:

> *You who go out alone, on tandem or on pillion,*
> *Down arterial roads riding in April,*
> *Or sad beside lakes where hill-slopes are reflected. . . .*
> *Refugees from cursed towns and devastated areas;*
> *Know you seek a new world, a saviour to establish*
> *Long-lost kinship and restore the blood's fulfilment;*[2]

and they also subscribe to a perfectly valid poetic myth, that is, the

1. Julian Bell: 'The Proletariat and Poetry: An Open Letter to C. Day Lewis' in Quentin Bell (ed.): *Julian Bell: Essays, Poems and Letters*, p. 326. The previous quotation is from p. 321.
2. *The Magnetic Mountain*, 32, op. cit., p. 115.

assemblage of metaphor, image, symbol and parable which is the poet's imaginative enactment of reality. *Revolution in Writing* is sounding out a part of this myth, an area of 'masked ethical intuitions'. Behind it lies the interior struggle of the renegade in his no-man's-land of disputing loyalties. The poetry often translates the certainty pretended in the essays into the delicate tensions of psychological and moral conflict. Day Lewis did carry a genuine imaginative impulse over to his poetry from the idea of making 'common cause with the revolutionary class'. His reply to Julian Bell isolates what it was.

His answer re-iterates the historical necessity of the poet's switching his class loyalties. A new metaphor gives the idea a scientific turn: the poet is a parasite; 'when one host ceases to provide him with the conditions he requires he will be attaching himself to another'.[1] Hence the transfer from *bourgeoisie* to proletariat; hence too (Lewis accepts Bell's criticism) much of their poetry must be tentative and uncertain: necessarily since there is no precedent for their attempt to create forms expressive of this new allegiance. 'In such a transitional stage a groping, unbalanced, exile poetry is inevitable.' This was not all to the bad. It was a frame of mind that could provoke the imagination at least to define its exiled estate; and in doing so 'to create for the class whose life we know . . . a revolutionary mythos . . . to present to the middle class their increasingly untenable position'. The frictions of estrangement from the past were part of this myth; so was their counterpart, the questing to identify with the new life 'which is forming and gathering strength'. The estrangement and the quest were willed, consciously undertaken. Both lines of reconnaissance were heroic in concept. Nothing in fact could be less appropriate to Day Lewis's version of the 'revolutionary mythos' than the metaphor of the parasite's involuntary drive to a more bountiful host. Its mood was of endeavour, of ethical venture into a terrain where even the proclaimed certainties were really untried. The heroic temper of this myth, unfamiliar in poetry since, comes from its assertion of the human responsibility to make moral choices and confirm them in action; and from its recognising the conflict inseparable from individual decision.

The poetic consequences were varied: satire on present dis-

1. 'A Reply' by C. Day Lewis in Quentin Bell, op. cit., pp. 328–34.

contents; phantasies of the utopian future; poems of dedication to
the hurly-burly of political action; and, informing any of these or
a separate theme, the subjective tensions stimulated in the poet.
The passage to another time has eroded the extraneous intellectual
and moral supports which carried many of these poems. There is
now no imaginative potency in:

> *Lenin, would you were living at this hour:*
> *England has need of you;*

in the appeal

> *to lovers of life, to workers, to the hammer, the*
> *sickle, the blood;*

in the peroration,

> *Raise the red flag triumphantly*
> *For Communism and for liberty.*[1]

They seem too glib in their passions, heedless of rhetorical
decorum. To resist this erosion the poet's sensibility must be
carrying out a more complex operation than arranging dressed-up
slogans to excite conventionalised emotions. The iconography of
the emotional process, in these 'public' topics especially, must consolidate two landscapes: the everyday social setting and the
private hinterland of the poet's sensibility. If not, object and
emotion are detached and inadequately defined:

> . . . there is a perpetual interplay of private and public meaning:
> the inner circle of communication—the poet's conversation
> with his own arbitrarily isolated social group—is perpetually
> widening into and becoming identified with the outer circles of
> his environment; and conversely, the specifically modern data
> of his environment—the political situation, the psychological
> states, the scientific creations of twentieth-century man—are
> again and again used to reflect the inner activities of the poet.[2]

Where language and image achieve this fusion the poems live up
to the pretensions of their heroic myth.

1. The first two quotations are from poems in *New Country*: Charles Madge,
'Letter to the Intelligentsia', p. 232; Rex Warner, 'Hymn', p. 256; and the third
from John Cornford, 'Full Moon at Tierz Before the Storming of Huesca' in
Poems for Spain, p. 29.
2. C. Day Lewis: *A Hope for Poetry*, p. 37.

The myth's frame of reference was primarily—at least most consciously—political. C. Day Lewis draws on the thirties dialect of public affairs and on the tangibles which this represents. Dictators, barons, petty *bourgeois*, the masses, people a gallery of Morality types: enemies of progress, victims of society, virtuous rebels, set against blighted rural and urban landscapes. Hammer and sickle are both objects and emblems. Their political connotations make left and right the diverging paths of choice to good and evil, Red the symbol of grace, power, victory. The imagery of revolution, warfare, spying and cloak-and-dagger intrigue extends the political factionalism to its destined outcome. Spain was not the origin of this imagery; it was the fulfilment of the imagery's portents. Thus heightened, epitomised and interpreted, the political scene itself supplied its own iconography, a poetic concentrate of reality. Here the poet was not employing ulterior analogues, such as the coming of Spring as a type of the Christian re-birth. His images are taken from political facts; they also act as emblems of the energies responsible for the facts and of their moral pattern.

This broadly political iconography shades into other figures of human dedication, effort, achievement: engineering, technical discoveries, flying, mountaineering, exploration—all the enthusiasms of the thirties *mystique* of a fresh and better equipped assault on the unknown. Their various kinds working together, the images make up a universe both exhilarating and exigent, requiring man because he is a rational being to act out his private moral drama.

This universe is common to all the thirties poets; Day Lewis's poetry treats it most consistently in heroic terms. As he puts it at the end of *From Feathers to Iron*, 'The march is what we asked for'. The march, its hazards, chimeras, ambiguities are his subject; his poems fill in its landscapes. One of the first to express the theme successfully is No. 29 in *Transitional Poem*:

> *Those Himalayas of the mind*
> *Are not so easily possessed:*
> *There's more than precipice and storm*
> *Between you and your Everest.*

It is a poem which acknowledges the pleasure of living in a

modestly solipsist world (the crowing cock 'Can signify a private dawn'), and simultaneously registers and queries the enchantment of venturing upon the inaccessible:

> *Another bird, sagacious too,*
> *Circles in plain bewilderment*
> *Where shoulder to shoulder long waves march*
> *Towards a magnetic continent.*

The 'magnetic continent' was to become 'the magnetic mountain', a symbol of the abundance that political change would lead to. Day Lewis saw it as a journey from a reactionary present to a communist future, from one class to another; in his poetry his 'second self' invested it with the ampler spirit of aspiration to travel from any present to any future.

III

Modern criticism assumes, helpfully on the whole, that the worth of a poem resides in its use of language. The only properties determining this worth exist within the poem itself, and they are properties of language. We cannot judge it, as poetry, by our response to its author's beliefs, by admiring the wisdom or maturity of its philosophy, its feelings or its myth, withdrawn by paraphrase from its own rhetoric. As T. S. Eliot argues, 'what is there to be communicated was not in existence before the poem was completed';[1] there is neither need nor justification to look outside it for feelings perhaps 'so numerous, and ultimately so obscure in their origins, that even if there be communication of them, the poet may hardly be aware of what he is communicating'. What is there to be communicated is the poem.

Persuasive though all this is, the reader, however mistakenly, will not cease to look in the poem for norms of feelings, behaviour, experience, recognisable to him from his own awareness of real life, actively engaging his own attitudes and perceptions. Eliot himself dissented (with his usual obliquity) from I. A. Richards's opinion that *The Waste Land* effects 'a complete severance between poetry and all beliefs'. The debate, whether it centres on the part of belief or other 'extrinsicalities' in the

1. *The Use of Poetry and the Use of Criticism*, p. 130.

relationship between poet, poem and audience, is between those who analyse the response to poetry as a response to form and those who admit the influence of 'non-aesthetic' values.[1]

Objects, ideas, feelings, beliefs, and their patterning in words are certainly inseparable in a poem, which is the outcome of

> *The maker's rage to order words of the sea,*
> *Words of the fragrant portal, dimly starred,*
> *And of ourselves and of our origins,*
> *In ghostlier demarcations, keener sounds.*[2]

The poet prompts and composes the traffic between the poem itself and its origin in 'real life'; between the paraphrasable content and the special identity given it by particular words. Each element influences all the others. The 'content' directs the search for words: the combining of words shapes and defines this content. The phenomenal event and its verbal rendering, the prose meaning of the poem and the reader's total experience of it do not simply 'add up'; they coalesce. As Wallace Stevens had said elsewhere, 'we protest against the abstraction of this content from the whole and the assessment of it by other than aesthetic standards'; but—'Form has no significance except in relation to the reality that is being revealed'.[3]

Few readers of poetry detach themselves from 'the reality that is being revealed' to contemplate exclusively the pure linguistic structure of a poem. The reader cannot, by an act of will, utterly extinguish as part of his experience of poetry the converse between his own beliefs and those informing the poem; nor can any poet be so completely impersonal that his poetry is innocent of his values. The greater the distance between the writer's and his audience's norms the less completely can he fulfil his purpose. The point is well made by Wayne C. Booth:

> . . . is it really true that the serious Catholic or atheist, however sensitive, tolerant and diligent, and well-informed about

1. The discussion here concentrates on belief and poetry; but as the first chapter argues, belief is only one aspect of the general relationship between poetry and the world around it.
2. Wallace Stevens: 'The Idea of Order at Key West', *Collected Poems*, p. 130.
3. Wallace Stevens: *Opus Posthumus*, p. 159.

Milton's beliefs he may be, enjoys *Paradise Lost* to the degree possible to one of Milton's contemporaries and co-believers, of equal intelligence and sensitivity? ... We must be very clear that we are talking now about literary experience, not the pleasure of finding one's prejudices echoed. The question is whether the enjoyment of literature as literature, and not as propaganda, inevitably involves our beliefs, and I think the answer is inescapable ... our convictions even about the most purely intellectual matters cannot help affecting our literary responses.[1]

It is foolish to suppose that the writer's audience is for the time magically insulated from its everyday convictions or the lessons of its commerce with everyday realities; and that these are therefore without literary relevance.

The problem is at its most acute where the writer is working from a particular scheme of beliefs. Here his fellow-believers will certainly have the completest access to enjoyment of his art, and also, no doubt, be in most danger of inferring artistic merit from the pleasure of having their own prejudices expressed. If the writer is to succeed at all, there must be a background of assumptions shared with the reader within which the writer can 'place' his personal tenets. The great works of literature in English assume the ethical values common to the Western tradition of speculative thought: the irony of Swift's 'Modest Proposal' depends on the values it does not have to state, equally credible to Whig, Tory, High or Low churchman, or whatever. By liberating beliefs from the demarcations of a particular system of ideas art becomes 'universal'. It can attain this condition only if it is dealing in values tenable within the broad area of consent open to artist and audience, the values common to the diverse creeds of its civilisation. Then, it is one function of the literary process to persuade the reader to assent to the writer's postulates.

Belief, whether a fully developed metaphysic or a complex of unformulated attitudes, is one of the links securing a poem to the experiences of ordinary human life. A similar relationship obtains

1. *The Rhetoric of Fiction*, pp. 139–40.

between the work of literature as aesthetic creation and the concrete reality around it—the source of Virginia Woolf's innumerable atoms of sensation which fall into the shape of Monday or Tuesday. The poet apprehends this reality more exactly than most men and has the unique ability to verbalise his perceptions. But he is dealing with a world jointly inhabited by him and his audience; it is this world, however transfigured, that his audience will expect to recognise: and more particularly the language, the habits, the unvoiced codes of feeling and behaviour of its own time and place. The idiom of literature responds to these properties: and the thirties poets insisted that it should, recording the realities of the time in a diction explicitly of the times. But not merely recording. The poet was also to judge. His statements would indicate a means of controlling to proper ends the world of experience which supplied his subjects. Correct, that is, a precisely contemporary, diction was an agent in the process of perception and judgment. There is nothing really new in any of this. Any innovating poet fashions a style relevant to new circumstances so far unapprehended by the imagination. The questions are whether the thirties poets were not embarking on a task already accomplished by Eliot, Pound and the later Yeats; and whether in fact they took innovation any further.

Certainly they claimed a radically distinctive manner. Its contemporary quality appears in specific details of linguistic connotation, perhaps not always too easily recognised now. The years between now and the thirties cover much more sweeping economic, political and social reorientations than the lapse of time might suggest. 'Arterial roads' is of course still a perfectly comprehensible phrase, and was long before the thirties. But it no longer has either the currency it had in the thirties or the same associations: with the first real era of popular motoring and the summer weekend exodus from cities by car; with highways being adapted to a fast and crowded flow of traffic, with reckless driving, multiple accidents, a habit of aimless release—at its most nightmarish the situation depicted in the last few paragraphs of Patrick Hamilton's *Mr Stimpson and Mr Gorse*. In Auden's 'Consider this and in our time', these associations translate the reader from the social particulars to their brusquely abstracted psychic underlay; from 'Escaping humming down arterial roads' to 'the prey to fugues' and 'the explosion of mania'. How superbly, in those lines, Auden has managed the shift to an intenser witness of his scene.

It is by just this use of particulars that poetry isolates the inwardness of a period; by this means, paradoxically, it achieves its necessary escape from a vision too narrowly vested in the assumptions of its times, like the depthless rhetoric of the quotations on page 97. As Johnson remarked in another connection, 'a man might write such stuff for ever, if he would *abandon* his mind to it'. Anthologies from Tottel to *Best Poems of 1920*, periodicals from eighteenth-century miscellanies to the 'little magazines' entomb, with its betters, verse that has not got beyond mere modishness. The difference between that and the apotheosis of a mode is the difference between Donne and Cleveland; between the conclusions of Pope's *Dunciad* (especially in its 1728 context) and of Otway's 'To Mr Creech';[1] between Eliot's 'taxi throbbing waiting' and Rupert Brooke's 'keen/Unpassioned beauty of a great machine'. Properly, the surface particulars are there, but as the basis of universalising images, fusing into one the poet's ideas and feelings, objective reality and his way of seeing it. The precipitate is myth, the total synthesis which dramatises the poet's vision of human life. Myth, in this sense, is clearly of the poet's own making; his rendering is its essence.

But certain situations, certain patterns of experience, certain conjunctions of circumstance and character—archetypal myths— seem to have an integrity and energy of their own, almost irrespective of the precise nature of their embodiment in a literary work. As George Steiner has said, 'Even a prose version in modern speech of *Antigone* or *Macbeth* holds the imagination spellbound.'[2] The dialect of a period and of the personal sensibility can stir one of these archetypes to life within a poem. It happens in Frost's 'Stopping by Woods' (the dark wood and the social haven); in Emily Dickinson's 'There is a morn by men unseen' (the return from exile on earth to the afterlife); and elaborately in *The Waste Land*. The poem thus opens out on a lengthened perspective of human experience; not just on acquired knowledge of mythical lore; on the mythical structures of the unconscious too.

1. J. C. Ghosh (ed.): *The Works of Thomas Otway* II, pp. 439–40, ll. 57–77.
2. *The Death of Tragedy*, p. 47.

The poets of the thirties may give the impression that they have constituted these resources into a composite myth, undifferentiated from poet to poet. They had much in common: their political thinking, their personal backgrounds, the society of their era. Their poetry contains a whole body of shared images and attitudes which makes sense of their being regarded as a 'school'—Auden, Spender and Day Lewis particularly—even if not one formally set up in the Continental manner. As both Spender and Day Lewis have pointed out, although each of the three poets knew the other two, the three never met until 1947, and so could not have legislated themselves into a kind of poetic commando. Their affinities are none the less undeniable. But the composite myth, as closer inspection reveals, has a protean constitution. Entered by way of different poets, it falls into the several alignments which their individual sensibilities determine. As I have briefly indicated, Day Lewis gives it a distinctively heroic cast. His 'Props of an English scene', as he calls them in *The Magnetic Mountain*, were partly the odds and ends of the standard décor; in his best poems they bring to life a scene disturbingly shadowed by the emblematic drama latent in its surface particulars.

Day Lewis's poems assemble a contemporary landscape with figures. Across it, in common with many of the thirties poets, he is given to saluting his personal friends. Auden and others turn up (unnamed but identifiable) in *Transitional Poem*, in the last poem of *From Feathers to Iron*, R. E. Warner and Auden here and there in *The Magnetic Mountain*. 'Wystan and Rex my friend', 'Wystan, lone flier', 'Wystan, Rex, all of you who have not fled' stand for the reformist band of apostates from their class, the clear-eyed elect 'Bringing light to the dark-livers'. Critics have found this practice offensive. It is certain rather naive, more self-conscious than its eighteenth-century precedents, in Swift, say: it rarely has the aplomb with which Yeats carried it off; perhaps because behind the author's friends the poems imply a bigger audience, the revolutionary masses. But though one might pretend, one had no assurance that the masses were really listening, while neither Yeats nor the eighteenth century had any such uncertainty of address. Auden, in re-working his poems, has eliminated the name-dropping, or replaced the Stephens and Christophers by cryptic pseudonyms like 'Maverick' and 'Pretzel'. But it was a harmless enough mannerism and in a small way perhaps added to the impression of a mysterious confederacy of initiates.

Day Lewis also recruits once-familiar names from the social history of the times, hired *bourgeois* apologists—'Professor Jeans spills the beans/Dean Inge tells you a thing'—or radical martyrs— 'What Wainwright wrote with his blood or Rosa in prison'. The anti-masque of villains also has the depersonalised cast of Morality types, mentioned in the previous section, who exhibit the stigmata of social privilege or neurotic distempers: politicians, press barons, clerics, middle-class suburbanites

> *At bay in villas from blood relations,*
> *Counters of spoons and content with cushions;*

and all the hostile or indifferent—

> *Lipcurl, Swiveleye, Bluster, Crock and Queer,*
> *Mister I'll-think-it-over, Miss Not-to-day,*
> *Young Who-the-hell-cares and old Let-us-pray.*

Complementing this grotesque pageant are the hero figures,

> *Sure-foot, Surveyor, Spark and Strong,*
> *Those whom winter has wasted, not worsted,*

the 'Wielders of power and welders of a new world', 'the doctor who is going to cure us'.

Current events as well as people move into the poems. The escapades of the Rector of Stiffkey (presumably), brought to light in 1932, feature in a montage of newspaper headlines:

> *Read about rector's girls*
> *Duke's disease synthetic pearls*
> *Latest sinners tasty dinners*
> *Plucky dogs shot Sinn Feiners*
> *Flood in China rape in Wales*
> *Murderer's tears scenes at sales.*

'A Time to Dance' tells the story of Parer and M'Intosh's 1920 flight to Australia, 'The Nabara' of a sea battle in the Spanish Civil War. A passage (expelled from *Collected Poems*) in 'A Time to Dance' chronicles a number of mining disasters:

> *Two hundred and sixty-one in the Dennis Deep—*
> *These are your latest ('the pit was hot for weeks*

Before'; meaning gas, and fire haunting their flesh
Invisibly measuring its leap. But they had to live
And some to show a profit),
Flame broke over them: they saw no further.
Senghenydd, Hutton No. 3 Bank, Ralton, Pretoria,
Wingate and Gresford—these are your battle honours.[1]

It is a simple catalogue without much imaginative intervention, nearer the raw material of art than art fully achieved: theory had it that facts could speak for themselves. One can see why Day Lewis chose to discard it, though its feeling, however ingenuous, is lively still.

This extensive use of actual events and people recalls the potted biographies and 'Newsreels' of John Dos Passos: the poet, in fact, was seeking to imitate the appearances of society in something the way of the novelist. So we find the generic thirties scene—or the aspect which seemed to dominate it—fixed in brief vignettes from city and countryside, capturing a mood from a scene in the manner we associate with the cinema, by abrupt caesuras of image as the viewpoint tracks over a landscape:

Consider the uniform foliage of roofs, hiding decay
And rain-fearing pests and all the diversities of loving:
Wind-screens dazzled by the sun: strip-built roads that stray
Out like suckers to drain the country; and routes familiar
To night-expresses, the fire-crest flyers, migrating south . . .

                              the two-faced traffic signs, the expensive
Flood-lit smile of civic beauties, the fountains that play
In limelight like spoilt children.[2]

The lines both focus the objects in exact, significant detail and characterise the spirit of the scene, marrying abstract and visual qualities: 'uniform foliage of roofs', 'expensive/Flood-lit smile', 'In limelight like spoilt children'—the drably utilitarian houses, roads, the slick municipal prettying-up, the rootless mobility. The critic can dismiss this succinct itemising of detail as taking 'phrases from that Thesaurus of Social Abuses so thumbmarked during

1. A Time to Dance, p. 56.
2. Noah and the Waters, Collected Poems, pp. 163, 164.

the thirties'.[1] It could become a routine patter. But so can the idiom of any sensibility, the graveyard paraphernalia of Jacobean melancholy, the selective 'wilderness' of Romantic nature, Augustan personification. At its best, this device in the poetry of the thirties mimed and judged a temper unwittingly transmitted to the artefacts and habits of the period.

This kind of 'location shot' gives body to what is really a generalised scene. If the poet had particular roads, a particular city centre in mind, it is more for their typical than their individual qualities. In the topography of the parody poems 'Come live with me' and 'Hush thee my baby' of *A Time to Dance*, the physical objects are pure types. The docks, the canals, the factory hooters are not meant to have any 'local habitation', made physically present by sensuous detail. Instead of by anatomising landscape, these poems disclose the pattern of a way of life by annotating the flat locutions, linguistically domesticated in the twenties and thirties, of Labour Exchanges, Means Tests and Depressed Areas. This new cant stood for shabby realities incongruously lodged in the setting recalled from the parodies' originals:

> . . . *we will all the pleasures prove*
> *Of peace and plenty, bed and board,*
> *That chance employment may afford.*

> *Thy mother is crying,*
> *Thy dad's on the dole:*
> *Two shillings a week is*
> *The price of a soul.*

Other registers of contemporary speech then disquieting the air accent the poetry too. The diction of Tin Pan Alley and broadcasting, American style, begins in *The Magnetic Mountain* to infiltrate the more formal language. Its most extended appearance was at the end of *A Time to Dance* in a sequence, now discarded, of mock-popular songs and radio announcements, partly lampooning the idiom they adopt, partly using it to express 'correct' political sentiments in a diction accessible to a mass audience. There was artistic precedent for the 'serious' use of commercialised jazz forms in Eliot's *Sweeney Agonistes* and in Brecht, though it

1. A. Alvarez: *The Shaping Spirit*, p. 94.

was easier to recognise the precedent than rival its superb achievement. Day Lewis's parodies are vigorous and have a place in the design of *A Time to Dance*, but they never take possession of their originals as Brecht (and Kurt Weill perhaps more) did. Here and there in 'Overtures to Death' there are still traces of these demotic styles, but in *Word Over All* they had disappeared. So, by then, had the thirties.

One may object that poetry is not sociology. But it can say more about the nature of a society than elaborate tables of statistics and questionnaires. In the various ways described, *From Feathers to Iron*, *The Magnetic Mountain*, *A Time to Dance*, *Noah and the Waters* and *Overtures to Death* create a poetic chronicle of their society. Is it consistent with the mythological interpretations it is called upon to support?

The subject of *From Feathers to Iron* is the anxieties and hopes of the prospective father and mother. The heightened sense of 'birth and death in our bones', of promise and threat, gives the experience its critical significance. Poem 27 opens with an oppressive scene of impending storm:

> Shallowly breathes the wind or holds his breath,
> As in ambush waiting to leap at convoy
> Must pass this way—there can be no evasions.
> Surly the sky up there and means mischief;
> The parchment sky that hourly tightens above us,
> Screwed to storm-pitch, where thunder shall roll and roll
> Intolerably postponing the last movement.

Images of mountaineering and warfare in the next section elaborate the suggestions of menace. The final part discloses the actual occasion, the birth itself, with the nervously intervening '*But if*' in Poem 27 finally allowed to complete its sense and the last lines accepting the possibility of death:

> So I, indoors for long enough remembering
> The round house on the cliff, the springy slopes,
> The well in the wood, nor doubting to revisit
> But if *to see new sunlight on old haunts*
> Swallows and men come back but if *come back*
> From lands but if *beyond our view* but if

> She dies? *Why then, here is a space to let,*
> *The owner gone abroad, never returning.*

The expected life is both rival and kindred, with the alien intimacies of a new relationship which may estrange, or further unite, the parents:

> *We must a little part,*
> *And sprouting seed crack our cemented heart.*
> *Who would get an heir*
> *Initial loss must bear:*
> *A part of each will be elsewhere* (5)

Analogous tensions attend the birth of 'a land which later we may tell of'. The first poem figures these ideas in a mode of imagery characteristic of the sequence. It is a poem about hope and resolution provoked by the speculative future:

> *Suppose that we, tomorrow or the next day,*
> *Came to an end—in storm the shafting broken,*
> *Or a mistaken signal, the flange lifting—*
> *Would that be premature, a text for sorrow?*

The moment is to be seized as a passage to the future, valuable because it has existed, not regretted because it is transient:

> *Over dark wood rises one dawn felicitous,*
> *Bright through awakened shadows fall her crystal*
> *Cadenzas, and once for all the wood is quickened.*
> *So our joys visit us, and it suffices.*

The first two lines pattern a movement of light and darkness, carried over into the third line with its climax of life emerging. This is a fugitive point in time captured from the 'Here-now we know' whose purpose is to renew itself perpetually as the individual journeys through experience:

> *Passion has grown full man by his first birthday.*
> *Running across the bean-fields in a south wind,*
> *Fording the river mouth to feel the tide-race—*
> *Child's play that was, though proof of our possessions.*

The sequence generally proposes the fusion achieved in this

poem of 'contemporary' and timeless images: 'the shafting broken', 'the flange lifting', 'Bright through awakened shadows', 'Fording the river mouth'. In poem 2 the constricted views of 'A city all suburb' where 'arc-lamps cramp/The dawn' give way to free expanses of countryside. In poems 19 and 20 the mood of liberation similarly appears in spacious skyscapes: 'The triple-towered sky', 'Sky-wide an estuary of light'. But it is not a simple antithesis in which nature supplies the images of liberation or the end desired and the thirties scene their anti-type.

One irresistibly attractive metaphor it threw up was that of the frontier. Europe was a continent of frontiers crossed by refugees, menaced by hostile powers, fertile in '*border incidents*', the climactic one staged by Hitler as the prologue to his invasion of Poland. In sympathy, the thirties poets, in their poems, travelled to, lived on or crossed a metaphysical frontier of intricate significance, now much derided by the critics. In *From Feathers to Iron* Day Lewis is either commanding its defence—

> *Patrol the passes alone,*
> *And eat your iron ration;* (18)

or seeking to get over it—

> *This is the frontier, this is where I change,*
> *And wait between two worlds to take refreshment;* (15)

or receiving *communiqués* reporting border attacks—

> *Is fighting on the frontier: little leaks through*
> *Of possible disaster.* (27)

The figure alluded to circumstances that were real enough—still are, though without the novelty they had then—and in spite of the derision it can be persuasive. Generally it signified an area of engagement between hostile forces (of progress and reaction) either objectively present or contending within the individual for his allegiance: the dubious region where choice is defined and settled.

The frequent images of journeying have this frontier as their objective, and associate modern and traditional occasions, from pioneer migrations—

> No mark out there, no mainland meets the eye.
> Horizon gapes; and yet must we journey
> Beyond the bays of peace, pull up our sweet roots,
> Cut the last cord links us to native shore,
> Toil on waters too troubled for the halcyon— (8)

to the exhilaration of machine-age transport—

> Tightens the darkness, the rails thrum
> For night express is due.
> Glory of steam and steel strikes dumb;
> Sense sucked away swirls in the vacuum. (4)

The poems are rich in images of growth (in dawns, flowering, the seasons) and movement (across causeways and oceans, through jungles, over mountains, from confined to open landscapes): lyrical expressions of energies released into new forms, nerve and will put to the test of extending their powers. The settings, typically, pose a challenge or embody an opportunity:

> Look how the athletic field
> His flowery vest has peeled
> To wrestle another fall with rain and sleet.
> The rock will not relent
> Nor desperate earth consent
> Till the spent winter blows his long retreat. (3)

> Now the young challenger, too tired to sidestep,
> Hunches to give or take decisive blow.
> The climbers from the highest camp set out
> Saying goodbye to comrades on the glacier,
> A day of rock between them and the summit
> That will require their record or their bones. (27)

Movement, crisis, choice are the *motifs* of the imagery: it is dynamic, enacting a drama of quest and challenge. The modern surroundings in which the hero faces his ordeal dissolve into the traditional terms and the traditional promise of the chiliastic myths: the Holy Grail whose recovery restores the land, the Hesperides or Earthly Paradise attained by suffering and struggle:

> Some say we walk out of Time altogether
> This way into a region where the primrose
> Shows an immortal dew, sun at meridian
> Stands up for ever and in scent the lime tree.   (1)

The Magnetic Mountain is recognisably the same world as From Feathers to Iron. Its political orientation is more overt and without the central private metaphor. The first of its four parts consists of five poems of which three celebrate the elation of flight, departure. The spirit thus emancipated glimpses the new lands commanded by the magnetic mountain. Its rich deposits transfigure the known universe; Arcadia here is a myth formulated in the concepts of pure and applied physics:

> Near that miraculous mountain
> Compass and clock must fail,
> For space stands on its head there
> And time chases its tail . . .
>
> Oh there's a mine of metal,
> Enough to make me rich
> And built right over chaos
> A cantilever bridge.

The other two poems diagnose the maladies of the present, a running-down of both psychic energies and technology. Poem 2 gives an interior view of emotional imbalance, a neurotic withdrawal which closes down communication:

> O you, my comrade, now or tomorrow flayed
> Alive, crazed by the nibbling nerve; my friend
> Whom hate has cornered or whom love betrayed,
> By hunger sapped, trapped by the stealthy tide,
> Brave for so long but whimpering in the end.

The literal state of society, in poem 4, is a metaphor of that condition:

> Can you keep the system going? Can you replace
> Rolling stock? Is everything all right at the base?

This poem surveys the outer tokens of social collapse, the habits which signalise boredom, frustration, lack of purpose—Eliot's world of 'restless nights in one-night cheap hotels'. The poet, jaunty where poem 2 is doom-laden, calls on his audience either to resign themselves to 'your bed-sitter at the station hotel' and 'feeling blue', or to join his expedition to the mountain. Parts two and three undertake what he here calls 'a last excursion, a tour of inspection' over this civilisation on the wane.

Part two centres on speeches by four Defendants vindicating the torpid resentment they feel for growth and change. A rebuttal follows each defence and the section ends with a poem condemning the Defendants' inertia:

> *Consider. These are they*
> *Who have a stake in earth*
> *But risk no wing in air,*
> *Walk not a planet path.*

This and the First, Second and Fourth Defendants' speeches appeared originally in *New Signatures* as 'Satirical Poems'. The titles then were, respectively, 'The Observer Speaks' (IV in *New Signatures*), 'The Mother Speaks' (III), 'The Schoolmaster Speaks' (II) and 'The Wife Speaks' (I). The only substantial changes are between 'The Schoolmaster Speaks' and 'Second Defendant Speaks'. Apart from a few inconsequential modifications the first six lines in each are identical; the following thirty lines are entirely different, though their intent is similar, to satirise the public-school mixture of arrogance and masochistic passivity. The Second Defendant's 'Kiss the rod, salute the quarter-deck' parallels 'The Schoolmaster's' 'Bending over, learnt that ignominy/Is the last privilege of the ruling classes' (to which the later version, 'Bend over before vested interests', gives a narrower political flavour). The school of the Second Defendant also seems more 'progressive' ('sex by charts') than the Schoolmaster's. The main difference, however, is that the original emphasises the personal satisfactions of the speaker; as re-written it concentrates on characterising the inadequacies he cultivates in his pupils. As the Mother's and Wife's are private complaints, this revision was presumably intended to widen the scope of the satire by making a social institution more evidently its target. It succeeds in this, but it is a pity to have lost the moments in the original poem where the schoolmaster's sentimentalities deepen into genuine emotion.

The First Defendant, a mother nostalgic for the child dependent in the womb, denies the life-force:

> *Warm in my walled garden the flower grew first,*
> *Transplanted it ran wild on the estate.*
> *Why should it ever need a new sun?*

But the child has 'crossed the frontier', abandoning her. The child's reply asserts individuality, which represents the universal urge to extend known horizons:

> *Bound by the limiting matrix I*
> *Increased you once, will not again.*
> *My vision's patented, my plant*
> *Set up, my constitution whole.*

Poems 9 and 10 are the two parts of a dialogue. A schoolmaster eulogises the 'public-school ethos'—

> *White hopes of England here*
> *Are taught to rule by learning to obey.*

A critic proposes contrary ideals in a parody of a prize-day speech (a favourite object of satire). Parts of it have a familiar ring. It is not always easy to make out what distinguished marxist virtues from fascist infirmities. We are evidently meant to deprecate the schoolmaster's 'obedience' and admire the 'discipline', 'the communal sense' advocated by the critic, who also warns, as earnestly as any schoolmaster, against 'Self-abuse. . . . Heroism in phantasy and fainting at blood'. The forbidden habits, though precise, have a suggestive vagueness, like the conditions imposed on a fairy-tale hero, the mysterious overtones of some runic spell. Poem 11 is a comminatory sermon admitting the decline of traditional faiths (the opium of the masses) and poem 13, rather in the style of the neurotic mother, the Fourth Defendant's plea that 'wisdom's best expressed in/The passive mood'.

The second of two intervening poems, as I read it, invokes a mystical community of love, the marxist brotherhood which, paradoxically, fosters the individual spirit:

> *There, as a candle's beam*
> *Stands firm and will not waver*

> Spire-straight in a close chamber,
> As though in shadowy cave a
> Stalagmite of flame,
> The integral spirit climbs,
> The dark in light for ever. (14)

What Mr Lewis had in mind, in fact, was his relationship with his wife, saying that there was one room in his self which even she might not enter. But in the context it is difficult to refuse the political inference: personal experiences so often took on such meanings involuntarily. In the first of these two poems a winter scene perfectly evokes the sense of suspended life:

> The winter evening holds her peace
> And makes a crystal pause;
> Frozen are all the streams of light,
> Silent about their source. (12)

This is the world of preparation for the movement into new life (spring, 'when primroses pave the way'), to achieve the energising fraternity of love.

This love, analogous to Christian charity, would consolidate the political and social unity of the socialist world-state and give individuality, in Christopher Caudwell's words, a 'new and higher realisation'. W. H. Auden had presented a similar argument in 'The Good Life'. Communism (at least 'in intention') would liberate the true essence of individuality, which is not self-subsistent. Elsewhere he said, 'That which desires life to itself, be it individual, habit, or reason, casts itself, like lucifer, out of heaven.' Edward Upward saw the ideal realised in Russia, where among other good things 'already writers are better off than anywhere else in the world'. And for Day Lewis the only work-able future lay in 'joining forces with the millions of workers who have nothing to lose but their chains' (which 'in the Soviet Union have been broken').[1] *The Magnetic Mountain* successfully

1. The references are to: Christopher Caudwell, *Illusion and Reality*, p. 293; W. H. Auden, 'The Good Life' in John Lewis and Karl Polanyi (eds.) *Christianity and the Social Revolution*, p. 49, and a review in *The Criterion*, January 1930, p. 571; Edward Upward, 'Sketch for a Marxist Interpretation of Literature' in *The Mind in Chains*, p. 54; and C. Day Lewis, 'Introduction' to *The Mind in Chains*, p. 15.

transmutes prose statements of this sort into poems divested of the political banality: but it was from politics that the inspiration came.

The third part has the same pattern as the second. Four Enemies, more purposeful than the Defendants, enunciate their designs to entrench the established order. The last poem forcefully categorises them:

> *Consider these, for we have condemned them;*
> *Leaders to no sure land, guides their bearings lost*
> *Or in league with robbers have reversed the signposts,*
> *Disrespectful to ancestors, irresponsible to heirs.*
> *Born barren, a freak growth, root in rubble,*
> *Fruitlessly blossoming, whose foliage suffocates,*
> *Their sap is sluggish, they reject the sun.*
>
> *The man with his tongue in his cheek, the woman*
> *With her heart in the wrong place, unhandsome, unwholesome;*
> *Have exposed the new-born to worse than weather,*
> *Exiled the honest and sacked the seer.*
> *These drowned the farms to form a pleasure-lake,*
> *In time of drought they drain the reservoir*
> *Through private pipes for baths and sprinklers.*
>
> *Getters not begetters; gainers not beginners;*
> *Whiners, no winners; no triers, betrayers. . .*

The First Enemy gives rather an enigmatic account of a seduction. Its edgy rhythms and snatches of dialogue recall 'A Game of Chess' in *The Waste Land*, another instance of the sterile lust which is one distortion of the ideal love. The rest of the Enemies have schemes to keep popular taste degraded—cheap newspapers, appeals to superstition, bullying geniality ('Now sir, now madam, we're all plain people here'); to make science the instrument of a tyrannous materialism ('God is a proposition'); to incite the retreat to self-absorbed phantasy ('I'm a dreamer, so are you'). The counterblasts exhort the unsuspecting victims—

> *Fireman and farmer, father and flapper,*
> *I'm speaking to you, sir, please drop that paper—*

and salute the forces of good—

> *Hammer is poised and sickle*
> *Sharpened. I cannot stay*

The final section, like the first, scrutinises these two conflicting worlds, the classless, property-sharing commonwealth, vibrant with life, imposing itself on the exhausted present. Again the tone varies from controlled lyric intensity to jeering lampoon. The poet whacks around him with a clown's bladder, perhaps not always too sure of his ground. It is fascinating to look back on the catholic anti-*bourgeois* venom, genuine or worked up, much of it consciously cheeky face-pulling. A good deal of it is salutary, a diatribe against smugness, indifference, mean-mindedness. These were the motives of 'appeasement' abroad and 'retrenchment' at home. They were policies much less studied, much more variously actuated, than appeared at the time—or in 1945; their authors were for the most part desperately improvising, though with appalling self-satisfaction. But their appeal was to self-interest. They made no demands that apathy could not fulfil. The satirists had their eye on legitimate targets, and *The Magnetic Mountain* picks them off accurately. Still, it is the work of a poet aware of a double-mindedness in himself. It comes out in the capricious treatment of his buffoons and mountebanks—are they victims or agents of 'the system'?—and in the images which unmistakably betray an attachment to the England whose rejection he urges. Poem 24 professes an assured stance in the struggle:

> *The poet's inward pride,*
> *The certainty of power.*

But really its mood is much less confident. The poet is aware of his own perplexities 'between two worlds' and of the indeterminacy of human vision:

> *Pity our broken sleep;*
> *For we lie down with tears*
> *And waken but to weep.*

Some of the best poems in *A Time to Dance* are on the same theme: 'The Conflict', 'In Me Two Worlds', 'Johnny-Head-in-Air'. The first two of these Day Lewis has called 'the only two political poems of any value which I wrote', an excessively modest verdict. Their intention is propagandist. 'The blood-red dawn', 'the red advance of life', the hosts that 'tap my nerves for power, my veins/To stain their banners red' are to obliterate 'private stars' and 'The armies of the dead'. But the emotional residue is of doubt, not triumph. Though the poet, as if from outside, rallies 'the red advance', it is he who is the object of the struggle. The 'tilting deck' of 'The Conflict', from which he 'sings/To keep men's courage up', is his own disequilibrium. In 'In Me Two Worlds' he is 'This moving point of dust/Where past and future meet', host to the 'armies of the dead' 'trenched within my bones', as well as to their antagonists, 'the men to come'. The imagery of both poems, its integrity poorly resumed by this kind of evisceration, sustains a metaphor of combat unresolved but precisely defined.

'Johnny-Head-in-Air' is an allegory, in ballad form, of the same conflict. A heterogeneous company of travellers/pilgrims struggles over a surrealistic terrain, limousines, a viaduct, telegraph poles incongruous in a folk-tale badlands. The language makes the same anachronous junctions. 'Leaden automaton', 'keen X-rays' consort with 'the frore and highest heavens', 'ferlies'; 'metaphysical' images with the stock ballad formulae: 'the crisis of the road' with

> Speak up, speak up, you skyward man,
> Speak up and tell us true.

The 'skyward man' describes two countries to which 'the cryptic way' leads. One ('to right, to right, comrades') has the eerie beauty of the Elflands which devitalise the human spirit. The other ('to left, to left, comrades') offers regeneration after toil. Asked which road to take, the 'skyward man' answers only,

> Traveller, know, I am here to show
> Your own divided heart.

Again the poem materially qualifies the implied political certainty, dramatising the emotional state of the 'divided heart'; and the ballad style, sensitively mimed and inflected, the haunting echoes of folklore, the hallucinatory settings, enlarge the relevance of the political dilemma which is their occasion.

As re-constituted in *Collected Poems*, *A Time to Dance* consists of these and other separate poems leading up to the title poem; 'A Time to Dance' is partly a narrative of the Parer-M'Intosh flight from England to Australia, partly an elegy on the death of L. P. Hedges, a fellow-schoolmaster. In the original volume it introduced a sequence setting depression England ('despair gathered together at street corners') against the airmen's spirited adventures and the 'radiant energy' of the dead friend, 'our dynamo, our warmth'. A chorus of the unemployed comments sardonically on 'flash talk of the spirit outshining death'; 'Two Songs' and 'A Carol' (given these titles in *Collected Poems*, where they precede the narrative) illuminate their plight. The poet then likens the 'radiance struck/From a deep mourning hour' of his personal loss to the strength accumulated in the martyrdoms of industrial life; and points the analogy which the pilots' technical skills and doggedness hold for the struggle of the workers. They are a metaphor of Engels's dictum, quoted in the poem, 'Freedom is the knowledge of necessity'. The remaining poems, in pseudo-jazz idiom, urge the poet's audience to love, unity, and the revolutionary spirit. The last thirty lines revert to the more formal manner, and *Collected Poems* retains these as an 'Epilogue'.)

The poems preserved are no doubt those that stand best on their own. Verses like 'Yes, why do we all, seeing a Red, feel small?'[1] and 'Revolution, revolution/Is the one correct solution' flourished in a climate which we can re-construct but hardly re-inhabit naturally. In the original arrangement, however, the sequence as a whole had an uninhibited aggressiveness which it is a pity to lose. But it was inseparable from its occasion and that has gone. The sequence lived off it rather than perpetuated its life; and it has not quite the dexterity that might have produced entertaining mockeries of the popular song. The narrative and the elegy are fine poems in their own right, celebrating the heroic spirit better than the directly propagandist glosses added to them.

Noah and the Waters is open to similar criticisms. The author's

---

1. The version in *A Time to Dance*, which ends, 'He is what your sons could be, the road these times should take', perhaps shades the odds a little compared with the original ending. The poem appeared in *Left Review* for November 1934, when it was called 'The Communist', and ended, 'He is what your sons will be, the road these times must take.'

foreword described it as 'something in the tradition of the medieval morality plays', dramatising in modern terms 'the choice that must be made by Noah between clinging to his old life and trusting to the Flood'. After the opening choruses three Burgesses plead with Noah to avert the Flood, then with the Waters of the Flood to undo the havoc they are causing. *The Voices in the Flood* ('Waters of the world, unite!') reject all entreaties: appeals for moderation, offers to compromise ('No doubt there was much that needed, that cried out for, destruction'), accusations of being foreigners, threats ('My poison-gas outfit will make them froth'). Noah sides with the Flood and they 'go out in a running fight,' with the Burgesses. The Second Chorus has bidden us

> *Consider Noah's fate,*
> *Chosen to choose between two claims irreconcilable,*
> *Alive on this island, old friends at his elbow, the floods at*
> *his feet.*
> *Whether the final sleep, fingers curled about*
> *The hollow comfort of a day worn smooth as holy relics;*
> *Or trusting to walk the waters, to see when they abate*
> *A future solid for his sons and for him the annealing rainbow.*
> *It is your fate*
> *Also to choose. On the one hand all that habit endears:*
> *The lawn is where bishops have walked; the walled garden is*
> *private. . . .*

The trouble, as Julian Bell observed, is that the action fails to dramatise the choice so delicately balanced here and elsewhere in the lyric passages. It turns a critical engagement of the emotions into roustabout farce; language surrenders its functions to horseplay. More might be salvaged from *Noah and the Waters*, but it displays that weakening of concentration which Day Lewis has attributed to the demands of his political chores.

The first ten poems of *Overtures to Death*, the last collection Day Lewis published in the thirties, exude an oppressive, despondent atmosphere. In 'Maple and Sumach', 'Regency Houses' and 'Two Landscapes' an autumn setting has the season's jaded melancholy, transferred to (or transferred from) and symbolising a debilitated human vigour. The landscapes and the Regency houses are the elegant but faded properties of a condemned society, evocative of loss, decay, not the triumph of their being supplanted. 'February 1936' makes a leaden winter day the portent of violence incubating:

> The unshed tears
> Of frost on boughs and briers
> Gathering wait discharge like our swoln fears.

In 'Bombers' and 'Newsreel' a 'womb-like sleep' resists the warning noise of aircraft in combat rehearsals.

'Overtures to Death', which follows, is a series of seven poems. They address, directly and with wit—the 'overtures' are preliminary negotiations—the death who is a menacing bystander in their ten forerunners. The first overture, without explicitly saying so, presents death as a 'remittance man', ignored by the family ('but in church sometimes/They seemed to be praying for you'), who 'had done well in the War', thereafter sought out by its survivors:

> Some of us went to look for you
> In aeroplanes and fast cars;
> Some tried the hospitals, some took to vice,
> Others consulted the stars.

In the second poem he is a bailiff,

> And he sits in our best room
> Appraising chintz and ornaments
> And the child in the womb.

The third poem pays tribute to 'one whose prowess in the bed and the battlefield/Have [sic] excited (and justly) universal comment'. Death has dominion over humanity, but a tolerable one: 'You are in nature.' To recognise and accept mortality is part of the human trial which only the elect—in another mountaineering image, 'Nearing the watershed and the difficult passes' (6)—can survive. But death alone has the right 'to deface the honoured clay' (4), not (the political moral) 'your free-lance and officious gunmen' (3), the despoilers of society who bring death prematurely to the weak. In the last poem the poor are the familiars of death ('We have come to think of you, mister, as/Almost the family friend'), waiting now to even old scores by becoming, in their turn, death's agents:

> When the time comes for a clearance,
> When light brims over the hill,
> Mister, you can rely on us
> To execute your will.

Most of the poems are in these sprightly quatrains. Their bouncy metre and laconically evasive personifications underplay the mordancy. The major theme of Day Lewis's poetry is engagements of mind and will in which death is the ultimate hazard to be faced. Characteristically, diction and imagery have an explicit and serious heroic tone. A different manner appears in 'Overtures to Death', where a number of the poems endow the hero with something of the wisecracking self-containment of Hemingway's heroes. Beneath the assumed nonchalance the same exigent challenge remains effectively present.

This sequence discharged the depressive mood of the poems that precede it. Among those which follow it are 'When they have lost' and 'In the Heart of Contemplation', both returning to images of glowing light, expansive scenes. 'The Volunteer' is a tribute to the Spanish War volunteers, in spirit recalling the idealistic poems written early in the First World War and like them contrasting the alien battlefields with remembered pastoral scenes in England. It introduces 'The Nabara', the very fine narrative of a sea battle off the Basque coast in 1937.

Each generation esteems its own disasters. Against the Second World War, the concentration camps, the Bomb, the momentous dangers of the thirties may seem diminished. But they prefigured all the rest. However, as the events recede, so the rhetoric which celebrated them is accounted bombast. Peter Lowbridge finds the 'archaic mock pastoral' and 'embarrassing sea-shanty heartiness' of 'The Nabara' 'unbearable reading today'.[1] In support he offers two brief quotations from the poem surrounded by his barrage of hostile comment. But not everyone finds the rhetoric of 'The Nabara' disproportionate or false to its theme. Kenneth Allott's Penguin *Contemporary Verse* mentions it as an example of Day Lewis's narrative gift. Frederick Grubb in *A*

1. 'The Spanish War' in *The Review*, number 11-12 (*The Thirties—a Special Number*), pp. 42–50.

Vision of Reality calls it 'the best poem about the Spanish Civil War from the pen of one who did not fight in it'. It is true that the conduct of heroes adds nothing to a poem written to honour them; but nor does any later debunking of their action's supposed importance or valour reflect on the artistic merit of the poem. Mr Lowbridge regards the sea fight as pretty small beer—'a souped-up predicate for these charismatic abstractions'; and this influences his verdict on the poem. But we are not sure why. Does the poet botch the souping-up, or was the occasion in some way unamenable to what he tries to make of it?

The poem certainly presents the battle in unabashedly heroic rhetoric: 'that oriflamme's crackling banner', 'the night dew fell in a hush of ashen tears', 'the battle's height/Raised it to love's meridian and held it awhile immortal'. Here was an actual event receptive to the heroic symbolism which embodied Day Lewis's view of the political dialectic, translating ideologies into the physical combat of shell fire and close-quarter fighting. The poem keeps the urgent movement, the physical details of scene and action at its centre:

> *Vague as images seen in a misted glass or the vision*
> *Of crystal-gazer, the ships huddled, receded, neared,*
> *Threading the weird fog-maze that coiled their funnels and*
> *   bleared*
> *Day's eye. They were glad of the fog till* Galdames *lost*
> *   position*
> *—Their convoy, precious in life and metal—and disappeared. . .*
>
> *For now, at a wink, the mist rolled up like the film that*
> *   curtains*
> *A saurian's eye; and into the glare of an evil day*
> Bizkaya, Guipuzkoa, Nabara, *and the little*
> Donostia *stepped at intervals; and sighted, alas,*
> *Blocking the sea and sky a mountain they might not pass,*
> *An isle thrown up volcanic and smoking, a giant in metal*
> *Astride their path—the rebel cruiser,* Canarias.
>
> *Slower now battle's tempo, irregular the beat*
> *Of gunfire in the heart*

Of the afternoon, the distempered sky sank to the crisis,
Shell-shocked the sea tossed and hissed in delirious heat.

As each man fell
To the deck, his body took fire as if death made visible
That burning spirit.

Particularly in these longer poems Day Lewis is not the poet of
the sudden electric phrase, the emotional or intellectual elisions of
Eliot and Auden. His method is discursive, gradually consolidat-
ing mood and tone and fixing an attitude, usually unequivocal. In
'The Nabara' as in 'Flight to Australia' his purpose is to establish
the actuality of the occasion and to locate the abstract significance
(heroism, the struggle of good and evil, resolution withstanding
physical defeat) in credible happenings. As in the above quotations
he makes the physical details participate in the epic quality of the
encounter. The poem succeeds because it synthesises the straightforward narrative sense and the poet's attitude to the events. In
the end, though, one's response is irreducibly a matter of taste. It
depends on one's still being able to allow the legitimacy of the
grandiloquent manner, and to disregard the fashionable esteem
for ambiguity and irony, rather than clarity and simplicity, as
desirable in themselves.

Overtures to Death reveals some of the outlines of Day Lewis's
later poetry. 'Passage from Childhood' delicately unfolds the
solitary evasions of a sensibility damaged in childhood. It antici-
pates the interest of 'Cornet Solo', 'O Dreams, O Destinations',
'Juvenilia' and other poems of youthful recollections issuing into
later life with a significance not grasped in the original experience.
There is a marked turning away here to a much more 'subjective'
area of consciousness. A number of the poems which conclude
Overtures to Death suggest the same switch of attention. 'Behold
the Swan' describes an October lake scene, its serenity abruptly
shattered by the sudden out-thrust of energy as a swan takes off in
noisy flight. At the end the poem says of the beating wings and
stretching neck, 'They are a prophecy'. But like 'Maple and
Sumach', 'February 1936' and 'Regency Houses' the poem is
primarily descriptive, with the 'moral' appearing very briefly as
a tailpiece. One can construe it politically only because of what

one knows from the poetry generally. The poet has responded to a quality in the scene which awakens a fundamentally personal emotion. Any ulterior social attitude it might be used to signify pulsates much more weakly than the immediate personal feeling. In this collection, too, the style has shed or modified most of the features that previously marked it: the elliptical syntax, the reminiscences of Anglo-Saxon models, the syncopated rhythms. And with these the frequent echoes of Hopkins, Wilfred Owen, Eliot have faded also.

The later poetry is both more personal than the poetry Day Lewis was writing in the thirties and, in a way, more general. That is, it reflects personal feelings and concerns which are more a part of common experience than the dedicated political commitment. Recollections of past life ('The Album'), marriage ('Marriage of Two'), landscapes ('Seen from the Train'): these are the subjects of the post-thirties poetry, which contains them in their private alignments. Day Lewis has much stronger affinities with John Clare than, as is often suggested, with the Georgians: in his deep attachment to the rural English scene and to domestic situations; his natural style is far less modernistic than the manner he cultivated in the thirties. Yet the poetry he wrote then bequeathed useful instruction to its successor. His novitiate came, happily, in a period which emphasised the astringency and the hold on sensuous reality which the Georgians lacked.

His later poetry retains a strongly public element. He writes with assurance about 'public affairs'—as in his war poems; and the communal world of extrinsic objects and events is firmly present, as in the scenery of *An Italian Visit*. The colloquialism is toned down, but its idioms and intonations still invigorate the cadenced, lyrical periods and set in relief the more elevated style. We hear this counterpoint in 'Two Travellers' and the sequence 'Florence: Works of Art' in *An Italian Visit* adopts the vernacular offhandedness fashioned in the thirties. One in particular of its poems, 'Perseus Rescuing Andromeda: Piero di Cosimo' re-enters the world of updated myth and fairly tale which had harboured the ogres of the thirties. Its prefatory initials, W.H.A., are intended as a clue to the reader that like the other Florence poems it is deliberate Auden pastiche. The later poetry also maintains the heroic stance of the political poems. The seasons, the individual's experience of life appear still in images of movement and crisis. And again, the modern setting assumes the exemplary patterns of myth—'The Image', 'The Revenant'—now without the specific political application.

Despite the evident differences between the two, the poetry Day Lewis wrote during and after the war is recognisably the descendant of the poetry he was writing in the thirties. The earlier verse does not fully represent his achievement—in translation, for example. But it is a distinguished body of poetry. It gives real emotional substance to the bickerings induced by marxist dialectic and the crude simplifications of the party line. The literary debate though solemn, was not uniformly edifying nor even very sensible. Day Lewis's poetry, however, gives the abstractions— art as propaganda, the *bourgeois* predicament, documentary realism—a flesh and blood presence. They exist in the events, personalities and appearances of the time: in the shabby towns of an industrial wasteland denied the machines of the new technology; in the sad landscapes of a countryside neglected or despoiled; in the heartless antics of the complacent or ill-disposed; and in the patterns of ideas and emotions which these formed in a troubled conscience not quite sure what was to be done but recording its dilemmas in terms of heroic conflict. The attitudes expressed are attractive; the passage of time has not obliterated their relevance. The poems uncover old myths in their images of the present; and refresh traditional forms—ballad, parable, narrative—with new techniques and contemporary language. It is not a 'communist' poetry; but it is a poetry which could hardly have existed without the communist entrance into the England of the thirties.

IV

W. H. Auden: The Island and the City

I

Auden's four contributions to *New Country* were: 'Prologue' ('O love, the interest itself in thoughtless Heaven'); 'A Happy New Year' (two parts—'The third week in December frost came at last', 'Now from my window-sill I watch the night'); 'A Communist to Others' ('Comrades who when the sirens roar'); and 'Poem' ('Me, March, you do with your movements master and rock').[1] These have a quite openly left-wing set, unlike his poems in *New Signatures*, possibly excepting 'Though aware of our rank' (*The Orators* Ode V), whose allegory has some darkly political scope.

The first three verses of 'Prologue' invoke the love which, possessing 'the ring where name and image meet', can order man's perception of reality. Its mediation will give his thought the instinctive sense by which starlings, 'Rising in joy over wolds unwittingly weave' their patterns of movement, bird flight and setting thrown into design. So Newton, watching the apple fall in England—'The mole between all Europe and the exile-crowded sea'—grasped from this momentous and casual conjunction the physical laws binding its parts 'in an eternal tie'. The next six verses lament the disruption of some evolutionary process which kept past and present, man and society, in vital connection. The present is a period of decline, stasis. In Dumbarton,

1. In *Collected Shorter Poems* respectively: 'Perhaps'; 'Not All the Candidates Pass' (Part II of 'A Happy New Year' retitled 'The Watchers' in the Penguin selection); 'Two Worlds'. See note p. 206 on texts used.

furnaces gasp 'in the impossible air'; on 'wind-loved Rowley', no steam-hammers shake the graves of the ancestors who created 'intelligible dangerous marvels'.

The old 'dream' has retreated, leaving 'impoverished, restricting acres', industry, countryside, spirit desolated alike. Its heirs, 'In bar, in netted chicken-farm', go inertly about their empty routines, each immured in the isolation of self: 'The ladies and gentlemen apart, too much alone.' This canker impedes the great upheaval which will release the dream, 'long coiled in the ammonite's slumber', destined to restore the concord of self and community. After calling upon the reader to think on this barren time, the concluding stanzas evoke the disciplining force of the dream, its 'military silence' laid 'on our talk and kindness'. It will restore the adventuring spirit of the age when Merlin and his lords 'into the undared ocean swung north their prow', and drive 'For the virgin roadsteads of our hearts an unwavering keel'.

'Prologue' is Auden at his happiest. Its images crisply outline objects and scenes, the phrasing perfectly blends the mood of oracular divination and exactly designated feeling. Marxian socio-historical 'laws' explain its 'thesis'. The language works it into a substantial 'here and now' whose past supplies the metaphors to prefigure its future.

'A Happy New Year' dates from the time when Auden was teaching in Helensburgh. Part I begins factually enough with the poet taking a walk in wintry sunlight through the Scottish countryside. As he climbs among lochs and moorland, the sky 'silent as an unstruck bell', a voice begins to issue mysterious injunctions and point out features in the landscape receding beneath, now a mosaic of actual ('the halt for the narrow-gauge motor train') and legendary ('the quarry where the lovers fell'). Suddenly he becomes aware of an army of 'The English in all sorts and sizes' converging upon the point where he stands. The rest of the poem is a boisterous narrative abusing Auden's favourite enemies of progress.

In the vanguard of the army are a troupe of boys and girls embarrassed by their ill-fitting bathing suits, a street band, a group of jazz musicians, a hymn-singing choir. The rag-tag main body is effete and foppish—lamed, stammering, giggling, drawling. Psychologically they deny the life force, inhibit positive emotions;

politically, they retard the advance to socialism. Either way, physical defects spring up to reflect emotional disturbance. Here the psychosomatic theories of illness expounded by John Layard and Homer Lane, which had taken Auden's fancy, intervene to confuse the strictly marxist selection of social wastrels.

Their commanders are a heterogeneous sampling from the leaders of banking, industry, politics, the arts, each acidly categorised as villain, buffoon or simply dupe: Ramsey MacDonald, Baldwin, Sir Montagu Norman, Sir John Reith ('standing aloof like a blasted tree/Was the gaunt Director of the B.B.C.'), 'Unhappy Eliot', the Sitwells ('giving a private dance'), Wyndham Lewis ('putting cascara in the still lemonade'). The motley crowd is engaged in something like a particularly fatuous cocktail party. There is a hubbub of inane conversation. Here and there little groups announce eccentric doctrines of salvation ('The colon we know is the seat of the soul'), pursue a deserter ('Dr Ernest Jones was well in the van'), amuse themselves by inflicting prep-school 'tortures'. Confusion spreads and the ranks mutiny. Secret police drag away the offenders; a General issues battle orders; 'The Tigers' head for Dumbarton. As snow begins to fall the poet is left musing on 'these blurring images/Of the dingy difficult life of our generation'.

Much of the poem is racily scurrilous, in a manner to which the eighteenth century was more accustomed than is the twentieth. Auden was letting himself go in designedly personal satire, an open blow not so much against (nor for) ideas and abstractions as against individual reactionaries and wrongheaded idealists. It still makes very entertaining reading, though now it is at a difficult stage, still too much of its time for its points to be readily taken, but not yet far enough away to mellow the personalities. In due course it will suffer resurrection, doubtless with notes to place its period allusions.

The second part of the poem is quite different from Part I, meditative, sinister in atmosphere, evocatively deploying Auden's private symbolism. Looking out at the quiet night the poet sees the school grounds ominously still—the lilac bush 'like a conspirator', the Great Bear 'a portent over Helensburgh'. In each sleeping pupil the coursing blood gives personal design to its inheritance, 'the long still shadow of the father', oblivious of the menace all around and the future of the individuals whose destiny it shapes. The season of the year, as the ice loosens, suggests quickening life. Unidentified agencies hasten their researches 'In scrubbed laboratories' and maintain a relentless surveillance: whether serving or opposed to 'the long lost good' it is hard to say. Less ambiguously presented in the next verse, the 'Lords of limit', who set 'a tabu 'twixt left and right', are the protectors to be appeased.

Literally they are the senior schoolmasters, 'whom the school-boy fears'. But they are more than that. Later verses associate them with armed gamekeepers, sleeplessly protecting 'Our peace . . . with a perpetual threat'. One must placate their moods, but their discipline can repair the devastation of 'the isolated personal life'. The poet is taking to heart his pupils' fate not only in examinations but in the world at large, the troubled, threatening society that awaits them after their schooldays. As he hears badminton players—the 'voices that I love'—come up the stairs, he thinks of the warning of 'the starving visionary', imagines their 'bodies kicked about the streets', and petitions that they shall not fall prey to the psychic disorders that would make them victims:

> Lunging, insensible to injury,
> Dangerous in the room or out wild-
> -ly spinning like a top in the field,
> Mopping and mowing through the sleepless day.

The Lords of limit are spiritual mentors, the apostles perhaps of a controlled and orderly moral system; but at the time and in *New Country*, the reference to 'left and right' could not have failed to carry a primarily political overtone.

The poem shifts confidently between its immediate concerns—the life of the school, of the small town—and its tenderly apprehensive forebodings of the claims made by a moral universe. Auden's mind is acting here among ideas that give his socialism a distinctly otherwordly cast, and not because of the transcendental fancies which the enthusiast can derive from marxism. The marxist prophecy ('the starving visionary') of inescapable violence is the cause for alarm, and certainly the poem sees it working itself out in society. But despite its castigating 'the isolated personal life', the poem makes the moral dilemma decidedly a matter of personal decision, a submitting to other than economic laws, or a pre-determined history, or any strictly materialistic frame of conduct.

It does not matter if, as Joseph Warren Beach argues, this toning of his marxism comes from Auden's familiarity with Gerald Heard's humanist philosophy of a 'higher consciousness' evolving from and subduing lower forms. Auden's thinking at the time was consciously secular. But whatever source, humanist philosophy or marxist politics, furnished him with ideas, he loaded them with suggestions that in the poetry burst through the secular framework of their origin. They emerge in images, symbols, myths expressing a mystical vision of human life which allows a role to more than human ministries. So the Lords of limit, 'training dark and light', because they are remote, exacting homage, and made palpably a presence in wordly affairs, become much more than the embodiment of humanly conceived ethical principles: though just what they represent Auden could hardly, at this time, have related to any one coherently defined doctrine. That was not to come until he embraced Christianity.

The conclusion of 'A Communist to Others' is in similar vein. It urges the masses to trust in a numinous love 'outside our own election'. For most of the poem, however, as in Part I of 'A Happy New Year', Auden is very much the declared propagandist, hurling abuse at his enemies, though here he names classes, professions, not individuals. The first four verses are a call for solidarity against the blandly superior bosses who 'For centuries have done you brown'; and whom the rest of the poem excoriates: the rich and cynical ('To whom our misery's a rumour/And slightly funny'); mystics who commend 'fasting, prayer and contemplation'; idealist philosophers (with a dig at psychiatrists, who blame all discontents on our being 'Jealous of sisters'); all the hangers-on of capitalism—professors, poets, bankers, brokers.

This is the poem that satisfied John Cornford's conditions for true revolutionary poetry. It was an essay in dropping the screen of phantasy and parable for directly partisan and easily comprehensible verse. It is impossible now to be sure whether its feeling was wholly and genuinely Auden's or, as Stephen Spender tells us, adopted as an intellectual exercise. The fact that, properly for a communist, it disparages psycho-analysis, does not tell us much about its good faith: some brands and some applications of Freudianism Auden endorsed, some he did not. Anyhow, the poem's readers would certainly have taken it as sincerely professed. We must presume that Auden was happy to have it so and to accept the role of activist poet dedicating art to the service of the revolution. As always when he writes in this manner, Auden is inventively and exuberantly outspoken. It is blunt, effective satire and worth reading, however callow its views. It is interesting too as a sample of one of the strategies adopted by Auden to give poetic form to the host of his intellectual curiosities.

'Poem' is the least successful of these four poems, though Auden thought well enough of it in 1950 to include it in *Collected Shorter Poems*, having left it out of *Collected Poetry*. It does not appear in the Penguin selection.

Amid propitious omens of spring, with a 'communist orator' landing 'like a sea-god' at the pier, and a general sense of well-being and power, two lovers agree to separate. All is not as well as it appears. A hawk above the town sees only the visual patchwork of landscape, not the opposing human loyalties of 'the Whites' and 'our Reds', 'which tends to become like a war'. The Reds (the lovers' party) are guardians of 'the carried thing', a unifying vision of life assembled from elements, shared between individuals, powerless unless fused in love.

The struggle to preserve this is underground, conspiratorial, menaced by danger. The lovers feel that dunes, mountains, once friendly, now are hostile: 'Strolling in the valley we are uncertain of the trees'. Hence their separation to pursue the struggle, divided from the world of those who 'Grow set in their ways'; and conscious of being under the malignant surveillance of 'the white death'. Like the hawk overseeing the town, but unlike it pitiless not indifferent, the white death wishes disaster upon them. Hope will keep their purposes alive; and the poem ends with a joyous dance in which everyone joins.

It is hard to make sense of the situation, even though trying not to be too nigglingly literal-minded. In this atmosphere of secret struggle, how can the orator make his far from clandestine entrance; or the dance (celebrating what?) be so public? The white death is presumably some emanation from the Whites, but its powers and function are obscure. Are we to associate it with the hawk, as Joseph Warren Beach does? Nothing in the poem warrants this. The 'For' that begins verse three and verse five has no clear relationship to its preceding verse: a fake transition. It is not often that Auden fails to bring off his chilling modern-sinister in the kind of trollish, watchful landscape we have here, 'Motionless, tense in the hope/Of catching us out'. But the parts of this poem do not coalesce. Some of the actors have moved on stage from a different play.

Of these *New Country* poems all but the first part of 'A Happy New Year' (never re-published) survived, with some alterations, into *Look, Stranger!* In their two appearances, these poems give a condensed view of Auden's political views between 1932 and 1936, and of what he was making of them in poetry. The revisions made for *Look, Stranger!* give no indication that Auden had radically modified his ideas and attitudes from the time when he wrote the poems. Their purpose is to tighten structure and sharpen phrasing; occasionally to shade a meaning. But because there is an occasional change of emphasis, the rather tedious process of describing the revisions, and trying to guess why he made them, is instructive.

Joseph Warren Beach's supposition is that Auden's ideological about-face around 1941 mainly accounts for his revisions and suppression of poems in the 1945 *Collected Poetry*. This now seems unarguable. There is more to it, however, than reverend maturity surreptitiously correcting the delusions of wrongheaded youth. And whether the process is quite the offence against moral and artistic propriety that Professor Beach maintains is another matter. In any event, when he presses his case to answer for Auden's tinkerings even within the thirties (as between *New Country* and *Look, Stranger!*), his zeal leads him to inconsistencies which the theory does nothing to reconcile. He proposes, for instance, that the 1933 edition of *Poems* dropped a couplet from the 1930 version because Auden wanted to palliate its indecorous statement of 'the psychological theory of corruption by sexual repression'.[1] Yet in the same volume Auden kept 'the distortions of ingrown virginity' (XXX); and in *New Country* the violent malediction of 'A Communist to Others', 'Their daughters sterile be in rut'. Auden's revisions pose tricky questions, and the critic does well at

1. *The Making of the Auden Canon*, p. 67.

least to entertain the possibility that his motives were as often artistic as ideological; and that we cannot easily separate the two reasons.

In 'Prologue', *Look, Stranger!* puts a comma in place of the full stop at the end of, 'The ladies and gentlemen apart, too much alone'. Hence the following line, 'Consider the years of the measured world begun', instead of apostrophising the reader makes a statement about the torpid, disinherited moderns. Perhaps, then, it allows them some understanding, or at least recognition, of their predicament. This is the only important change in pointing, 'which', Auden says in *Letters from Iceland*, 'I don't understand. I can only think of them as breathing indications.' The *New Country* line, 'Some dream, say yes, long coiled in the ammonite's slumber' becomes 'Some possible dream . . .'—no unachievable phantasy, 'And called out of tideless peace by a living sun' becomes the more literal and positive, 'And out of the Future into actual History'.

Look, Stranger! corrects a few misprints in 'Now from my window-sill' and omits verses 11–13 of the *New Country* version. These pay lighthearted tribute to life in the small town of Helensburgh, at once corporate and individual. Auden may have thought that their whimsical tone diminished the poem's broader reference. The later history of the poem is curious enough to be worth summarising here, though it takes us well beyond the Auden of the thirties.

Collected Shorter Poems excises another two verses (12 and 13 in *Look, Stranger!*). These solicited gifts of skill and character for the pupils, particularly the badminton players, whose names are mentioned. When he removed this, Auden abstracted a bit more of the original setting and the personal rudiment. In the Penguin *Selected Poems* the surgery is even more radical. Only eight verses remain; the last line of the first reads 'The lights of near-by families are out' for 'The jets in both the dormitories are out'; the school has completely disappeared. In this final condition the poem is entirely an appeal to the Lords of Limit, supreme tutelary powers in the ominous circumstances now briefly set out in the opening and closing verses. Among other casualties, the intricately devised stanza on the coursing blood has gone: there is no longer anyone in particular to whom it can refer. In the penultimate verse the 'bodies kicked about the streets', which used to be the boys', can now only be those of the Lords of Limit, which does not make very good sense. By extricating the poem from its private detail, Auden was presumably trying to isolate its cosmic myth of exiled, despairing man's redemptive homage to the Lords of Limit, now unequivocally spiritual beings. Even in its truncated form the poem keeps some of its eerie power. But the new ending confuses the controlled ambiguity of the mysterious guardians in the original, which if a more discursive, was a less freakish composition.

'A Communist to Others' drops its title in *Look, Stranger!*, which also changes 'Comrades' in the first line to the less explicit 'Brothers'. One might read some portentous recantation into this, but it is hardly significant. The poem is still an unregenerate statement of class antagonism. The disappearance of verses 6, 16–17 and 20–22 in no way reduces the poem's vituperative power or its leftist feeling: it retains, for instance, the indelicate stanza calling down fever, sterility, cancer and madness on the *rentier* families. The omitted sections respectively avow the proper contempt for the sportsman-playboy's elegantly useless splendour; expose the 'idealist' philosophies and their exponents, whose sophistries disarm protest and anger; and trounce the introspective poets, abdicating their responsibilities, 'whose only/Real emotion is feeling lonely', but who 'could help us if you chose'. All this eliminates some re-statement of ideas already more forcefully expressed. Verse 22 in the original closes the poem with an appeal to the love which 'Holds us in unseen connection.' The new ending, in which the parasites of capitalism 'fade away like morning dew/With club-room fossils', makes a fittingly tart (and marxist) conclusion. But the amputation of the three verses that originally ended the poem was a real loss.

Auden seems to have been trying to censor his involuntary twitch of sympathy for the 'change of heart', the willed emergence of a 'higher self', which would redeem man's baseness and with it society—the 'New styles of architecture, a change of heart' in 'Sir, no man's enemy'. The love invoked by the original ending had suspiciously theological overtones, rather at variance with the earlier gibe against 'personal regeneration'. It came out to absolve the poet of inconsistency, and to arrive at a less lyrical finale.

'Poem', when it became No. XV in *Look, Stranger!*, lost its two opening lines of pastiche Hopkins for a more soberly phrased itemising of scenes observed on a 'blue March day'. The new third line converted the 'communist' to the 'political' orator; the party of the lovers in the political struggle became 'the' not 'our' Reds. Verse 8 is omitted; verse 9 has a different first line in which the lovers instead of standing on 'the bone-rich soil of England' 'ride a turning globe' and 'stand on a star'. The local allegiance gives way to a sensuously weaker—but ideologically purer?—internationalism.

The eclectic nature of Auden's thought appears in a number of prose pieces which he wrote between 1930 and 1936, particularly during the three years between *New Country* and *Look, Stranger!* These pick through the teachings of Christianity, communism, humanist philosophy and various schools of psychology for ideas between which he might find common ground. In the 1930 *Criterion* review of Dibblee's *Instinct and Intuition: A study in mental duality*, Auden is engagingly at play with a highly technical patter: 'The motor-control is cortical and the memory-reserves of the hemispheres are dependent upon the sensory-receptor mechanism of the thalamus for their supply.' Scientific matters briskly disposed of, Auden turns to contentions that are his own. Properly regarded, reason is merely an instrument which operates upon desires and can co-ordinate them or make one modify another. Any change that takes place is a change in the whole self, as for example in a man before and after a religious conversion. A theory of autonomous parts, 'of a higher and lower self, of instinct and reason, [is] only apt to lead to the inhibition rather than the development of desires, to their underground survival in immature forms, the cause of disease, crime, and permanent fatigue'. Yet the 'higher consciousness', for Auden at this stage of his career, must have had a secular origin, not like the Grace of a revealed religion. It was, then, part and parcel of all human feelings, although, without being autonomous, superior to them all: the distinction is a fine one.

The *Scrutiny* review of December 1934 is categorical that, though physical violence may be necessary to bring it about, only a 'change of heart' can save people and civilisations; and 'The Good Life' (1935) places the 'change of heart' at the centre of

Christian teaching. It is 'fundamentally non-political' because 'it regards all institutions as a product of the heart, the form of which can be changed, and only changed by a change in the latter'. On the other hand, communism and Christianity may work together. Christianity is not 'a quietist religion'. It sees the human environment as dynamic and holds that 'a change of heart can, and must, bring about a change' in it. Auden is now, however, even more doubtful of the Social Democrat belief that the possessing class may voluntarily abdicate, or allow itself to be peacefully dispossessed. Communism may in fact further the Christian ideal, for example by depriving the family unit of economic power, leaving it 'free to be what it should be—an emotional bond—instead of what, as psychologists or common-sense observation can testify, it, at present, so often is—a strangling prison, whose walls are not love, but money.'

The imagery of 'Psychology and Art Today' (1935) presents Freudian psychology almost as a surrogate religion. Its therapy removes guilt feelings, 'in the forgiveness of sins, by confession', and gives 'absolution' by enabling the patient to understand the significance of his experience. Freud and Marx are the two great diagnosticians of modern society. Though each is rather hostile to the other, both of them, Auden concludes, 'are right. As long as civilisation remains as it is, the number of patients the psychologist can cure are very few, and as soon as socialism attains power, it must learn to direct its own interior energy and will need the psychologist.'

All these essays pre-suppose a complex, industrialised society, which Auden looks on as a desirable corporate body. *Letters from Iceland* praises Byron 'because he was a townee, a European, and disliked Wordsworth and that kind of approach to nature'; and describes Byron's Muse as 'a good townee'. The much later essay in *I Believe*, when Auden was still a socialist, explains why he set so high a value upon a sophisticated, urban community. Society is the natural condition of man, and the individual is 'the product of social life'. The best society is the one which offers the individual the greatest variety and the greatest potential of function. Urban life offers the 'townee' fuller opportunities of using his powers than peasant life did, and so it is an advance. Extension of choice, in fact, equals moral improvement, or at least the opportunity for it.

Auden's ideal is 'social' man and the community, the city not the desert, the settler not the nomad.

Finally, Auden was at this time developing his ideas about the role of poetry in society, along the lines described in chapter 1. The belief which in 'The Good Life' he attributes to psychology is a recurrent theme in his remarks about poetry: 'You must never tell people what to do—only tell them particular stories of particular people with whom they may voluntarily identify themselves, and from which they voluntarily draw conclusions.' As he puts it in 'Psychology and Art Today', the writer's aim is to advance from 'uncontrolled phantasy, to deliberate phantasy directed towards understanding'. Such is the aim of his own poetry, which fully realises it: to tell 'particular stories of particular people and experiences, from which each according to his own immediate and peculiar needs may draw his own conclusions'.

The ideological constant in the *New Country* poems, as in these essays, is in their various shelvings into marxist thought. In the poetry it may emerge at an openly propagandist level of drumming up class antagonism, or proletarian unity, and instigating revolution. 'Prologue', more distantly, arises from the historical theory that new social forms and relations evolve from frictions set up by the established system: the new will subsume the old. The cause of these changes is purely materialistic, not finer ideals of truth and justice, but shifts in the means of production and exchange which demand new strategies if man is to retain control of his environment. The crisis is the point at which the old appear to threaten a stalemate, or make a last stand against the foreordained triumph of the new. At that juncture, the new society may erupt through a spontaneous collapse of the existing order into economic chaos; or direct revolutionary action may administer a final push. These concepts, as well as being part of the poems' meaning, generate the sense of crisis and imminent violence that pervades them all. It was supposed, wrongly but not altogether without reason, that the final crisis had come.

Isaac Deutscher has an interesting account of his introduction to Marx's writings. He notes that *Das Kapital* attempts no explanation of the principles of dialectics, which Deutscher compares to the rules of grammar: one's mastery of them appears not in reciting laws but in creating lively speech. Similarly, '*Das Kapital* is the supreme example of the dialectical mind in action, of the dialectical mind using all its power of abstraction to plough up layer after layer of empirical social experience . . . a creative imagination which had harnessed reasoning and research for one of its tremendous leaps'.[1] This is very much what Auden and the others recognised and responded to in Marx, though of them all perhaps only Caudwell and Cornford, possibly Madge, read Marx with Deutscher's total and passionate acceptance.

Auden's revisions of his *New Country* poems seem to mark a conscious attempt, which the prose pieces reflect, to harden their attachment to the materialist and revolutionary tenets of communist doctrine. But it is quite evident that in his poetry the marxist-derived ideas display excrescences appropriated from other pet systems of thought. An appeal to proletarian unity was a sympathetic host to the selfless, all-encompassing love, somehow diffused amongst individuals and yet extrinsic to them, the path to release from 'the isolated personal life'. It was a function of the 'higher consciousness', a future stage of spiritual evolution, to which the present should aspire: not just a new socio-economic structure but the hoped-for 'change of heart'. The marxist theory of social change was also congenial to these notions, provided one re-construed its materialist principles. The id, ego and super-ego of Freudian psychology provided analogies too; and its account of the perversions and repressions of love in actual human relationships diagnosed anti-types of the supreme, unifying love. As Auden, via Groddeck and Homer Lane, extended Freud's analysis, these, and any other, emotional impairments were the cause of physical disabilities. And all these iniquities characterised the *bourgeois:* neurotic, sick, and politically moribund, the last impediment to the evolutionary advance.

The identifiably marxist thesis that most occupies Auden in his earliest poetry—up to about 1933—is that each historical/economic period is a direct outcome of the conditions of its predecessor. We see this, for example, in 'Prologue', in Poem III of *Poems* (1930) and in the witty Chorus towards the end of *The Dance of Death*. In the writings of Marx and Engels this theory is the nucleus of a whole cluster of ideas about human motivation and the individual

1. *The Listener*, 3 August 1967, p. 140.

psychology and about the 'deterministic' and 'materialist' explanation of the historical process.

Adapting Hegel, Marx analysed this development as 'a process of realisation of a human species-self',[1] expelling God or any spiritual being outside man. The modern industrial economy was a positive step towards this, and achieved by capitalist expansion with its sophisticated apparatus of law, technology, distribution and so forth. Capitalism, however, ceases to be concerned with 'The simple circulation of commodities . . . the satisfaction of wants'; and it creates a labouring class whose employment is to sell itself as a commodity. The aim of the capitalist is 'The restless never-ending process of profit-making alone.' Unlike the individual owner in a more primitive system, the capitalist is out not to satisfy needs but to accumulate money—like a 'rational miser . . . [not] by seeking to save his money from circulation . . . by constantly throwing it afresh into circulation.'[2] This purpose—the 'profit-motive'—is not an innate principle of human behaviour. Nor is it even, in origin, a psychological element. It is a social objective prescribed by the total framework of monopoly capitalism and rationalised by the Judaeo-Protestant morality.

No rationalisation, however, can eliminate the 'division within the life of each individual, in so far as it is personal and in so far as it is determined by some branch of labour and the conditions pertaining to it'.[3] That is, the socially prescribed exercises separate the personal and the functional lives of the individual and are the cause of his alienation. It is therefore a social, not a psychological, problem and thus demands the mass therapy of reforming society's institutions, not treatment of the individual alone. The family, which according to Freud determined the individual's psychology, is itself a unit in this society, whose pressures it embodies and transmits. More generally still, marxian psychologists argue, the capitalist system, through its elaborate institutional machinery, its laws and property rights, exerts a 'surplus repression',[4] beyond what is a necessary part of any organised society, to protect the

1. Louis J. Halle, 'Marx's Religious Drama', *Encounter*, XXV, No. 4 (October 1965), pp. 29–37.
2. K. Marx, *Capital*, I, pp. 169–71.
3. K. Marx, *The German Ideology*, p. 76.
4. H. Marcuse, *Eros and Civilization*, p. 34.

property-owning class. This too produces the *'socially induced neuroses, largely described by the concept of alienation'*;[1] and afflicting the *entrepreneur* as well as the worker.

Present-day communism, as Norman Cohn points out, has paid hollow respect to these carefully reasoned, patiently documented socio-economic theories. The 'quasi-apocalyptic fantasy' which Marx 'as a young man . . . had assimilated from a crowd of obscure writers and journalists' makes better politics. This is the vision of 'capitalism as a monstrous realm whose masters have both the cruelty and the hypocrisy of Antichrist—capitalism as Babylon, now about to go under in a sea of blood and fire so that the way shall be cleared for the egalitarian Millenium'.[2] These inflamed images have warrant enough in the marxian classics to have become the staple of communist rhetoric. They endow with popular appeal—and distort—Marx's much more complex propositions about the historical moment.

Being a controversialist, Marx at different times lays more or less stress upon the materialist nature of man and of the historical process of which he is a part. Man consists of matter and so has no immaterial properties, history is a product of physical circumstances and events, of the impersonal forces of environment. It is true that man by inventing new techniques, discovering new materials, can affect the course of history. But it is his surroundings that determine the discoveries and inventions open to him and decide the use to which they will be put. Man's activity is in the most radical way the creation of his environment.

Marx none the less recognises that there is no creating entity, 'history': 'It is not "history" which uses men as a means of achieving—as if it were an individual person—*its* own ends. History is *nothing* but the activity of men in pursuit of their ends.'[3] This is at the root of Engels's dictum that 'Freedom is the appreciation of necessity', that by 'knowing' his environment, seeing through to the natural laws which operate in it, man changes what he thus knows. The natural laws are fixed: 'What can change in

1. John O'Neill, 'Marxism and Mythology', *Ethics*, LXXVII, No. 1 (October 1966), pp. 38–49, a paper to which this account of marxism and psychology is much indebted.
2. *The Pursuit of the Millenium*, p. 311.
3. K. Marx, *Selected Writings in Sociology and Philosophy*, p. 63.

changing historical circumstances, is the form in which these laws operate.'[1] Compare 'I Believe', where Auden says that the 'history of life on this planet is the history of the ways in which life has gained control over and freedom within its environment'; and that 'in so far as [man] is able to understand the laws of his own nature and of the societies in which he lives, he approaches that state where what he wills may be done'. There is hence constantly in operation, according to both Auden and Marx, a two-way process of modification between man and matter, man and his environment, subject and object. Capitalist society, at its climacteric, will have brought into being the conditions within which the proletariat must violently intervene to cast down the old order.

Like Yeats's 'system', Auden's eclectic use of marxist and other ideas triumphs in the poetry; however useful a knowledge of Marx may be as 'background', in that form it sheds all the colour, vivacity and coherence given it by its poetic statement. The poems set going a fable of journeys whose ends, though known, are perplexed by conflicting instructions. They are poems of enquiry or oracular reply, of postulates and suggestions, not dogma. The myth of C. Day Lewis's poetry is heroic—the satisfactions simply of challenging the ordeal or initiation; Auden's is daedelian, fascinated by the intricacies of the journey from the maze. The outlines of this world, partly apparent in the *New Country* poems, would have been already familiar to their readers from *Poems* (1930) and *The Orators*.

II

The rare 1928 volume of Auden's poems, privately printed by Stephen Spender and limited to about forty-five copies, did not bring his work within the public domain. The 1930 Faber collection, his first 'professional' appearance, included nine poems from the Spender printing; of these the 1933 edition eliminated five, which with another two from 1930 Auden replaced by new poems. Thus the contents of the 1930 *Poems* are not identical with those of the 1933 edition. In the latter, and now much more easily accessible, volume, numbers II, VI, IX, XIII, XXV, and XXVII

1. Marx to Kugelmann, London, 11 July 1868, *Selected Correspondence 1846–1895*, p. 63.

are therefore outside the scope of this discussion, whose purpose is to discover the geography of Auden's poetic world as it appeared to his first general audience.

Most of the 1930 (and 1933) poems are boldly modern; or 'modernistic': allusive, oblique, arcane in imagery and diction; in fact, 'difficult' in all the ways usually ascribed to modern poetry. Some of the poems, however, quite plainly state ideas and feelings elsewhere indirectly denominated. XXII, for example (excluded from *Collected Shorter Poems*), needs little by way of explanation.

In brisk Locksley Hall fifteeners it enjoins its audience, presumably those of the poet's own class, to look at the industrial wasteland, graphically pictured in the first six verses, which is now 'the land you once were proud to own'. Once the proprietors, they let themselves go under to the new and caddish entrepreneurs: 'These were boon companions who devised the legends for our tombs.' The siren voices of philosophers and artists lured the old *rentiers* from their traditional powers and responsibilities into an escape-world—'Better join us, life is worse'. Now their latest heirs, the poet and his contemporaries, either put up a futile defence against any critic of 'Perfect pater. Marvellous mater;' or head off into mindless opposition—do 'the reverse on all occasions' till they 'catch the same disease'. Their world is like 'an isolation camp', a dingy seaside town from which, in a striking image of forlorn confinement, they 'Stare out dully at the rain which falls for miles into the sea.' Organised opinion vilifies and destroys the Seers and Healers—Lawrence, Blake, Homer Lane—whose vision might bring salvation. Scenes of terrified flight through a winter landscape, of mob violence, show how, meanwhile, revolution simmers. The poet's class must either start to live or its members resign themselves to death.

The poem has every appearance of a call to action: curt orders, urgent rhetorical questions, abruptly cut-in scenes of pursuit and ambuscade. In the end, though, it is not at all precise about the form of action that Auden is urging. Just what must he and his friends do if they 'really want to live'? Nor among all the names it mentions, does the poem refer to Marx. But it is evidently predicating its argument on marxist assumptions: the class war, the revolution, the decline of the *bourgeois* tradition. We infer that the poet is demanding that his class should in some way throw in its lot with the masses; and we see that the sickness which this course of action is to remedy has psychological as well as social causes; or, according to Marx, psychological causes produced by social and economic conditions. In stating these themes as it does, the poem is a kind of skeleton key to the whole volume, in which the condition of *bourgeois* society is a recurrent *motif*.

Inherited characteristics seem to have fascinated Auden. Poem XXI is explicit: the 'Roman nose/Is noticed in the villages', the family sign of a carefully preserved stock. III ('that shape for your face to assume'), XVI ('conformity with the orthodox bone'), XX ('the ancestral face'), XXVIII ('the well-shaped heads/Conforming every day more closely to the best in albums') similarly represent a continuity of family line. All these poems, like XVIII, XXVI and XXIX, are ringing the changes upon the theme of the degenerate breed still transmitting its genetic insignia, now with no more real meaning than heraldic coats of arms. The distinctive features entomb a dead power and spirit. In *Collected Shorter Poems* Auden gives No. III the title, 'Venus Will Now Say A Few Words', but Venus seems a less appropriate speaker than the Life-Force, the Evolutionary Principle, the Dialectic—whatever determines the origin and decline of species. Man, 'whose cleverest invention was lately fur', has come far. Now his dominant culture, though outwardly assured, is past help. The time has come to 'Select another form, perhaps your son'. For the older generation it is too late 'to begin today', either to adapt to new conditions or to abdicate. 'Holders of one position, wrong for years', their destiny is extermination, like the 'Lizards my best once who took years to breed' but 'Could not control the temperature of blood'.

XVIII, XX and XXVI all concern an ancestral presence, in XX actually conjured up by ritual—'the initiating ceremony/ That out of cloud the ancestral face may come'. The attitude to the ancestors in each poem is different. XX represents the family tradition as an 'assaulted city' bent on 'Recovering the archaic imagery'. The heirs, who appear to be the speakers, take some kind of comfort from the approval of the past, 'Filtered through roots of the effacing grass'. But they are doing no more than 'turn away the eyes' from the reality of 'Massive and taciturn years, the Age of Ice'. XVIII is about the pretensions of decayed gentility in inferior clothes, 'a cheaper house', 'mortaged lands'. They keep up appearances, stick to the forms. But

> This gracious greeting
> 'Good day. Good luck'
> Is no real meeting.

No. XXVI, the fine 'Taller today', also points the question of just how we are to take the poems' various enigmatic narrators.

The speakers ('We') seem to be taking farewell of a past whose irrelevance they recognise. In their family house they revive memories of their lives there; and re-calling crises of family history now admit defeat:

> Nights come bringing the snow, and the dead howl
> Under the headlands in their windy dwelling
> Because the Adversary put too easy questions
> On lonely roads.

The Adversary, like the speaker now called 'Venus' in III, is not identified: fate? evolution? death? In any case, the ancestors have failed to meet his challenge—'too easy' because their pride concealed their vulnerability from them. Now the latest heirs find a moment of 'peace/No bird can contradict: passing, but is sufficient now'. The poem's beautifully composed landscapes set the tone of elegiac leave-taking. The protagonists, 'though no nearer each other', have a sense of 'something fulfilled this hour', the prelude to a still undefined new way of life. They are, then, within and part of the tradition they now reject.

XXVIII certainly suggests that a recusant *bourgeois* is the speaker, an initiate who knows what's in the wind. He and his friends, 'Sharers of our own day', respond to the exciting necessity of change and all its signs and portents—'drums distant over difficult country'. They thrill to acts of daring—

> Can plunder high nests; who sheer off from old like gull
> from granite,
> From their mind's constant sniffling,
> Their blood's dulled shuffling.

In thus denying their inheritance they seek to cut themselves off from the 'ancestral curse', which haphazardly 'repeats its potent pattern'—in, it would appear, monstrous births. They live with their ignorance of what is going to happen:

> *What industries decline, what chances are of revolution,*
> *What murders flash*
> *Under composed flesh;*

they know that the new life will come, and

> *Escaping cannot try;*
> *Must wait though it destroy.*

Structurally the poem is tightly knit. The 'difficult country' of verse one is the 'which' of verse two, where that setting introduces the friends who are the 'Sharers of our own day' in the third verse; and join the 'we' of verses four and five. Despite this precision of development, the poet's attitude is open to question. Are the speaker and his friends true revolutionaries? Might not the poem be the reckless *apologia* of one of the rebels in XXII who blindly 'do the reverse on all occasions till they catch the same disease'? There is really no way of telling. The poem takes its place with the other dilemmas of loyalty at a crisis in social evolution.

Mystification, indeed, is urged upon the enlightened as part of their necessary subterfuge. They must seem to conform, hide their true allegiance. 'Wear no ruffian badge', poem I advises, but 'Salute with soldiers' wives/When the flag waves'. No. XXIV discommends 'temptations/To skyline operations'. The unregenerate *bourgeois* too is a dissembler. His poise is a pose, his assurance a device,

> *. . . poised between shocking falls on razor-edge*
> *Has taught himself this balancing subterfuge*
> *Of the accosting profile, the erect carriage.*   (IV)

In No. VII,

> *Calling of each other by name*
> *Smiling, taking a willing arm*
> *Has the companionship of a game.*

But the real purpose of these little ceremonials is to preserve a precarious balance on the familiar and known, which may tip into disaster:

> *On neither side let foot slip over*
> *Invading Always, exploring Never,*
> *For this is hate and this is fear.*

The participants in these rituals may be either the 'progressive' initiates or the 'reactionist' enemy. The conditions are the same for both parties, who appear throughout the poems as 'we', 'you', or 'they' indifferently.

Auden's poetry makes its images of these brief social encounters: the 'gracious greeting' of XVIII; 'Laugh warmly turning shyly in hall' in III; the 'dextrous handling of a wrap' (IV); 'The shutting of a door/The tightening jaw', 'Voices explain . . ./ Still tap the knee' (X). The poems vibrate with these casual gestures, involuntary habits, commonplace usages, which they turn into symbols of unrest, tension, dispositions of the mind. In X, for example, which is about love shut off from communication, these reflexes carry the strain and effort, the sublimated aggression of the love which in this society cannot come completely to union. Even between couples—though this seems to be looked on as a lower form—love is partial:

> *Another I, another You,*
> *Each knowing what to do*
> *But of no use.* (VIII)

Poem **XXIX** brings together this and other themes in a panoramic view, 'As the hawk sees it or the helmeted airman', of a society dislocated by internal hostilities. Its wealthy, leisured class is a faction which, destroying itself, sows its neurotic illness broadcast. In random glimpses of fashionable occasions—a garden party ('cigarette-end smouldering on a border'), the dining-room of a Sport Hotel ('admire the view of the massif/Through plate-glass windows')—the poem displays the upper class about its pleasures, 'Dangerous, easy, in furs, in uniform'. They are 'Supplied with feelings by an efficient band', which is relayed to remoter outposts 'in kitchens in the stormy fens': the properties of the scene are made to hint at the sinister extent of their control. Despite this, they are themselves victims, unwitting accomplices of the 'supreme Antagonist', to whose comments (as to the Adversary's questions) 'the highborn mining-captains,/Found they no answer'; and died. Now the modern *bourgeois* follow the same path to destruction. A coming day of general reckoning may settle their fate (flight is useless, they are told); or personal collapse into mania or 'a classic fatigue': 'The game is up for you and for the others'.

Auden's spokesman in No. XVI knows this, though he is a member of the same class and to some extent afflicted in the same ways. Auden wrote the poem after his visit to Germany in 1929, over fifteen years after Rupert Brooke's meditations of another 'homesick foreigner', in the Café des Westens. The poem shuttles in time between Christmas, Easter and late summer; and in place between Germany and England. Presumably it is from the latter, an England very different from Brooke's folksy Cambridge, that the speaker looks back on his German winter.

He is living in a segmented world where ducks in a city harbour

> . . . *find sun's luxury enough,*
> *Shadow know not of homesick foreigner*
> *Nor restlessness of intercepted growth;*

where a friend, 'Talking excitedly of final war/Of proletariat against police', only confuses his emotions. An exile from home, he is an exile in a larger sense too. Growing up brings knowledge of otherness, of intensifying isolation within the self. Yet as he stood on a hill at twilight, absorbing impressions of the scene, he felt 'absolute unity of evening' and an impulse

> *To love my life, not as other,*
> *Not as bird's life, not as child's,*
> *'Cannot,' I said, 'being no child now nor a bird'.*

The third and fourth sections return him in August to England. In a superb passage describing a woodland walk as autumn approaches, the speaker's reflections take shape in a flurry of sensuous detail from his surroundings:

> *Startled by the violent laugh of a jay*
> *I sent from wood, from crunch underfoot,*
> *Air between stems as under water;*

As I shall leave the summer, see autumn come
Focussing stars more sharply in the sky,
See frozen buzzard flipped down the weir . . .

Seeing this he is able, with the companion whom he addresses in the fourth section, to accept a future whose birth demands the 'Death of the old gang'. A future spring will keep its promise and they will see 'the destruction of error'. In the 1930 volume this ending includes sixteen lines elaborating the wretchedness of frustrated love which the speaker and his friend endure with the rest in their repressive society. These lines disturb the tone of the conclusion. The speaker can hardly see things so clearly and be at the same time so utterly a creature of his circumstances. In 1930 the reader would probably have taken the passages simply as part of the general condemnation; but when Auden removed them in 1933 he made the poem's development much more coherent.

Like No. XXIX, this poem makes its successive scenes completely present, condensing some tangible property of each in a phrase. The observation of passing moments snatches on detail that is exactly right; and for all their variety of locale, the details assemble a country of origin of which they are all organic parts. They lead the eye past a city centre to its outskirts, along modern highways to ports, harbours, 'stately homes', and a bleak, remote countryside, between them composing the topography of a single country. Its character is distinctively modern, rather twentieth-century Scandinavian in style. But it is not its dams, power-houses, railway-stations, factories, Grand Hotels and arterial roads which make it modern. These appear discreetly, and the urban scenes are in fact much more infrequent than the distant, timeless rural settings.

The modernity comes from the lyric intensity of observation and from the manner of its expression. Auden conveys the freshness of contemporary experience and allies it venturesomely with a diction whose effect, in an urban civilisation, is archaic. His land is one of moors, fells, barrows, fens, coombs, becks, scars; its beauty is austere, silhouetted in clear-cut outline: by the starlings of 'Prologue' rising 'over wolds'; in poem XXIV by

The slow fastidious line
That disciplines the fell.

149

Individual words, recondite in themselves, make the reader look anew at the things they name. Startling combinations of words—'a polar peril', 'valves of laughter', 'neural itch'—re-cast the outlines of what they describe.

Poems (1930) sets out to 'tell particular stories of particular people and experiences'; and advance them into phantasy and parable which suggest interpretations of reality to the reader: commonly a marxist interpretation. Whether Marx's theory is right or wrong is irrelevant here. It is a serious and substantial body of thought, and from the scheme of ideas outlined in the second section of this chapter Auden withdrew a potently unifying epistemology. The function he assigns to poetry in *The Poet's Tongue*—'to reconcile the unwilling subject and object'—is analogous to the relationship Marx postulated between man and his environment. Auden's poetic method is a mode of this relationship, in its use of social encounters, gestures, mannerisms, tricks of deportment, and in its anthropomorphic landscapes. These metaphors of active contact with the social and material world reveal man's identity, though one cannot say to what extent Auden's knowledge of Marx thus directed his imagination.

What is demonstrable, even in these early poems, is a marxist interpretation of psychological freaks. Torpid, decaying landscapes are images of the exhausted minds that can no longer contend with their environments. In Poem III it is 'your conviction'—the whole *bourgeois* ethos—which will 'Cause rather a perversion'. The 'free one' of Poem IV has only the sham freedom of *bourgeois* civilisation ('dextrous handling of a wrap . . . the beggar's envy'). He is in consequence straining to survive, 'poised between shocking falls on razor-edge', both socially and psychologically. In all the 'family poems' the family is essentially a social unit. Its neurasthenia is a failure of social function—living 'in legend' when 'We in legend not,/Are not simple' (XXIII)—psychologically disastrous for its members ('mind's constant snuffling' in XXVIII). Auden, then, is borrowing freely from the whole marxist chain of reasoning, the dynamic of historical epochs that accounts for the final state of capitalist society and the condition of its dominant class, no longer playing its part in the two-way relationship with its environment.

But his application of the ideas is not an orthodox one, partly because of the more bizarre intrusions, such as the Homer Lane psychology, or the rollcall of victims admitting quite private and un-marxian categories (see the various lists in *The Orators*). More important, as we have seen, Auden implants alien concepts—the 'change of heart', the Grace-like unifying love—which offer his creatures of circumstance avenues of escape denied in the strictly marxist reckoning of their dilemma. Constantly they are urged that by their own will they may regenerate their world. Auden does not always pull off a synthesis. Some of the poems make the reader aware of a collision of incompatible values. But the successes are many more than the failures, and constitute the triumphs of Auden's first volume: the wide, confident sweep of the vocabulary, the dramatic human encounters, the exactness with which these embody ideas, feelings, attitudes. The directness of Poem XXII does not touch the subtler nerves which the elliptical encounters and fugitive *tableaux vivants* of the other poems excite. Broadly, themes and subjects are the same: the fated evolutionary decline of the *bourgeois* tradition (as in the *New Country* 'Prologue'); their habits as a species; the identity of the 'initiates' and their enemy and the struggle between the two; the dangerous inhibitions imposed upon the self by a sick community. All, with few failures, are called into unity by marxist assumptions.

The Orators is like a manifesto of some contemporary Lord of Misrule, in which the spirit of 'A Happy New Year' and 'Get there if you can' is let loose and given wider scope. It has more imaginative coherence than one might expect of such a document, and than it is often credited with. Like a high-spirited *Waste Land*, it assembles characters, incidents, maxims, outlines of principle— diagrammatic and verbal—contemporary allusions, spare, definite images of place and action, into a surrealistic montage of realities from the life of its times. In its three 'Books'—*The Initiates*, *Journal of an Airman* and *Six Odes*—*The Orators* enunciates a pathology of English society, 'this country of ours where nobody is well', and an equivocal prognosis that might be surmising either cure or deterioration.

Book I of *The Orators* consists of 'Address for a Prize Day', 'Argument' (three parts), 'Statement' and 'Letter to a Wound', all but Part II of 'Argument' in prose. The 'initiates' are those voices in *Poems* (1930) which admit the need for, in the words of

Poem XXX, 'New styles of architecture, a change of heart', and work to bring this about. So the four declarations of 'The Initiates' should be 'reliable' statements of an edifying viewpoint. 'Address for a Prize Day', delivered with the sanctimonious heartiness characteristic of the style, exhorts its audience to resist the temptations of distorted love, both in themselves and in others. The speaker has the manner to perfection, the initiate's protective colouring among the enemy. He chooses his diction—'rotters and slackers'—and his examples—'at games they are no earthly good' —largely from the experience of public-school adolescence. Then at the end he stirs up the boys—one of the practical jokes recommended in *Journal of an Airman*?—to lock a number of their masters in the stoke hole; and takes his leave.

A more resonant, suggestive phrasing persistently disturbs the schoolboy idioms: 'crouching for hours among sunlit bushes like a fox'; 'Habituees of the mirror'; 'With odd dark eyes like windows'; 'complaints less heard than the creaking of a wind pump on a moor'; 'dust settles on their unopened correspondence and inertia branches in their veins like a zinc tree'; 'Each hour bringing its little barrowful of unacted desires'. At these points the speech looks into the world where an object, a situation, becomes a sympathetic emblem of queer, unsettling dispositions of the human mind. The serious import of the speech is its attack on all the expressions of morbid love and the spiritual inertia which is a type of the death-wish. The attack is not a frontal one. The piece deliberately masks its real intention. Most obviously it is a send-up of the speech-day oration; but under that it is using the form to state ideas which we are meant to take in earnest. The imagined situation of the initiate-spokesman enables Auden to exercise a highly complex irony and makes sense, once we have got inside it, of the apparent contradictions.

Parts II and III assume the existence of a conspiracy directed by a mysterious 'Him' ('writing reports for Him in the copper-green evening'), who though unidentified has the character of a semi-fabulous Leader. 'Argument', which has a vaguely narrative core, describes the landscapes in which the struggle is waged, imbuing with a mood of danger and expectation every apparently commonplace scene and incident, His presence immanent in them all. Its second part invokes popular heroes—Ferrers-Locke, Poirot,

Dixon Hawke *inter alios*—to eradicate the negative emotions and protect the people of good will.

'Statement', with a fine eye for the range and eccentricity of human behaviour, and a superbly comic fancy, lists the gifts ('One can do cart wheels before theatre queues'), the disasters ('one is despised for wearing stiff collars'), and the successes ('One discovers a new variety of sneeze wort') of individual destinies. A new bestiary suggests correspondences and differences between human and animal life; the section ends with another register of the employments and qualities of individuals and a sibylline reckoning of the powers of sun, moon, earth, light and dark. In sum, it is a witty and provocative account of the initiate cosmology, where the outlandish, the outré, the *acte gratuit*, seem much more to the poet's liking than any ideological scheme.

The sickly, neurotic indulgence of 'Letter to a Wound', like the fatuous buffoonery of 'Address for a Prize Day', might at first appear to be out of place, the secret conference of a demoralised invalid, not an initiate. Its author's 'wound', which is incurable, has become his fondling, his 'dear'. The letter illustrates their relationship with a good deal of morbid ingenuity ('Once, when a whore accosted me, I bowed, "I deeply regret it, Madam, but I have a friend"'). But through this strange intimacy he has 'come to see a profound significance in relations I never dreamt of considering before'; and he sees that he is ineluctably bound to his sickness. That is to say, he is an initiate because of his acquiescence in a deserved sentence of death, in his unfitness for any 'healthier' world; his acknowledgement that, in the words of Poem XXVIII,

> *Escaping cannot try;*
> *Must wait though it destroy.*

'Journal of an Airman' is a prose diary, irregularly interspersed with poems, in which the diarist sets down the principles of his fellowship, recounts their training for war and derides mothers, parsons, newspaper peers, the aristocracy: the Enemy—smug, conventional, playing for safety ('insure now'; 'don't kiss your baby on the mouth'). There are instructions for identifying the enemy and tests that will betray him. The Airman's party suffers losses—accidents, nervous collapse—and the Airman himself is prey to a mysterious weakness which he tries in vain to resist. 'A cold bath every morning', he decides, may help him control his hands, the agents of his sin. If his infirmity is kleptomania, as a few remarks suggest, this is an odd remedy, more usually recommended in boarding schools as a specific for 'self-abuse'. The Airman also has an uncle-fixation ('my real ancestor', he calls him), perhaps associated with homosexuality and certainly with hostility to the mother. The flying sequences enact phantasies of escape, the urge to destroy, the temptation to be destroyed.

While the Airman and his comrades are disciplining themselves, the Enemy strike. The form of their attack closely resembles the sort of skylarking recommended and practised by the Airman: 'bombardment by obscene telephone calls', 'the boys, out of control, imbibe Vimto through india-rubber tubing, openly pee into the ink-pots'; and by a curious anticipation of the popular myth of 1940, they arrive 'disguised as nuns'. The Enemy's victory demands 'absorption of, *i.e.*, infection by, the conquered'. The Airman has 'three days to break a lifetime's pride'; and at the very end can claim, 'Hands in perfect order'.

The *Journal* is an exhilarating performance, a weirdly reasonable miscellany of nonsense-definitions, psychiatric and biological hocus-pocus and occasional staider intervals, as in, ' "We have brought you," they said, "a map of the country" ', in context a sombre reminiscence of the pressures to conform in the Airman's upbringing. Like Ludendorff's *The Coming War*, which in part inspired it, the *Journal* and the Airman are both 'very dotty'.[1] But if it exhilarates, it also bewilders. Why should 'ancestor worship' be a counter attack against the Enemy as described; why does nothing like the predicted results of an Enemy victory—'impotence—cancer—paralysis'—occur?

The poems omitted from *Journal* in the latest edition of *The Orators* (1966) do not seem crucial to understanding. They are: (1) 'After the death of their proud master'; (2) 'Well, Milder, if that's the way you're feeling' (also omitted from the 1934 edition); (3) 'Last day but ten'; (4) 'Beethameer, Beethameer, bully of Britain'; (5) 'The draw was at five. Did you see the result?' (omitted in 1934); (6) 'I'm afraid it sounds more like a fairy story'. (2) reads like a heartening address to a prospective recruit; (3)

1. W. H. Auden: Foreword to *The Orators* (1966).

chronicles a novice's failure to stay the course; (5) celebrates the events and the spirit of 'graduation day':

> *The town seems stiller, our greetings quieter than usual.*
> *O charged-to-the-full-in-secret slow-beating heart,*
> *To-night is full-moon;*

(4) promises the newspaper peers, 'Leading the lost with lies to defeat', 'the thrashing you richly deserve'; (1) concerns 'the circle's after-image of itself exploited for private ends'—that is, the survival of a propertied élite, 'poops and smarties', on the vanished strength of their ancestors, 'Denying weakness by believing legends'; and (6), very obscure—'There is a lot about the Essay Club and Stephen', as it rightly says—seems to be a bumbling attempt at persuasion which—deliberately—completely loses its thread.

These poems did make a quite material contribution to the wholesale sweep of the *Journal*'s irreverence, and to placing the Airman's attitudes in particular contexts. 'Beethameer', for instance, is the clearest and most extended statement of their political application. But while they are not essential to its meaning they may distract attention from its psychological basis, much clearer in the 1966 *Orators*, which plays down the politics.

We suspect that the Airman is like the writer of 'Letter to a Wound', though less passive; that his nervous disorder is hysteria, of which his diary exemplifies the primary symptoms: dissociation and susceptibility to autosuggestion caused by conflict and repression. Its 'inconsistencies' are part of his condition. Everything he records, Enemy attack and all, is an acting-out in his own mind of psychological trials (especially his antagonism to his Mother), though we are to understand as well that these have objective social analogues: part of the Airman's trouble is his refusal to accept the conventional 'map of the country', to 'keep their hours and live by the clock'. The *Journal* is in fact an impressive attempt to synthesise marxism and psychoanalysis.

Book III comprises Six Odes, of which the 1966 *Orators* reprints five. The omitted Ode is Number II, dedicated to Gabriel Carritt, captain of Sedbergh School XV, Spring, 1927. It is a rollicking tribute to the victorious team, outlining the virtues of each of its members rather in the manner of a school magazine report, but understandably with more imagination. The boys are full of spirit and energy, not 'Dark fearers, dreading December's harm'. Three other Odes are addressed to friends of Auden: III ('What siren zooming') to Edward Upward, IV ('Roar Gloucestershire, do yourself proud') to John Warner, (infant) son of Rex and Frances Warner, V ('Though aware of our rank and alert to obey orders') to his pupils; and I ('Watching in three planes from a room overlooking the courtyard') contains references to Wystan, Stephen and Christopher.

The purpose of these poems, though this is a rather drab and stuffy way of describing them, is to insinuate Auden and his circle of friends into the situation of the initiates set out in the first two books. Wystan, Stephen and Christopher, 'in cold Europe, in the middle of Autumn destruction', confront precisely the same hazards—

> *The fatal error,*
> *Sending the body to islands or after its father—*

and at the end look for a new leader to resist these evils. II suggests some kind of training camp:

> *We are here for our health, we have not to fear*
> *The fiend in the furze or the face at the manse.*

III represents the young Warner as the longed-for Leader who will restore 'The directed calm, the actual glory'. It castigates just about everyone who could be castigated in the England of the time, from trimming politicians like Baldwin and MacDonald to the apathetic workers—'Poofs and ponces,/All of them dunces'. Now excised is an Envoi of considerable charm setting the poet in a delightfully visualised Helensburgh domestic scene. The Ode's success comes, again, from its high spirits and the flamboyant versatility of its diction: 'rufflers or mousers'; 'the mawmet and the false alarm'; 'ducked in a gletcher'; 'lovely quarrons' (an association daring in a way somewhat reminiscent of Eliot's 'liquid siftings').

The soldiers of Ode V belong to an army sustained by legends 'About the tall white gods' and halcyon days 'When love came easy'; kept in ignorance of why they are fighting; pitted against an enemy with all the Vices—Fear, Lust, Gluttony: or so they are told. Now they are due to parade for ecclesiastical blessing in the struggle. Across the frontier the enemy similarly prepare themselves. Four verses indicate that despite their supposed corruption and demoralisation the enemy are tough, skilled and dedicated. More mysterious still, the soldiers seem to recognise among them people suddenly vanished from their own ranks. But on the verge of revelation the soldiers retreat from these thoughts and half-suspicions:

> *But careful; back to our lines; it is unsafe there.*

Without much hope they entrain for 'The headlands we're doomed to attack', leaving us to wonder, to adapt the title now given the poem, whose side we are supposed to be on.

Its aim seems to be just to raise that question. It is an allegory of the confusions which cause the question to be asked and discommode any attempt to answer it. The poet's party—which might be either side of the frontier in this poem—are inextricably implicated in the system they wish to destroy, whether it is the class society or capitalist economics, and vulnerable to its ills, of the spirit and the flesh. Victory may mean—may require—their own destruction of a part of themselves. The frontier and the battlefield are within each individual psyche, where habit, the genetic inheritance, the individual psychopathology mask the conflicting forces. The soldiers whose thoughts the poem gives us are on the 'wrong' side, misled by their newspapers, kept in the dark by their leaders (but do their enemy's 'scarecrow prophet' and 'bitter psalm' sound any better?). They are, however, potential initiates, at times glimpsing the truth of their situation, like those of their comrades who have deserted. But by attempting to represent simultaneously an 'exterior' and an 'interior' enemy, the poem over-complicates its ironies.

The final Ode ('Not, Father, further do prolong') succinctly and more directly resumes this idea of self-immolation. The poet and his friends—and the *caste* they represent—pray for 'Our necessary defeat' in syntax that parodies the convoluted structures of the desperate hymnist. In this Ode the best hope is that the Father, instead of having to destroy them, may mystically impart a Grace that will exalt them—'Illumine, and not kill'. *Collected*

Shorter Poems simplifies the elliptical third verse—

> These nissen huts if hiding could
> Your eye inseeing from
> Firm fenders were, but look! to us
> Your loosened angers come—

by substituting 'hide we' for 'hiding': it remains a *Bay Psalm Book* construction. The Father is the Leader for whose advent *The Orators*, privily and openly by turns, is a cry. Auden and his confidants are not so much the governors of destiny; more humbly, they are the agents through whom the Leader may work, the seekers after a passive role. It is easy now to see why Auden suspects fascist leanings in the book. For all its exuberance and the positiveness of its abuse, it expresses a yearning to be made one with some outside Power.

Yet we cannot take this too seriously: not so seriously as we take Lawrence's phantasies of power in *Kangaroo*. The wit, the constant re-statement of apocalyptic alarms as gleeful absurdities (the Prize Day, the Airman's war, the infant Warner as Saviour) keep Auden's, and the reader's, feet on the ground. So, for example, does the distorted syntax of Ode VI. Though many of its implications may be distasteful, *The Orators* none the less sees most perceptively into the illness of its society: its phoniness, pretensions, and desperation. In a way, it is an extended treatment of the masks, disguises and subterfuges intermittently practised by the characters of *Poems* (1930). Auden has called *The Orators* a 'fair notion fatally injured'. It is much better than that. The dual reference points, social/political and psychological, land it in occasional difficulties; it tempts the critic to expend ingenuity in establishing a consistency that simply may not exist. But more often, the rhetoric, the 'oratory', when we have grasped its design, consolidates Auden's viewpoints.

Unlike Eliot, Auden in these two volumes draws heavily upon the immediate, the ephemeral, and has in consequence been belittled for journalistic cleverness. Yet his achievement is that he invests his topicalities with an exemplary power, or derives that from them, without impairing their singularity. Auden produces a satirical newsreel of the thirties, variously mordant and good-humoured, in which the sinister vision of German expressionist cinema can suddenly assume control and the people, the events, of the thirties take on nightmare proportions. As Geoffrey Grigson has said, the 'frontier' in Auden's poetry is not 'the consequence *only*, and the expression *only*, of Auden's middle-class position'. It is 'the line between the known and the feared, the past and the future, and the consciousness and everything beyond control, the region of society and the region of trolls and hulders (and Goebbelses)'.[1]

Poems (1930), *The Orators* and the *New Country* poems, the earliest itineraries of this world, represent a remarkable accomplishment, not only for their pliant idiom and sensuous re-creation of experience. The movement of ideas within the experience gives it intellectual design. Throughout the thirties, Auden never ceased to return to the affairs of the day: very often his immediate subjects were indeed exactly those of the newspapers, including the society columns. But increasingly the matter, the ideas, the images begin to find their place in a more disciplined symbolism. Donne is much praised for his ability to fuse his eclectic pickings. Auden has not always been so fortunate in his critics, though his situation and his successes are comparable.

III

Auden's early work includes his poetic dramas, of which the first, *Paid on Both Sides*, appeared originally in *The Criterion* for January 1930, then in *Poems* (1930). Described as 'a charade', it is the story of a feud which on the verge of reconciliation fails to achieve it. The characters are doomed to endless, futile struggle in their bleak, northern homeland. The setting is contemporary: 'shops/Open a further wing on credit', gears break down for want of maintenance. Other properties (a boy 'born fanged like a weasel') and the blend of styles in both prose and poetry, Auden Ancient and Modern, refer the situation back to the world of the sagas, 'a society with only the gangster virtues'. The play's techniques are expressionistic and its characters marionettes plucked through tragedy and farce. They love, die, are wounded; and when the

1. 'Auden as Monster', *New Verse* (Auden Double Number), November 1937, pp. 13–14.

doctor comes he 'takes circular saws, bicycle pumps, etc., from his bag', and conducts a vaudeville dialogue with his 'Boy'.

The villain of the piece is the Mother, who engineers the continuation of the feud. The speech by the Man-Woman, who makes a parenthetical appearance as a prisoner of war, associates impotence and auto-eroticism with generally purposeless action:

> I tried then to demand
> Proud habits, protestations called you mind
> To show you it was extra, but instead
> You overworked yourself, misunderstood,
> Adored me for the chance. Lastly I tried
> To teach you acting, but always you had nerves
> To fear performances as some fear knives.

Both social and psychological disorders afflict the characters and their community: all the activity of the feud is unreal, a vacant expense of energy for a bogus 'good'. Yet the play's treatment of these themes is neither didactic nor heartless. Its people are 'marionettes' because they are players in a charade: not individualised characters but universal symbols of anguished human resistance to the weaknesses and follies of the self. We may discern in this a debt, at several removes, to Marx and Freud: the neurasthenic dependence on the past which obstructs emerging forms of life and thought. But the play enlarges these scholastic concepts into forceful images of archetypal experience. Its superb lyrics, stitched together by the narrative line, are all movement, unrest, animated by the vivid, vigorous images. They are an intensely moving expression of the timeless human quest for assurance amidst haunted, shifting landmarks,

> Where rifts open unfenced, mark of a fall,
> And flakes fall softly softly burying
> Deeper and deeper down her loving son.

Other plays sound the marxian message more clearly. *The Dance of Death* (1933) presents the death-wish acting itself out in little pantomimes of what are almost entirely social and political phenomena. The *bourgeois* 'Audience' dream of a new life ('Rise and make a workers' state') but their instincts drive them to destructive action ('I was a Black and Tan/I was always there when the tortures began'). In a series of cabaret-like 'interludes' they acclaim an English revolution 'to keep the race pure', beat up the Manager ('A dirty Jew') and debate the paths to Utopia. The Dancer mimes their fickle urges—as Sun God, Demagogue and Pilot. When he falls paralysed the Chorus sing his Will, which surveys the successive declines of Greeks, Romans, feudal barons and acquisitive Calvinists, all victims of economic forces they failed to understand. At the end, Karl Marx pronounces the Dancer dead: 'The instruments of production have been too much for him.' It is a lightweight piece of work, episodic and disjointed. Professor Replogle discounts its marxism because of the play's antic mood, but it is a large assumption that you cannot write humorously about ideas if you really believe in them. Despite its stating so much more naively the same 'progressive' ideas that brood within the poems, *The Dance of Death* makes intelligent entertainment of them. One has only to look at the complacent dreadfulness of *MacBird* to recognise the incomparably defter talent of Auden's popular satire, and the intelligence with which it makes its fun from ideas.

Auden wrote *The Dog Beneath the Skin* (1935), *The Ascent of F.6* (1936) and *On the Frontier* (1938) in collaboration with Christopher Isherwood. They collaborated, no doubt, because they were friends; because each of them, the poet and the novelist, wanted to attach the other's art to his own in a form that could absorb something from both, and perhaps carry their ideas to a popular audience; and one can imagine Auden's being attracted by the spirit of the Mortmere phantasies of which Isherwood gives so engaging an account in *Lions and Shadows*. Isherwood's exact contribution to the plays is a matter of guesswork. It would have been largely to the prose speeches and dialogue; one can detect his hand in the medical patter of the hospital scene in *The Dog beneath the Skin*, perhaps in details like the poor articulation of Martha Throvald, in *On the Frontier*, whose 'false teeth fit so badly' —a Mr Norris-like touch. It may be—see Isherwood's essay in *New Verse*, where he speaks of Auden's fancy for 'choral interruptions by angel voices'—that whatever formal circumspection the plays have comes from Isherwood.

F.6 and *On the Frontier* differ from all the others in having a more or less naturalistic plot. The former concerns a mountaineering expedition whose success would establish British dominance over the superstitious Sudolanders. Through this situation the play explores both the futility of power politics and the psychological problems of the expedition's leader, Michael Ransom. His discreditable motives include jealousy of his brother (whose motive, equally discreditable, is political power) and some kind of obscurely delivered mother fixation. The speeches of Mr and Mrs A from the audience reveal the irrelevance of the expedition to the needs and desires of ordinary people, cynically humbugged by their leaders. In the final Chorus, Ransom's death represents the dissolution of those 'Whom history has deserted' and so offers, not too persuasively, to knit together the double significance of the argument.

The Chorus tells us that 'At last the secret is out, as it always must come in the end', and in three verses sounds out the sinister, the innocent, even the beautiful, appearances that are the reticent signs of a 'wicked secret'. This proceeds, however, from Ransom's personal 'secret', his unacknowledged motives, and so one of the play's few poetically heightened moments, though it illuminates the private, occludes the political, allegory. Perhaps Auden and Isherwood recognised the confusion of this duality, of the free-for-all of naturalistic and expressionist manners, and the arbitrary cuts from mysticism to satire and farce (one stage direction enjoins the characters to 'behave in general like the Marx brothers'). Whatever the reason, their next play disciplines its themes more severely.

On the Frontier chronicles the nationalist ill will, culminating in war over a border incident, between fascist Westland and monarchist Ostnia. Its spirit is pessimistic. Neither side is any better than the other. The people are the dupes of chauvinist leaders, the leaders of profiteering industrialists. The losers are the workers, the poor, the ordinary soldiers of both sides, who towards the end rise against their bosses. There is no happy ending, however. The last we hear of the revolt is from the reports in five English newspapers which have reconstructed the facts into propaganda, the communist as corruptly as the rest. A number of *chansons populaires* by workers, political prisoners and soldiers (the last an inspired imitation of the sardonic songs of the First World War) very successfully find words to pay more than perfunctory witness

to left-wing ideas: that the capitalists and their hangers-on hope
to contain and profit by fascism, that only the union of the exploited can prevail against it. The inspiration is marxist and undoubtedly the play owed to the marxist view of contemporary
Europe the timeliness of its analogies: Hitler was well set on his
hysteric rampage and a second world war clearly in prospect.
What could prevent it but the united action of those who stood to
lose? But the play as a whole strongly implies that Parties corrupt
principles. It moves beyond marxism and timeliness both. The
ideal that survives to the end is the love between Eric Thorvald of
Westland and the Ostnian Anna Vrodny, a love that inhabits
persons but is more than personal, that may 'build the city where/
The will of love is done'. *On the Frontier* is a compassionate
affirmation of humane beliefs: that war is evil, that each person,
as Auden put it in a *Scrutiny* review some years earlier, is more
interested in his own wellbeing than he need be and does less for
others than he could.[1] As bald generalisations these are platitu-
dinous. Of all Auden's plays this comes nearest to reducing the
general platitudes to specifically dramatic truths.

The first Chorus of *The Dog beneath the Skin* originally appeared,
in part, in *The Listener* of 12 July 1933, under the title 'The Witnesses' and with an introductory narrative discarded in the play.
It announces the theme of the quest in terms—recalling 'Now from
my window sill' and Poem XXVI—which the hero's escapades
never adequately put in action. This Chorus warns the young men
of Pressan Ambo of the dangers of the quest and appoints two
'guardians of the gate in the rock./The Two'. Their world
screens its dangers in the most innocuous of settings: 'the green
field comes off like a lid'; the woods 'come up and are standing
round/In deadly crescent'; mysterious agents prepare Gestapo-
like abductions:

> Outside the window is the black remover's van.
> And now with sudden swift emergence
> Come the woman in dark glasses and the humpbacked
>   surgeons
>   And the scissor man.

Like the Lords of Limit and the Adversary, 'the Two' are as much

1. Vol. IV, No. 2, September 1935, p. 200.

arbiters to be appeased as guardian angels, demanding the observance of certain rituals to avert their wrath. The quester/pilgrim is to be constantly in danger and under surveillance.

The Chorus is a telling evocation of uncanny disquiet, slyly unsettling, unclear in its application—why should the quester conform to the kind of stodgy routine repudiated by the Airman —'Trim the garden, wind the clock'? The events of the play supply no answer and in fact ignore the purchase given by the Choruses, rather as Marlowe's *Faustus* does.

The action is much less seriously formulated than the verse commentary. Alan Norman sets out with a dog to find Sir Francis Crewe, the missing squire of Pressan Ambo, and bring him back to the village. On their return the dog, who has revealed that he is Sir Francis, denounces the village and with some kindred spirits goes off to join 'the army of the other side', whereupon the leading villagers perform an animal masque which reveals their true characters. Alan's adventures in Westland and Ostnia, 'Products of the peace which that old man provided', are a frolic. Scenes in a Red Light district, a lunatic asylum, an operating theatre, the Grand Nineveh Hotel, provide Auden with occasion for lively cabaret and music-hall songs, a spirited satire of the decadence and vacuous frivolity of Europe, where 'You may kiss what you like; it has often been kissed before'.

These episodes and the Choruses deal with the same actualities, though in totally disparate styles. The Choruses are gravely meditated, close to the facts of Europe which the action travesties and caricatures. Together, the Choruses constitute the most sweeping reconnaissance in all Auden's poetry of the contemporary urban scene: 'The summer holds'; 'You with your shooting sticks'; 'Happy the hare at morning'; 'Night. And crooked Europe hidden in shadow'; 'Now through night's caressing grip'. These, more discursively than Auden's short lyrics but with the same incisive detail, mount an oppressive exhibition of elegant buildings and complex technology alongside wretched slums, sophisticated art alongside desperate want; of human activity totally deprived of rhythm or pattern, change, crisis, migration (unlike those of the animals) entirely random and without due season. Through all, through cities disrupted by the visible evidences of their arbitrary class divisions, through love betrayed, ideals degraded, intelligence perverted, 'corruption spreads its peculiar and emphatic odours/And Life lurks, evil, out of its epoch'. It is these, not the body of the play, which prepare for the concluding exhortation: repent, unite, act; and the final maxim— 'To each his need: from each his power'.

The plays are a public disbursement of Auden's intellectual stock-in-trade, which in all of them but *On the Frontier*, Justin Replogle argues, owes more to Freudian psychology than to marxism. Yet Auden constantly resists isolating psychological ills within the individual as an outgrowth of autonomous private experience, an alienation susceptible of solitary relief. Ransom's problems, like those of the Dancer, and of Francis and Sir Alan until they come to see more clearly, are a consequence of their society's having the forms and institutions it does, and of their failure to recognise its realities. While the plays do not very successfully keep up the correspondence between the personal neurosis and the social structures, their intention is to demonstrate a relationship: see, for example, the commentary of Mr and Mrs A. The alienation is in concept as much marxist as Freudian.

It would be wrong to take Auden's plays lightly because they are not solemn. The verbal fireworks, the wit, the parodies and the farce have an undertow of serious meaning which we should not look for only in the graver passages. But it is the case that none of the plays achieves dramatic unity. They cobble together individual scenes as a setting for what are often detachable poems and other pieces more or less integrated with a tenuous action. For Auden, the plays were a permissible outlet for his felicitous 'light verse'; and they enabled him to lay a series of landmines assembled out of materials from many intellectual sources. They explode under unexamined, conventional ideas (of family relationships, class-based politics, nationalism and so on). There the metaphor must halt, since landmines do not replace what they destroy and Auden, if he is not explicitly stating, is writing on the assumption of, alternative hypotheses.

The poems of *Look, Stranger!*, which share these hypotheses, integrate them much more persuasively than the plays. As well as the tender lyrics celebrating personal love ('Let the florid music praise', 'May with its light behaving', 'Fish in the unruffled lakes'), the volume contains a number of seriously ideological poems (of which XXI is a love poem as well), the great majority of them published in 1933 and 1934.[1] The *New Country* poems are representative of these. *Look Stranger!* No. XVII takes more fully into the present scene the marxist view of England that informs 'Prologue'. In a Europe 'anxious about her health' after 'a banker's winter', the Cotswolds landscape utters a warning. The poet (like the Airman) must get his 'nerves in order' and make his will effective, 'For men are changed by what they do'. Man is to recognise the limitations he arrogantly ignores. Though he can modify, he is limited by, his environment: machines are not 'our hearts' spontaneous fruit'. So far, so marxist. But even here Auden projects the human environment from a purely materialist determination of choice into analogies of ethical or spiritual decision. The directing impulse comes from submission to 'the disciplined love which alone could have employed those engines'. To be 'changed by what they do' men must first change within.

Unlike 'Prologue' (and other poems), No. XVII is not setting a vagrant present against a past achieving itself. The contrast is between an ideal 'what-should-have-been/What-might-be' and the dreadful 'what-is'. Running through *Look, Stranger!* is the image of the city unachieved: 'these starving cities', 'unhappy cities', 'the policed unlucky city', 'the starved city', 'our city—with the byres of poverty'. This is a composite of the actual cities of the times. Auden is very good on their mean employments, coarsened splendours, their flashed-up dowdiness, spilling thinly into the countryside. Behind them is the spirit of statism—'The total state where all must wear your badges' (IX)—and its exponents—'Hitler and Mussolini in their wooing poses' (XXI). There are contrary movements. 'Epilogue' (XXXI) speaks of 'the neat man' in the east (Lenin) 'who ordered Gorki to be electrified'.

The city as image grows from the cities of fact. It takes further substance from the infiltration of the personal experiences and

---

1. In addition to the four *New Country* poems there are: Nos. II ('Out on the lawn I lie in bed'); VII ('Hearing of harvests rotting in the valleys'); IX ('The earth turns over, our side feels the cold'); XVII ('Here on the cropped grass of the narrow ridge I stand'). These first appeared in, respectively: *The Listener*, March 1934; *The Criterion*, July 1933; *New Verse*, February 1934; *New Oxford Outlook*, November 1933. Their *CSP* titles are: 'A Summer Night 1933'; 'Paysage Moralisé'; 'Through the Looking Glass'; 'The Malverns'.

feelings of the poet and his friends. XXI fully realises the bride's presence ('A pine tree shadow across your brow') and the love of the young couple under the sombre 'sixteen skies of Europe'. No. II, while violence is done 'Where Poland draws her Eastern bow', evokes the companionship of the poet's group. They enjoy a leisured English summer, evenings 'When Death put down his book', though aware that 'through the dykes of our content/The crumpling flood will force a rent'.

The abstractions work out from concrete situations and events. The city takes on visionary qualities. Its fullest single expression is in Poem VII ('Hearing of harvests'). Here the dream, of 'evening walks through learned cities', is side-tracked into a wild goose chase after 'islands'. The quest is folly. No idyllic 'otherwhere' will remit the proper task, set out in the climax, which resolves the earlier 'Lotus Eaters' rhythms:

> *Ah, water*
> *Would gush, flush, green these mountains and these valleys,*
> *And we rebuild our cities, not dream of islands.*

This poem's images discharge a myth of aspirations frustrated yet kept alive, of a quest after mirages that charm away the reality under the quester's noses.

The antithesis of the city is the island, an emblem of isolation, illusion, self-regard. The 'favourite islands' of the people in XXX are the 'showy arid works' of mass entertainment, bringing them no closer together in understanding of 'the dangerous flood/Of history'. We have 'islands of self through which I sailed all day' in No. IX, a poem (addressed to Love or a loved one) which I take to be using an allegory of art as illusion. Art is bound to be a cunning make-believe of reality—no 'painter's gifts can make its flatness round'. It puts familiar figures into grotesque roles ('My mother chasing letters with a knife'), makes what it wants of flesh and blood. But it is no more contrived than the world it imitates, 'Love's daytime kingdom'. There as well, in a memorable personification, facts, emotions

> *organised and massed*
> *Line the straight flood-lit tracks of memory*
> *To cheer your image as it flashes by.*

The lover loves no one but himself. Better relationships require an 'untransfigured scene' where love could be truly itself, and art presumably a truer mirror of it ('My mother at her bureau writing letters').

The ideas of the poem and their organisation, which this account much attenuates, are complex, oblique, interesting. So they are in XXI, which seems to touch upon the same theme. The wedding photographer—or is it Auden?—conjuring 'a camera into a wishing rose', can transfigure a Europe of 'terrifying mottoes' into 'worlds as innocent as Beatrix Potter's'. But this does not really alter facts, of which the love of the couple is one. It may follow any one of a number of paths, perhaps become a source of the unifying love that may redeem the time and which 'through our private stuff must work/His public spirit'. But it may equally ('A choice was killed by every childish illness') satisfy hatred, vanity, power-lust, all the evil desires of solitary growth.

The poems of *Look, Stranger!* cover the years 1933-6, almost half of them from 1933 and 1934. Their mood is troubled, not disheartening. Their anxieties had real and substantial cause, yet they keep their hopes alive, though under assault in the crisis of choice. Auden's revisions for the volume suggest, as we have seen, an attempt to strengthen its marxist activism and its materialist philosophy. Together with the plays, *Look, Stranger!* confirms what his earlier poetry had made obvious enough, that Auden accepted many of Marx's propositions as a valid account of what had happened in history and what was to come; and as at least partly illuminating individual human behaviour and motives.

The remaining collections of the thirties indicate no real change of premiss. None of them is negligible. The patchiest is *Another Time*. It contains the fine poems on Yeats and Freud, 'Spain 1937', '1 September 1939' and 'Dover'. With these it includes a number of rather trivial pieces which Auden has not preserved in *Collected Shorter Poems*. In *Letters from Iceland* (with Louis MacNeice) Auden's mockery is at its most genial. 'Letter to Lord Byron' stands with the best of English light verse, combining autobiography, politics, social history, aesthetics, gossip, in a witty exposition of ideas elsewhere seriously deliberated.

Journey to a War is an account of Auden's visit to China with Isherwood during the Sino-Japanese war. Its sonnet sequence and verse commentary ('In Time of War') make of the experience another solemn marxian instance. They are a history of human development. Man, having outstripped the lower animals, in different ways 'to his own creation became subject'. He has failed to create 'the Good Place' because he has failed to see that 'We live in freedom by necessity'. Hence a restlessness that usurps action rightly directed, a deep-rooted maladjustment which is the source of social impotence and psychological instability. Once more a particular curiosity of modern life gives Auden a symbol, like his 'arterial roads' loaded with factual associations, for the spiritual condition of its people: 'Anxiety/Received them like a grand hotel'. The commentary ends with an eloquent plea for men to 'construct at last a human justice,/The contribution of our star'.

Here again, Auden is working towards the creation of myth, the set of images, situations, characters which, while having a particular relevance to a particular society, involves archetypal human experience and suggests an interpretation of it. Auden's myth places its insights with great assurance in a marxian framework. It is marxism which assists him to his powerfully comprehensive statements of society as the 'carrier' of spiritual and psychological predicaments. The symbols which define these metaphysical conditions grow from sensuous images, from 'the data from the outer world'. These translate us to a world recognisably an image of the phenomenal world, yet at the same time exciting hidden associations of ideas and feelings from its familiar outlines. Inanimate nature stirs into life and becomes an actor in dramas of the human exploration of the self and its relationships to others and to its environment. The landscapes harbour powers whose guidance may assist the travellers; or if they judge wrongly ensnare them:

> It's in its nature always to appear
> Behind us as we move
> With linked arms through our dreams.[1]

The goal is a political union of mankind, a world-state; more largely, a moral-spiritual resolution of the conflict between ego-centred energy and the thwarted impulses of disinterested love. In

1. 'Poem', Poem XV, *Look, Stranger!* p. 40.

this early poetry the reader is conscious of intelligence and imagination working harmoniously among a wide scope of ideas and feelings, seizing upon exactly the objects to represent them, exactly the language to represent the objects.

The poetry Auden wrote after his religious conversion does not renounce either the manner or the matter he was developing in the thirties. He is working amongst many new analogies and within a new vision of human life. His interest is still in man in society, man alone seeking not to be alone, now firmly entering the perspective leading to immaterial reality, the revealed God, shadowy before. The island and the city remain the poles of human experience, though it is no longer a city that man can build in the temporal world. The 'Good Place' of *Journey to a War* becomes the 'Innocent Place where the Law can't look' of Rosetta in *The Age of Anxiety*; and on earth there can be no such place. Love is still the unifying force; now it is unequivocally a divine love. The love of the couple in *Look, Stranger!* No. XXI, the type of a secular communion, becomes the love of Ferdinand and Miranda in *The Sea and the Mirror*, the imperfect type of a godly love which, without God, it can never attain. Ideas, echoing from the past, strike new resonances. The 'mother love' of Mary's lullaby in *For the Time Being* can only 'tempt you from His will', as before it obstructed the collective human will. And 'His will', more generally, faces man, to other ends, with the Christian version of the Freedom-Necessity paradox; see *New Year Letter*, part III, and 'Criticism in a Mass Society'.

New Year Letter is the first long poem written in the new dispensation. It has been called a 'a pretentious farrago of facile rhymed octosyllabics' and as having 'dropped to a nadir of dullness'.[1] It is neither facile nor dull and later opinion has rightly thought better of it. It develops its ideas, in lucid verse and aphoristic definition, at a punishing pace. Though neither economics nor psychiatry now give Auden final answers he is still solicitous how man may mend the economic disasters of his society ('An earth made common by the means/Of hunger, money and machines') and the unhappy relationships born of

---

1. Henry Reed, 'W. H. Auden in America', *Penguin New Writing*, No. 31, pp. 124–30; Ronald Mason, 'W. H. Auden' in Denys Val Baker (ed.), *Writers of Today*, No. 2, pp. 105–16.

childhood experience:

> *The state created by his acts*
> *Where he patrols the forest tracts*
> *Planted in childhood, farms the belt*
> *Of doings memorised and felt*
> *And even if he find it hell*
> *May neither leave it nor rebel.*

Auden's Christian poetry is not a withdrawal into abstract contemplation of the poet's own spiritual state. His conversion has prompted a re-examination of the scene that has always occupied his imagination, finding now in Christianity alone a sufficiently comprehensive explanation of human experience. The two later works which rise to this new and demanding opportunity are *The Sea and the Mirror* and *For the Time Being: A Christmas Oratorio*.

The Sea and the Mirror is a projection from *The Tempest*, developing hints and situations from the play into a commentary upon: the play itself, the relationship between art and life (like Poem IX of *Look, Stranger!*) and the ineradicable self-will (Antonio) that refuses reconciliation (as achieved by Prospero). *For the Time Being* is written around the events from Christ's birth to the Flight into Egypt. Through these Auden dramatises the traditional agnostic doubts, the Faith which brings the endless Charity of revelation accepted; and their present-day relevance. The references and the imagery extend the Christian story into Auden's own time, where there are 'bills to be paid, machines to keep in repair,/Irregular verbs to learn'; and which is the 'Time Being to redeem/From insignificance'.

What is new in both these poems is their use of a 'given' framework. Auden uses it to integrate his lyrics, his songs in popular idiom, his penetrating satire and the sustained and exalted expression of belief. The Fugal-Chorus in honour of Caesar is an expert demolition job on the dafter complacencies of technical and intellectual progress in philosophy, science, mathematics, economics; and on dictatorships that pretend to manage them to the end of human happiness. It takes its place harmoniously with the final Chorus identifying Christ as Truth:

Seek Him in the Kingdom of Anxiety;
You will come to a great city that has expected your return for years.

He is the Life.
Love Him in the World of the Flesh;
And at your marriage all its occasions shall dance for joy.

The integrity of Auden's work is too large a subject to be undertaken here. Perhaps, though, even this inadequate postscript on his post-war writings may suggest that he has not reversed direction. His understanding of his early beliefs brought him to the point where they were no longer serviceable. At that point he could make the new assumptions that led him to a journey's end satisfactory for him—'the greatest discovery that we can make', Henry Reed has said, 'if we can make it'.[1] Our concern is with the brilliantly composed looking-glass world in which he has re-enacted his journey. He has continued to meet Geoffrey Grigson's criterion for *New Verse* that a poem should take notice 'for ends not purely individual, of the universe of objects and events'. The ends have changed. But the later poems still create from their objects and events a dramatic myth that extends their bearings beyond local and immediate relevancy. So it was with his 'marxism'. Of all the thirties poets he was most at home in the poetic fable he constructed from it. A knowledge of Marx enlightens many of Auden's poems; Auden's poems create their own luminous after-image of marxism.

1. 'W. H. Auden in America'.

V

Louis MacNeice and Stephen Spender:
Sense and Sensibility

I

VIRGINIA WOOLF'S 'The Leaning Tower'[1] assailed the left-wing poets of the thirties for technical incompetence, their 'poor little rich boy' self-pity, their suicidal attack upon the sort of society that had produced and continued to support them (and which in her view was a pre-condition of any literature worth having that she could imagine). In the next issue of *Folios of New Writing* Edward Upward, B. L. Coombes and Louis MacNeice answered back. MacNeice remarked on the assumption 'by the undiscriminating —among whom for this occasion I must rank Mrs Woolf—that all these writers of the Thirties were slaves of Marx, or rather of Party Line Marxism.' (*i.e.* Stalinist policies?) Indeed if slavishness implies uniformity, there was little of it evident either in the sort of political accommodation these writers made with communist beliefs and practices, or in their transference of marxism to poetry. Madge, Caudwell, Day Lewis and Auden arrived at quite distinct poetic statements of marxist ideas.

Louis MacNeice would have appeared particularly well qualified to question the assumption of intellectual surrender. Critics think of him as the least political of the political poets of his generation. He was never a Party member nor a self-proclaimed communist. He professed no intellectual attachment to marxist

1. In John Lehmann (ed.), *Folios of New Writing*, Autumn 1940, pp. 11–33.

theory nor is his poetry ever propagandist in the manner of
Cornford's, nor habitually a poetic transcription of marxist
thought. He was wary both of parties and of systems. 'You,'
Portright accuses his tormentors in MacNeice's play *Out of the
Picture*, 'want to set the psychologists on me to dig me to pieces
with scalpels. Or you want to set the communists on me to make
me a cog in a gear-box. Or you want to set the stormtroopers on
me to make a man of me with truncheons.' He honestly enjoyed
the material pleasures of his class and wrote most attractively about
them. Still, his political colour was deep pink/liberal. He thought
of the great issues of the day—the rise of Hitler, mass unemployment, the Spanish War—as Auden, Day Lewis and Spender thought
of them. The subjects of his poetry were similar and so was his
notion of the right poetic methods: 'the poet's first business is
mentioning things. Whatever musical or other harmonies he may
incidentally evoke, the fact will remain that such and such things
—and not others—have been mentioned in his poem'.[1]

One might object that the statement would make just as good
sense if reversed: 'whatever things he may incidentally mention . . .'
That MacNeice put it as he did in *Modern Poetry* briefly indicates
the procedure he and his contemporaries endorsed. His earlier
essay, 'Poetry Today', optimistic in tone, argues the consciously
sought and increasing popularity of poetry, and the adherence
(beneficial) of poets to 'cliques; they identify themselves with
economic, political or philosophical movements'. These aims and
conditions decide where the poet is to find the 'things' his poem
should mention: the world of affairs, the shared life of society,
pubs, streets, the fabric of cities, domestic interiors—observed by
the politically 'aware'. The essay stops far short of saying that this
awareness equals being a communist, or that a 'communist' is the
only alternative to a *bourgeois* poetry. MacNeice notes, in fact, the
'inverted jingoism' to which their communism encouraged Auden
and Day Lewis. The essay does not dogmatise poets into permitted
categories of subject. However, it has the period emphasis on the
value of reporting and public subjects. It accepts a 'narrowing' of
range because this will keep the poet and his audience together in
an accessible world where his verbal symbols have shape and
substance.

1. *Modern Poetry*, p. 5.

A poem will give its reader the pleasure of recognition. In the clarity of a new context he will identify scenes and objects inexplicitly familiar to him. MacNeice himself wrote to achieve this recognisability. He is a poet of the shape and substance of what is actually happening around him. This is more consistently his subject than it was Auden's or even Day Lewis's, whose poems also have often the same kind of social documentation. It interests MacNeice, too, for itself, not as the staple of myth, so that we do not very often find his pictures of people, places and events disintegrating into surrealistic riot or phantasy-parable, as Auden's characteristically do.

Modern Poetry re-affirms and elaborates these arguments on the essentially social character of language, which properly used must link poetry to, not abstract it from, communal experience. Politically, *Modern Poetry* is rather more contentious than 'Poetry Today'. It must have been wellnigh impossible for anyone of liberal sympathies not to feel and to say that the thirties poets were making 'less feeble protests' than Eliot, and accepting 'a world where one gambles upon practical ideals, a world in which one can take sides'. In the circumstances of the time it was easy to believe that consequently, if support for 'those forces which at the moment make for progress' did not guarantee, it was at least a necessary condition of producing, 'literature on a large scale'. Auden, Spender and Day Lewis, MacNeice now allows, do not on the whole 'state such beliefs more explicitly than is warranted by their own emotional reaction to them'; and by the facts of life, as the events of the three years between the two essays would have seemed to confirm. He would agree with Death in 'Eclogue by a Five-Barred Gate' that poetry is not only the surface vanity,

> *The painted nails, the hips narrowed by fashion,*
> *The hooks and eyes of words.*

Yet these views read like brave avowals of what ought to be, not of what MacNeice found personally congenial. A dialogue between himself and his Guardian Angel in *I Crossed the Minch* probably gives a truer statement of his feelings. G. A. proposes the moral splendour of virtuously challenging class and privilege. MacNeice recognises how admirable such resolution is, though with some misgivings about its 'masochism of the puritan'. His respect for John Cornford was an exception to his agreement with the working-class Birmingham student who 'thought nothing was so funny as the Oxford and Cambridge proletarianisers'. For himself, he confesses that he prefers to satisfy his own cultivated appetites. Most of his poetry comes into being between perfectly sincere humanitarian sentiment and honestly selfish pleasure in a world irreconcilable with altruistic ideals:

> *in order*
> *To preserve the values dear to the élite*
> *The élite must remain a few. (Autumn Journal, III)*

One trouble with this thesis was that much of what counted as the élite was distinctly unprepossessing; and, seemingly, both arrogant and inept, not even very well able to secure its privileges. This is the burden of the satirical *exempla* of looks and behaviour that MacNeice draws from his life and times. Tweedy matrons, 'bright young things', *grandes dames* and hunting fathers don their masks and go through their expressionistic paces. The Eclogues 'For Christmas', 'From Iceland' and 'Between the Motherless' have them drinking, swanking, whistling hounds, hunting, jazzing, serving elegant teas, 'keeping up' farms and gardens, homes, conservatories and appearances, seeing but ignoring the spread of slums and factories. Briefly and acidly characterised, they are marionettes enacting their involuntary rituals. In 'The Brandy Glass' the human actor, dehumanised, occupies a chilling dream scene. Snow falls from the chandeliers in an empty dining hall and ruin forms around the solitary diner, who sits 'like a ventriloquist's doll/Left by his master'.

In 'Eclogue Between the Motherless' the predicament of A and B, more commonplace, is middle-aged solitude in unhappy families. They parrot the phantasy joys of marriage which fact has disappointed and which A has sought once more. He has written proposing to a woman with only a year to live. With the neurotic pulse of this hopelessness, their conversation falls into broken sentences, disregarded responses, vacant repetition of each other's phrases, dying falls of rhythm. Of the poems mentioned, 'An Eclogue for Christmas' most frequently returns to the human fauna of town (observed by speaker A) and country (observed by speaker B), equally afflicted with 'the mad vertigo of being what

has been'. Again, their daily round of action is made up of
mechanistic tremors independent of the will. Like the street
hawker's tin toys, they 'move on the pavement inch by inch/Not
knowing that they are wound up'. His liveliest and most celebrated
exercise in this vein of satire is 'Bagpipe Music', a jaunty sequence
of mad, yet somehow prosaic, disasters:

Annie MacDougall went to milk, caught her foot in the heather,
Woke to hear a dance record playing of Old Vienna.
It's no go your maidenheads, it's no go your culture,
All we want is a Dunlop tyre and the devil mend the puncture. . .

It's no go the picture palace, it's no go the stadium,
It's no go the country cot with a pot of pink geraniums,
It's no go the Government grants, it's no go the elections,
Sit on your arse for fifty years and hang your hat on a pension.

It's no go my honey love, it's no go my poppet;
Work your hands from day to day, the winds will blow the profit.
The glass is falling hour by hour, the glass will fall for ever,
But if you break the bloody glass you won't hold up the weather.

For all this stylisation, the scene is real enough. The rural landscapes open into common scenes made present to the senses.
Squireens go 'hunting in the heavy shires'. 'Sunset like a line of
pyres . . . smoulders through the ancient air'. Farmyards have 'the
smell of dung' and ducks draw 'lines of white on the dull slate of
the pool'. On the open downs, 'eyelashes stinging in the wind',
sheep are 'like grey stones'. Now, however, industry and its
technical accoutrements make their inroads on the pastoral setting.
The air is 'hazed with factory dust', traversed by 'the thrumming
of telegraph wires in an east wind'. In the incoherent cities, 'red
lights sullenly mark/The long trench of pipes'; the 'black
streets' are 'mirrored with rain and stained with lights'.

Within such finely observed scenes the revolutionary vapours
again afflict the poet, who wonders

What will happen when the sniggering machine-guns in the
*   hands of the young men*
Are trained on every flat and club and beauty parlour and
*   Father's den?*

These sound like the same mettlesome and engaging young men who in Auden and Day Lewis plot and battle against the system; like Spender's 'young men', 'young comrades', who 'advance to rebuild and'—curiously—'sleep with friend on hill'. MacNeice, a good deal less enamoured, looks sourly enough at those destined to take over. Though the doomed classes are 'like palaeolithic man', what is in store is 'some new Ice Age or Genghiz Khan', or 'the Goths again come swarming down the hill'. Faced with this— if A and B in the Christmas Eclogue speak for him, as they appear to do—MacNeice forlornly longs that

> . . . *the cult of every technical excellence, the miles of canvas*
> *in the galleries*
> *And the canvas of the rich man's yacht snapping and tacking*
> *on the seas*
> *And the perfection of grilled steak . . .*
>
> *Be somehow permanent like the swallow's tangent wings.*

So, while like Day Lewis 'Between two worlds' he both ridicules *bourgeois* decadence and confesses his own attachment to its tradition, he lacks the heady confidence that its successor, and those who would bring it into being, are an inviting prospect. He is in the unhappy position of A and B. More perceptive than their fellow 'tin toys', they know that the clockwork is 'running down'.

MacNeice's poem 'To a Communist' testifies to his unregeneracy. After some ironical praise of the beautifully methodising power of marxism it repudiates the philosophy because its symmetry depends on abstractions—much what he thought of Platonism. Nevertheless, MacNeice often seems to be writing from a quite thoroughgoing acceptance of the marxist account of social change. Perhaps it stemmed from a sympathy between the marxist philosophy and the Aristotelian, which MacNeice found congenial. *The Strings Are False* offers an ingenious translation of 'Marx's basic thesis' into Aristotelian: '*energia* can only be achieved by the canalisation and continued control of *kinesis*'.[1] Aristotle, he pointed out, was 'among other things a zoologist' and unlike

---

1. *The Strings Are False*, p. 154.

Plato intent on the real, the shifting, mutable world of active matter:

> *watched the insect breed,*
> *The natural world develop,*
> *Stressing the function, scrapping the Form in Itself.*

Aristotle, he says elsewhere, more marxian still,

> *was right to think of man-in-action*
> *As the essential and really existent man*
> *And man means men in action.*

And finally, making the connection explicitly, he speaks of the Greek thinkers 'long before Engels'—but like Engels—being conscious 'of necessity/And therein free'.[1] Marxism too, as he acutely observed, 'while it attacked human individualism, it simultaneously made the cosmos once more anthropocentric . . . asserted purpose in the world. Because the world was *ours*'.[2]

In the thirties, the class in which power was vested seemed to have lost the understanding of its nature and the energy to apply it. MacNeice assented to the idea of a dynamism of the human will whose workings regulate man's control of his environment. 'An Eclogue for Christmas' calls the city—a perfectly marxian conceit—'this vast organism grown out of us'. Now *accidie* enfeebles the 'man-in-action' who created it. The necessity of their 'angry circumstance' eludes them; they will die of 'moral self-abuse', addicts to impotent routine; and, like 'the lady of the house' serving tea, 'cannot do otherwise, even to prolong my days'. In the words of *Autumn Journal*,

> *Spiritual sloth*
> *Creeps like lichen or ivy over the hinges.*

MacNeice, then, was not just 'reporting', and among the attitudes his poems express is a sort of reluctant marxism which accepts the premises but has no enthusiasm for the conclusion: a mark of the recurrent melancholy, insufficiently recognised, within

---

1. This and the two preceding quotations come from *Autumn Journal*, *Collected Poems*, pp. 145, 157, and 138.
2. *The Strings Are False*, p. 169.

MacNeice's high spirits. *The Strings Are False* is full of memories of the macabre dreams and waking nightmares that afflicted him.

As the critics observe—S. Wall is notably captious[1]—Mac-Neice's poetry does not much develop its range of ideas or method over his career: 'a small talent and a limited achievement', the *Times Literary Supplement* pronounced, reviewing his *Collected Poems 1925–1948*, when, of course, much that *was* new had still to come. John Press gives a more generous and a truer assessment. Still, it is true that all the poetry MacNeice wrote during the thirties clusters around the ideas, and sticks to the manner, apparent in the few early poems discussed here; though the interest of this account, it's fair to add, diminishes the personal matter, and the gaiety that flashes through all his writings. This gaiety, the doubts, the play of ideas and circumstance, the sparkle of words, find their happiest composition in his best and most representative poem, *Autumn Journal*.

It is not free of MacNeice's artful dodges. He has a glib way with clichés inset to point up more ingenious fancies:

> *And the critic jailed in the mind would peep through the grate*
> *And husky from long silence, murmur gently*
> *That there is something rotten in the state*
> *Of Denmark but the state is not the whole of Denmark,*
> *And a spade is still a spade;*

and with inverted clichés: 'I loved my love with a platform ticket'; 'till life did us part'; 'Glory to God in the Lowest'; 'hark the herald angels/Beg for copper coins'. The lists can begin to sound ominously like BBC Radio *Scrapbook for 1938* material. At times he will not leave wit enough alone. The section on the irrelevence of the philosophy he read at Oxford—and of Oxford —is hardly worth its eighty lines of elaboration on quite a hoary joke. But these defects do not force themselves on us. The poem's language is generally as free of trickery as its sentiments.

One might begin reading the poem at any point. It does not impose any tight structure on the themes of its twenty-four sections, which are diversified also in form. The only locus in its irregular progression is the various points of origin in MacNeice's

1. 'Louis MacNeice and The Line of Least Resistance', *The Review* (11–12), pp. 91–4.

past and present experiences which occasion the discourse of ideas. It is his strength that the ideas attend upon events, whether the matter of public journals or private diary. Seven separate sections turn upon three political episodes, two of them major, and obvious choices. Sections VI and XXIII (the Spanish War), V and VII to IX (Munich) and XIV (the Hogg-Lindsay by-election at Oxford), attach to their particular subjects a general mood of doldrums and spleen, febrile crisis, fearful precautions against death still kept—is it shamefully?—abroad.

The physical detail is memorable. In London 'the rain comes pimpling/The paving stones with white'; on the felled trees of Primrose Hill 'The wood is white like the roast flesh of chicken'. But just to evoke the scene is not MacNeice's purpose. The grace-less heterology of a city preparing for war it wants to avoid—'the raw clay trenches' and protest meetings 'in the sodden park'— disturbs his conscience. Wryly, he confesses his own timidity of purpose, his assent to sophistries, the comfort of an easy way out, all concurring in honest perplexity with recognition of bad faith.

Section V acknowledges that

> *it is no good saying*
> *'Take away this cup';*
> *Having helped to fill it ourselves it is only logic*
> *That now we should drink it up.*

But it pleads too the difficulty of choice:

> *. . . the individual, powerless, has to exert the*
> *Powers of will and choice*
> *And choose between enormous evils, either*
> *Of which depends on somebody else's voice.*

The ending of VIII is a sardonic summary of the consolations of Munich:

> *And negotiation wins,*
> *If you can call it winning,*
> *And here we are—just as before—safe in our skins;*
> *Glory to God for Munich.*
> *And stocks go up and wrecks*
> *Are salved and politicians' reputations*

> *Go up like Jack-on-the-Beanstalk; only the Czechs*
> *Go down and without fighting.*

But the section as a whole avouches the pleasures of a life that colluded with indifference, and which Munich now secures again. It is a marvellous re-creation of leisure on £700 a year, when MacNeice was a lecturer at Birmingham: troubled, but not too sharply, by 'the queues of men and the hungry chimneys'. 'Sun shone easy, sun shone hard', and

> *. . . roads ran easy, roads ran gay*
>   *Clear of the city and we together*
> *Could put on tweeds for a getaway*
>   *South or west to Clee or the Cotswolds;*
> *Forty to the gallon; into the green*
>   *Fields in the past of English history;*
> *Flies in the bonnet and dust on the screen*
>   *And no look back to the burning city.*

In IX 'we are back to normal', eight years after Birmingham. Term begins again, in London now, and MacNeice returns as 'impresario of the Ancient Greeks'. 'The Glory that was Greece' is not a lie. But the conventional picture excludes

> *. . . the crooks, the adventurers, the opportunists,*
>   *The careless athletes and the fancy boys,*

the noise of market-place and cheapjack orators, superstition, 'trimmers' at Delphi, 'dummies' at Sparta; and the slaves. The totality, whatever bits and pieces of wisdom we may resurrect from it, is irrecoverable—'It was all so unimaginably different/ And all so long ago'. The last echo of Munich in section X dies into a reminiscence of 'the halfway house of childhood', school-days in England and the distant war then being waged. In a way not normally argued, school was indeed a model for life, insisting on conformity, compliance, the line of least resistance to 'the order of the day'.

With a kind of inverted bravery, and no pretension to revolutionary élan when extremism was the fashion, the only personal act of rebellion MacNeice lays claim to is his tiny and ineffectual part in the Oxford by-election. But it makes a point:

> *this crude and so-called obsolete*
> *Top-heavy tedious parliamentary system*
> *Is our only ready weapon to defeat*
> *The legions' eagles and the lictors' axes.*

Even these homely chores demand an act of the will which, as the Spanish War most dramatically reminds him, he and others have 'thrown away' along with conscience. Visiting Spain before the War he had not realised that

> *Ideals would find their whetstone, that our spirit*
> *Would find its frontier on the Spanish front,*
> *Its body in a rag-tag army.*

There, unlike Oxford, 'the people's mind' has issued in deeds, and 'these people contain truth'.

Time and again the poem returns to 'the seeds of energy and choice' (XVIII), the precedence of will. In the world at large it no longer acts. Society has drawn for too long on the reserves of its ancestors. A scene graphically verifies the moral:

> *And still the church-bells brag above the empty churches*
> *And the Union Jack*
> *Thumps the wind above the law-courts and the barracks*
> *And in the allotments the black*
> *Scarecrow holds a fort of grimy heads of cabbage*
> *Besieged by grimy birds*
> *Like a hack politician fighting the winged aggressor*
> *With yesterday's magic coat of ragged words.*
> *Things were different when men felt their programme*
> *In the bones and pulse, not only in the brain,*
> *Born to a trade, a belief, a set of affections.* (XVIII)

MacNeice's personal history too seems to corroborate the communal frustration. Sections IV and XI turn movingly upon memories of a tempestuous love-affair, perhaps the one he alludes to in chapter XXXIII of *The Strings Are False*, shortly after his wife had left him. In its failure he sees the same incapacity in private as in social relationships to apply the truth that 'action makes both

wish and principle come true'. The blame is his that affection
lapsed to 'narrow possessiveness', could not then and cannot now
salvage what was good:

> *For suddenly I hate her and would murder*
> *Her memory if I could*
> *And then of a sudden I see her sleeping gently*
> *Inaccessible in a sleeping wood*
> *But thorns and thorns around her*
> *And the cries of night*
> *And I have no knife or axe to hack my passage*
> *Back to the lost delight.* (XI)

Like the sections rooted in public experience, the passages of
personal memory too excite and give body to ideas. Conversely,
in the more directly 'philosophical' meditations, ideas assume the
forms of what, then and there, was MacNeice's world of fact.
Section XII, for instance, set in an autumn day and finding that
Plato's 'world of capital letters, of transcendent/Ideas is too bleak',
enlivens the argument from the day itself:

> *Now it is morning again, the 25th of October,*
> *In a white fog the cars have yellow lights;*
> *The chill creeps up the wrists, the sun is sallow,*
> *The silent hours grow down like stalactites . . .*
> *And no one Tuesday is another and you destroy it*
> *If you subtract the difference and relate*
> *It merely to the Form of Tuesday. This is Tuesday*
> *The 25th of October, 1938.*

The poem's logical inconsistencies are obvious. Though
MacNeice is against war, and very movingly suggests its pathos in
a 'wistful face in a faded photo' (XIX), his sophisticated 'pacifism'
cannot resist Spain and Czechoslovakia. Against all systems, he
wants to replace the existing one by a better. The satirist of urban
ugliness, he is also the poet of the city, which he acclaims in 'An
Eclogue for Christmas':

> *But yet there is beauty narcotic and deciduous*
> *In this vast organism grown out of us:*
> *On all the traffic-islands stand white globes like moons,*

> *The city's haze is clouded amber that purrs and croons,*
> *And tilting by the noble curve bus after tall bus comes*
> *With an osculation of yellow light, with a glory like*
>   *chrysanthemums.*

What attracts him is the eccentric, the out of the ordinary, the outpost, of region or of character. When he leaves the city it is, typically in the poems, for the Hebrides, for Barra, for Carrickfergus, Cushendun, Galway; or to characterise the gentle, feeble-minded Orangeman in 'The Gardener'. MacNeice was Anglo-Irish and the fact is important. He grew to feel for the world what, like many another, he felt for Ireland: an aversion that could not extinguish love, complicated for him by memories of a lonely childhood in the County Antrim Rectory, and later the Bishop's Palace, of his father. *The Strings Are False*, according to his sister, makes more of the loneliness than the facts perhaps warrant. But the account must be true to his feelings and temperament. This, and an Irish gloom, may lie behind the nightmare visions that disturb certain poems. His 'Postscript to Iceland' has deeper personal roots than its passages of Auden-pastiche would suggest:

> *Watched the sulphur basins boil,*
> *Loops of steam uncoil and coil,*
> *While the valley fades away*
> *To a sketch of Judgment Day . . .*
>
> *Great black birds that fly alone*
> *Slowly through a land of stone,*
> *And the gulls who weave a free*
> *Quilt of rhythm on the sea.*

But he liked 'putting on the Irish' too, and the individualism still cherished in a small country—though 'It is self-deception of course'. If *Autumn Journal* has any consistency it is the esteem in which MacNeice holds the individual human being, for no matter what the system,

> *Nothing whatever can take*
>   *The people away, there will always be people*
> *For friends or for lovers.*

The contradictions and the sense of incompleteness are truthful.

It is a record of ideas forming, not resolved, in the 'débris of day-by-day experience', ending only with the hope that

> *there will be sunlight later*
> *And the equation will come out at last.*

More than Day Lewis, whose background is similar, MacNeice seems to be slightly outside the scene to which Auden and Spender belonged, a difference apparent even in his 'marxism', whose will is markedly an individual's, not a collective, possession. In the London chapters of *The Strings Are False* he often appears a detached, sardonic observer, diverted by the earnest day-dreams of the left. His own compassion was independent of theory. It kept him from assisting in the stratagems, the expedients, the evils which marxism does not forbid to marxists—'allows and even encourages',[1] MacNeice said. All the same, there was that in it to which he was receptive and for which his poetry found a place among what he later called its

> *waifs and wraiths of image*
> *And half-blind questions that still lack their answers,*
> . . . *Which was the right turning?*

II

In 1936 Stephen Spender published *The Burning Cactus*, a collection of five short stories written mostly between 1933 and 1935. The earliest is 'By the Lake', based on an account drafted in 1927 of a 'passion' which Spender had conceived in Lausanne for an English boy of his own age, 'well-bred and ignorant, delicate and uncultivated, beautiful and vapid'.[2] The title story was written in 1933; 'The Dead Island', 'The Cousins' and 'Two Deaths' in 1935. They are all studies in neurotic character. Each of them to a different degree establishes the neurosis as an image 'of chaos, of aimlessness, of hysteria in everything', of a kind of social *fugue* whose destiny is to annihilate society as it is.

The style of the stories, mannered, nervous, decisively penetrates the disorder of its subjects. Observed by the two protagon-

1. *The Strings Are False*, p. 161.
2. Spender, *World Within World*, p. 30.

ists of 'The Dead Island', the sea takes on their instability, moving somehow with the jerky action and angular, frozen moments of silent films:

> The black flatness of the sea was shattered, as though an age of ice were unlocked with rushing streams. This transformation made the land seem steady while the immoveable iron sea bounced into wrinkling hills, shaken with a light like the diffused light of mists. The plunging lights from the fishing-boat lamps were now shot sometimes downwards at an oblique angle into the water and sometimes aimlessly into the air. The fishermen, standing in the bows of their boats against the dull smoke of spray and a riding sea, assumed the archaic gestures of heroes, became whalers aiming harpoons, or Romans about to effect a landing. But the spell that magnetised the heaven-pointing fish was broken . . .

These touches are partly a tribute to another vogue of the thirties, that of 'cinema', which promised to link art and the people. It meant silent films rather than talkies; and Continental, French and Soviet particularly, rather than American, although the public remained obstinately content with Jean Harlow, Clark Gable and the other stars of the Dream Factory. In an otherwise adverse review of Aragon's *The Red Front*, Spender praised 'its effective cinematographic imagery'. His own short stories often attempt the same transposition. Another 'cinematic' sequence in 'The Dead Island' describes the man as looking 'as if a quick pair of scissors had cut his silhouette into pointed black and white, giving him the starred select features of a genuine hero'; and behind him and the woman, the 'two islands merged into the continent of their gigantic close-up kiss'. It is no more infallible a method than any other, but Spender uses it discreetly and with point. Generally, the stories are beautifully written; the form, as well as the discipline of prose, seems to have enabled Spender to get more fully outside himself than he does in his poems.

The setting of 'By the Lake' is a *pensionnat* for the nervous or retarded sons of wealthy families. Richard Birney makes a few tentative advances to Donauld, a fellow-boarder, whose ignorance conceals their sexual significance from him. At the end of the story he feels that he has brought Richard within sight of a religious conversion; while Richard, still trapped in his self-regarding miseries, 'was imagining an existence in which people behaved differently from Donauld'. 'By the Lake' solidly establishes its trappings of male adolescent tantrums and bitchiness, the meandering, ill-informed talks about sex and poetry. Within this glows the crisis, ultimately unresolved, of a period in the two youths' lives made up of 'little closed-in beads of lust that ran on a chain of days and weeks for years; till now, that which had been hidden and furtive, cried to be let out, would burst its way through'. The story confines its definition of the crisis within the strictly personal boundaries of the relationship which it inspects. At one point Richard is allowed, gratuitously for all one can see, to contrast their frivolous complaints of privation with the serious plight of 'slum mothers and of unemployed people living on fifteen shillings a week'. What is said of him later, that 'at every moment of crisis he was condemned to think only of his isolated self', is more consistent with our knowledge of him. The slum mothers are cant.

'The Burning Cactus' makes more of the social correlations to which 'By the Lake', in a perfunctory manner, gave the obligatory acknowledgement. As an unsavoury 'companion' in the Spanish home of a rich German, Till is convinced that he is being thrown over for a new favourite, Conrad. Without being markedly explicit about their homosexuality, the story makes it clear that these relationships are morbid, perverted, and beneath the urbane forms of the household corrupting into jealous rage. Till's phantasies of persecution have some basis in fact. Conrad appears to be plotting the disclosure to Till's relatives of the shoddy parade of his male lovers. But the phantasies would exist anyhow. Their real cause is his sick dependence on 'explosive individual feelings, which shot one like an aimless but hot rocket across an expanse of space in which the sun was cooling and the world running down . . .'

Till's confidants are an English couple, Pearl and Roger, in whose company, one hot summer day, he fecklessly sets a cactus field ablaze. Roger is conscious of a latent ferocity in Till. It resides in the coarsening elegance of his looks, something 'violent which threatened in time to alter the whole face'; in a dislocation of act and motive; in an insane autonomy of self, 'giving the whole body an expression of excluding mountains, port, sea and sky, while pointing singly to the speaker's own personality'. The story reiterates Till's 'I, I, I, I', the fiery particle at the centre of a whole web of relationships, urgent to destroy—itself, others, indifferently. It is this in Till which gives Roger the sense 'of chaos, of aimlessness, of hysteria in everything'.

Till is much more than the stock homosexual, though he is that too, with his epicene mannerisms and impedimenta, 'his powder, his lipstick, his gold chain, his scents, his hair-oil, his hand looking-glass and magnifying looking-glass', his letters from Pierre, Hans, Erich, Christopher. Though little happens in the story, Till's baleful qualities, his face 'lined but expressionless as a sheet of paper', his willed detachment from any demands but those of his own ego, effectively deliver an unremitting menace. Till suffers and luxuriates in his suffering. The 'tireless flames that consumed and shall consume him endlessly' reach out to, and are fed by, the society of whose incoherence his derangement is a symptom.

'The Cousins' invents a situation that allows a directly political reading. Werner, a young, rather solemn German socialist, visits his two upper-class English cousins. There are light comedy elements in their encounter, but underneath are antagonisms and on the English side a certain mistrust and malice. Werner's passionate and earnest advocacy shatters on indifference or hostility. He succumbs to 'an infinite air of reference to institutions more or less vast', to 'the entire machinery'—family, sport, entertainment, cars—of his hosts' happiness; and in the end makes a stealthy departure, undecided ' "Which of us exists, and which is dead?" '

On the face of it the disagreements are purely political—about colonial rule in India, for example. The story powerfully suggests that these are but the most superficial displays of nervous tensions secretly discharged. It is not a simple antithesis between Werner and his cousins. Though there is frustration in Bob's 'blurred eyes', a hint of 'impatience and hysteria', in Tom 'the aristocracy and beauty of his mother seemed to have triumphed without producing any conflict'. While the story mocks the English cousins and implies sympathy with Werner's humane ideas, it does not make Werner an invulnerable hero. Though his is the voice of reason, his past disturbs him, 'filled with horrors of the divorce court, the cemetery and the asylum'. He guesses at abstruse fields of force in society which govern the individual. They none of them *decide*, *act*, exercise their wills, but are 'pitchforked like the hay'. Hence his final questioning of what had been his certainties.

The dispute about British administration in India borrows from an argument Spender had with his uncle, J. A. Spender, famous for his 'balanced point of view'. That is, he could counter any un-orthodoxy with unshakeable nineteenth-century Liberal op-timism. The Weinberger family in the story, too, securely a part of the governing class, resembles Spender's own and is given the same part-Jewish origins, which they likewise, as Spender recalls of his family in *World Within World*, 'passed over in silence or with embarrassment'. Yet we are not made to feel that the story was written as an ejection mechanism for these pieces of auto-biographical débris. The narrative takes them up into its own logic, just as it does the socialism, though the significance of that too has remote echoes in Spender's personal questioning of marxist infallibility.

Spender's European travels furnished the basis of most of these stories. With Isherwood he would have seen the prototype of Till and his patron in Berlin, where he absorbed 'a sensation of doom to be felt in the Berlin streets . . . a permanent unrest, the result of nothing being fixed or settled'.[1] Austria, which Spender was visiting during 1934, was similarly distraught. In February of that year Dollfuss shelled and hounded the Viennese socialists to extinction. The following June, a few miles from Vienna, Spender read of Dollfuss's assassination and felt 'the waves of excitement . . . in the crowds surging through the streets of Vienna'.[2] The first of these events is the subject of his poem, *Vienna*; the second the offstage climax of his story, 'Two Deaths'. An old socialist dies in hospital of wounds from the February fighting. No friend or relative dares claim his body. At the end, the narrator hears over a hotel wireless of Dollfuss's murder. Behind the well-staged posturings of Government and Church dignitaries, society is succumbing to a rule of violence. The two deaths are equally its signature. In the crises of Spender's world, the individual is typically the acted-upon, not the doer; at best an involuntary in-strument. Even if he acts, as Dollfuss acted and in turn his assas-

1. Spender, *World Within World*, p. 129.
2. ibid., p. 192.

sins, the consequences are unforeseeable and beyond the actor's control.

The longest story in the collection, 'The Dead Island', makes the most ambitious attempt to signalise in a neurotic character the general social morbidity. A woman separated from her husband fails to arrest a youthful dancer's manic-depressive cycle. Her failure is inevitable. He is beyond help. One of the characters is allowed to explain that the youth's madness 'expresses an intuition of a destructive spirit which really exists in the world in which we live'. Retreating from that world, 'he *is* the world ... in him a very important part of our world reveals itself ... the moment when a civilisation really begins to lose grip'. His behaviour is a working-out of 'the poem, the dance, the madness, which he apprehends from the world around him'.

The story could perfectly well do without these rather laboriously stage-managed interpretations. Their point is implicit in the cross-cutting sequences of action, the disordered chronology, hallucinatory settings which gradually accumulate ulterior meanings, the islands in particular. They are, literally, an escapist playground, in which the dancer's refugee spirit seeks 'The calm vision of the islands', 'the peace of the islands'. Under their influence—'the translucent symbol of his wasted future'—he claims to care for the woman—'more than I care even for my illness'. But the real attraction for him is the Dead Island offshore, then the innumerable islands beyond, then Egypt, in endless irresponsible flight.

Set against these stations of escape are the absent, remembered cities of Northern Europe. The woman thinks of them, at first, as 'circles of the Underground railway filled with faces of clerks or shopping women, circles round a sunlit court of high flats where rich women with lapdogs met for tea, the interior of one of her own drawing-rooms ... surrounded by the circle of her yearning friends': the circles of an inane hell. In the final paragraph, in the illumination of exhaustion, she has 'the sense of cities lying to the North under the all-covering European night, cities domed by an opaque atmosphere smudged through by artificial light, cities hammering with their traffic against their own foundations'. They are the epicentres of social change which one must understand if one is to join the living, who 'are being continually forced to alter their lives'. This the woman now sees, though to what consequence the story leaves unsaid.

In all these stories, social organisation has built up a 'cage of institutions', of which marriage and family are as much a part as its bigger, more impersonal mechanisms. Together, they compose 'a machinery of anxiety' whose operation affects all individuals while remaining beyond their control. Each of the characters is thus, in the widest meaning of the term, 'a purely political mentality'. The stories state the condition without releasing any of their protagonists from it. They are diagnostic not prescriptive, at most suggesting the need to understand the condition.

III

The Burning Cactus fully possesses itself of its marxist and Freudian ideas and absorbs into them the particles of Spender's personal experience. The reader of the early poems, however, exposes himself to much more raw sensibility, what Allan Tate reviewing *Poems* (1933) called 'a kind of rambling accumulation of sensitive perceptions'.[1] At times 'sensitivity' is more apparent than perception. Some of the poems give the impression that it is enough for the man of feeling to utter, however slackly, a fine sentiment; or describe, however inattentively, an incident or scene. Joseph Gurnard's 'Poets' Excursion' acidly hits off this characteristic. As the train carrying Louis MacNoose, Don Layman, Dick Chapel and other notables pulls out of Paddington, the susceptible Stephen Spendlove is moved to verse:

'Listen,' said Spendlove delicately.
We listened.
'She leaves the station,' said Spendlove, with gentle lowing insistence, 'like a queen. First . . .' (his voice trembled) . . . 'the powerful plain manifesto, the black statement of pistons . . .'
'Black, Stephen?' we said.
'Black,' he repeated, starry-eyed.[2]

The contribution of the period was to advise what sentiments

1. *New Verse*, No. 3, May 1933.
2. Joseph Gurnard (G. W. Stonier) in J. Lehmann (ed.), *Penguin New Writing*, No. 194.

were fine, what scenes and episodes significant. Once again Geoffrey Grigson's remark comes to mind, that Spender's period saved him from Rupert Brooke's particular kinds of ineptness. Yet in fact when Spender is bad he seems quite often bad in very much the ways that Brooke was. He displays the same linguistic banality and the skiddings from romps to sentimentalism. The notorious pylons 'like nude giant girls' would not be out of place in Brooke's breezy humours. The mood of 'My parents kept me from children who were rough' (the sort of confessional piece that the thirties brought into fashion) is as self-consciously stoical as, say, Brooke's 'Unfortunate', which is about unrequited love, modish then as *bourgeois* guilt was for Spender.

As Louis MacNeice noticed in 'Poetry Today', Spender is also inclined to fall for the 'floating' associations of words that need to be circumspectly used. His innocent enthusiasm, not any identifying vision, produces the comrades who 'step *beautifully* from the solid wall', 'the *beautiful* generation' of the future, 'the young men *splendid*'. Some of the settings are recalled from personal experience, as in Poem XVIII, about a parting from a friend on a morning of

> *Expansive sheets of blue rising from fields*
> *Roaring movements of light discerned under shadow.*

Others are purely emblematic. XXII urges the 'young comrades' to

> *. . . count the sun and the innumerable coined light*
> *sparkling on waves and spangling under trees.*

XXIV visualises a land of the future.

> *Where light equal, like the shine from snow, strikes all races.*[1]

Whether actual or symbolic, the scenes tend to vanish in the nimbus generated by a cluster of favourite words: fire, stars, light, bright, brilliance, bronze, azure, haze. Odd scraps of outmoded diction surface amidst the modernistic phrasing: 'that charmed moon', 'the pale lily boys flaunt their bright lips', 'the swarm of stars and flowers'.

These features are as typical of the good poems in Spender's

1. *Collected Poems* (where these poems are differently numbered), pp. 39, 46 and 49 respectively. The numbers used in this chapter are those of *Poems* (1933).

first collection as of the bad. Except in a few brittle Audenes-queries like:

> *An 'I' can never be great man,*
> *This known great one has weakness.*

Spender habitually converts into glowing, ethereal sight images the intense emotions that experience excites in him. The process goes wrong when it leaves the reader unpersuaded that the quiverings of the poet's sensibility justify the incandescence of the imagery. One can understand, and often sympathise with, Cornford's irritation at an egotism that shoulders through tragic events to put the poet at the centre of the stage where he draws admiring attention to his own heartache. Poem XXI, 'Without that once clear aim', abominates the 'tortures and wars' of a new Dark Ages because this 'century chokes me', 'I suffer'. The solace is to be a poet: 'The writings are my only wings away'. Not exactly like Keats, to 'leave the world unseen'. The sphere to which Spender wings away lets in, as well as personal griefs of love and parting, the greed, pain, fatigue, killing of the world at large. He observes the unemployed 'turn their empty pockets out' (XVI). The wrongs of a martyred class 'cry out as raw as wounds' (XXX). Brutality and murder are the argument of politics. From such miseries the poems, true to marxist theory, infer hope: 'from hunger/We may strike fire' (XXIV). Death is the prelude to life (XX, XXXII, XXXIII). The worse things are, the nearer their violent consummation. Though 'our graphs through History' (XXX) bring no present relief, their prophecy of triumph is assured. Poem XX puts the *bourgeoisie* in its usual place. They are the prisoners of the title, deaf to the poet's compassionate warning, impotent, doomed to extinction. So, as one of them, is the poet, 'When our bodies are rejected like the beetle's shard' (XXXII)—a transfiguration, not a death. Meanwhile, he exhorts his comrades:

> *No spirit here seek rest. But this: No one*
> *Shall hunger: Man shall spend equally.*
> *Our goal which we compel: Man shall be man.* (XXXIII)

Yet a marxist might with some justice have complained that the poems are dreamlands where 'I wish' becomes 'It is'. Spender might have taken nearer home his criticism that in Eliot's poetry impressions 'seem important for what they impress upon the mind, without regard for the reality which is doing the impressing'. Rarely out of our sight, more in front of than between the lines, he gestures and makes it so. None of Spender's contemporaries was freer with the first person singular; more effectively, in his poems, the agent of change: 'I must have love enough,' he claims, 'to run a factory on/Or give a city power, or drive a train'; 'I've signed his release'; 'My healing fills the night'; 'I build'; 'I say'. The poetry becomes a sort of magic which, quite traditionally, eases a particular emotional stress, or more generally, defies the imperfections of life and the sad erosions of time.

One of the best poems in the volume, No. XIII, 'What I expected, was', concerns this polarity of art and life. Like Cornford's 'As Our Might Lessens', Day Lewis's 'Sonnet for a Political Worker', and the 'Today' section of Auden's *Spain*, it finds that experience soon puts paid to any fond notions of sudden and decisive combat. It calls instead for irksome resistance, with little to show for it, to

> the gradual day
> Weakening the will
> Leaking the brightness away.

Only art, and some freaks of nature, achieve a beautiful finality of form. The fact is no solace. The essence of such creations is that they are unlike life, where there is no purpose in

> Expecting always
> Some brightness to hold in trust,
> Some final innocence
> Exempt from dust,
> That, hanging solid,
> Would dangle through all,
> Like the created poem,
> Or faceted crystal.

The language is subtly organised to make the poem's point. 'Exempt from dust' recalls 'The pulverous grief'; the 'faceted crystal' the cripples 'With limbs shaped like questions'. While the poem gives art the last word, so to speak, the questionings of life echo past it.

Three other poems give particular distinction to Spender's first major collection: IX ('Beethoven's Death Mask'), XIV ('In 1929') and XXIII ('I think continually of those who were truly great'). The first and last of these succeed with just the kind of diction that in other poems befogs its subject. In XXIII the images of light, fire, blossoms, snow, sun properly celebrate the theme of aspiration achieved and imparted to the future. The superb climax joins abstract and concrete in an image of striking visual force, quite independent of its chance and moving association with the vapour trails of 1940:

> *Born of the sun, they travelled a short while toward the sun*
> *And left the vivid air signed with their honour.*

'In 1929', quite contrary in tone, starts from a 'whim of time' that allows friendship between the poet and two Germans, one a *bourgeois*, the other a communist clerk. Twelve years back from this moment, or (more arbitrarily) forward ten, and war or revolution has undone the bond of love. The second part of the poem, in language of unusual restraint, grave, ceremonial, solemnises this 'now' which has exorcised ancestral passion:

> *Our fathers killed. And yet there lives no feud*
> *Like Hamlet prompted on the castle stair;*
> *There falls no shade across our blank of peace*
> *We being together, struck across our path,*
> *Nor taper finger threatening solitude.*

The poem ends comfortlessly. The past no longer torments, but neither will the pasts ceaselessly accumulating be any help. The last line precisely simulates the final act of burial, the utter extinguishment of the living spirit, past and present for ever disjoined:

> *Lives risen a moment, joined or separate,*
> *Fall heavily, then are always separate,*
> *Stratum unreckoned by geologists,*
> *Sod lifted, turned, slapped back again with spade.*

It is a haunting end to a poem notably animated and dramatic, which, like the other three mentioned, stands with the best work of Spender's contemporaries.

The dilemmas that exercised Spender in his political activity, chronicled in *Forward from Liberalism*, clearly have their analogues in his poetry. There it was cause and conscience, communist end and communist means, Soviet Constitution and Soviet policy: incongruities that withstood his most indulgent regard; in the poetry 'socialist realism' and self-expression, mass communication and high-flying sensibility, Agitprop and Bloomsbury. Spender was naturally disposed to ornately mounted tours around his own emotions, however inbred. He was less in need of encouragement to spiritual autobiography than of the marxist instruction—whatever its sophistry in practice—to deal with 'pieces of external reality'. The poems in fact come off when they give an object, an event, an idea sufficient presence to account for the feeling it generates. His next poetic work, *Vienna*, with a specific political happening as its subject, gave this opportunity.

World Within World acknowledges that Spender had this in mind. He wanted to state 'a public emotion which had become a private one' (though 'it invaded my personality rather than sprang out of it') and 'to relate the public passion to my private life'. *Vienna* was one such attempt—'the most ambitious', Spender says, '—and perhaps the least successful'. Its main subject is the Dollfuss Government's suppression of the Viennese socialists. According to Spender, it was also 'concerned with a love relationship', and 'fails because it does not fuse the two halves of a split situation, and attain a unity where the inner passion becomes inseparable from the outer one'.

While the author's opinion has special authority, one is really hard put to it to uncover much trace of the 'love relationship' in the poem. It begins ('Arrival at the City') with rather a tortuous elaboration of the idea that the *bourgeois* 'living' embody death and the workers who die, life. T. S. Eliot's influence is generally apparent in the death/life paradox (according to Marx) and here and there in its phrasing:

> *Whether the man living or the man dying*
> *Whether this man's dead life, or that man's life dying*
> *His real life a fading light his real death a light growing.*
> *Whether the live dead I live with.*

It is not always crystal clear who is who, as in a conscientiously gruesome medical image and a surrealistic deathmask/landscape. The patient here (putrifying *bourgeois* or fecund worker?) bears some resemblance to Eliot's Sweeney:

Whether this man's dead life stinking, like an open wound decaying,
Or the other's life stinking, and his real life decaying
His wound a wound, his life a life, his death
Opening to life like a flower him overarching—
Yes, the tube stuck in his stomach, and the rotten waste
Dripping in flasks; eyes red, jaw dropped, his mouth
A printed o; his kind hair flourishing
Wild above the wreck, like grass tall on a ruin;
Beard tufts from crannies of experience bristling.
Unroll this death, and flowers revive and rain
Like hair strokes on the faces of his girls.[1]

Part II ('Parade of the Executive') is a sardonic commentary on Dollfuss, Fey, Stahremberg, 'the whole bloody lot', and the despotic alliance of Church and State: 'the volleys/Of gunfire hammered with the Holy Ghost'. Part III ('The Death of Heroes') sets down the workers' memories after the week's fighting in Vienna, and tells the story of one of them, Wallisch, betrayed to the Government and executed. In Part IV ('Analysis and Statement'), the carnage over, five voices, all of them presumably Spender's, place his concerns, his background, his personal anxieties, against the wider disaster. In a *reprise* of earlier phrases, the poet again recalls, perhaps from the love relationship, a woman 'With dark eyes neglected, a demanding turn of the head/And hair of black silky beasts'. The poem concludes of the martyred workers, continuing the meditation of I and III, 'These are/Our ancestors'. They are more vital than the individual cares and inherited ways of life familiar to him.

Part IV begins, with no doubt unintentional appropriateness, much in the style of Prufrock:

> *Fading fading the importance*
> *Of what was said*
> > *by so many voices*
> *Between the sunset and the coffee;*
> *So many faces, so many invitations.*

---

1. Like the grotesque portrait of 'Sweeney Erect':
> This withered root of knots of hair
> > Slitted below and gashed with eyes,
> This oval O cropped out with teeth.

Spender lived for long periods in Europe. He was a witness of what was happening. Where Day Lewis is a poet of the English scene, Spender is, by intention, a poet of Europe. Yet, like Prufrock in his situation, he remains a spectator. Vast national upheavals, the polity agonistes, do not feed his imagination. He remains on the outside, like a tourist suddenly involved in an obscure tribal dispute which is not at all like its 'profile' in the liberal weeklies. His attention turns easily from Anschluss, pogrom, civil war, to the ebb and flow of love and friendship, the misfortunes of people whom he knows. So in Spain 'for several months . . . my life was dominated' by anxiety for a young Welsh friend who, having discovered that war meant killing, incompetently deserted from the International Brigade.

There is nothing abnormal in any of this. Human beings are not long moved by remote and impersonal distress. However, unlike Prufrock ('No! I am not Prince Hamlet') Spender magnifies his role in *Vienna*, undertakes to speak for the dictators and their mass of victims. But without plausibility. *Vienna* remains obstinately outside the tragic experience that is its subject, for all its toughening up of style and attitudes. Perhaps the hardboiled mannerisms were a response to criticism like Cornford's ('the poetry of revolution as a literary fashion, not as an historic reality . . . an idealist romantic affair'), cultivated to undo any suspicion of high falutin aestheticism. But they carry no conviction. This, and a sporadic incoherence of delivery (the prolocutors discourse from confusingly mobile premisses) impair the poem. The failure is in style and address with an uncongenial subject, a background interference from other voices, like Eliot's, jamming his own.

Psychologically, Spender seems to have turned to marxism, as he later underwent psychoanalysis, in the hope that it would 'resolve the problems'—moral, spiritual, intellectual—'for which I sought a solution'.[1] Spender's enquiry was painstaking, but neither system answered his credulous ambition. He was too keenly aware of his troubles, as *World Within World* makes clear, to suppose that they had vanished. Between 1934 and 1938 he continued his debate with marxist theory and communist policies mainly in his prose writings, *The Destructive Element* and *Forward from Liberalism*. The former, much the more sensible of the two,

1. *World Within World*, p. 255.

examines marxism as an instrument of literary criticism—and in
part so uses it—and as 'a system of values' useful to the creative
writer. He emerges with a formula—the synthesis of marxism and
psychoanalysis—for the writer 'who wishes to write about
society as a whole, and not about the individual severed from his
background'. Spender himself shared this wish—'to relate the
public passion to my private life'. But the technicalities of
marxist thought did not help him fufil it in his poetry. It was in
The Burning Cactus alone of his imaginative writing that these
ideas both supplied the substance of his argument and penetrated
the form and symbols of its expression. The poems which attempt
statements of comparable scope and import, like 'My parents
quarrel in the neighbour room' (*Poems* XI), 'Without that once
clear aim', 'In railway halls', seem to be asking us to take rather
tepid vapours as great, universalising tempests of passion.

A recurrent theme in Spender's poetry is in fact the comprehen-
siveness of the self, the Whitmanesque ego that 'contains multi-
tudes', all experience, all creation. The journey inwards, so, is as
ample a path as any that sets more by the sensible world. The
sequence *Explorations* (1944) takes up the idea. Its final poem says
of the 'one' that

> *Within his coils of blood,*
> *Drumming under his sleep, there moves the flood*
> *Of stars, battles, dark and glacial pole.*
> *One is all that one is not. On his dreams ride*
> *Dead ancestors. All spaces outside*
> *Glitter under his ribs.*

Earlier, *The Still Centre* has a number of poems, written after
Spender's return from Spain, in which he 'tried to state the condition of the isolated self as the universal condition of all existence'.[1] 'Darkness and Light' and 'The Human Situation' ('This I
is one of') are of this kind, poems at once anguished by the solitary
inquisitions of self ('My territories of fear') and exulting in its
boundless potential:

> *What's inside my bowels and brain,*
> *The Spring and the volcanoes,*

1. *World Within World*, p. 255.

> *Include all possibilities of development*
> *Into an unpredictable future,*
> *Full of invention, discovery, conversion, accident.*

The theme encourages Spender to his diffuse and bodiless rhetoric. The poems depend heavily on exclamation, apostrophe, repetition, paradox and pun: 'lucid sailing shine', 'A lucid day', 'my sight hid from my sight' (*The Still Centre*); 'far far far from these wars', 'blind walls that blind/Their eyes', 'I who say I call that eye I'. 'O life, O death' (*Explorations*). All the weaknesses of *Poems* are let loose. The glittering sea, skies, horizons, stars, flames, exist purely, we are all too aware, to silhouette the poet, like arty photographic effects:

> *Dreaded light that hunts my profile!*
> *Dreaded night covering me in fears!*   ('Darkness and Light')

Even in the Spanish War poems, ostensibly to do with particular scenes and situations, the events and settings are as abstract as the abstractions they symbolise. Before their physical outlines register, they thin into allegories of some interior drama or transcendental convulsion that the poet keeps assuring us is in progress. The sensibility is too easily thrilled to discriminate among its excitements, too taken up in the mere fact of their existence to discover the words that would give them reality for an audience.

Spender has assumed many of the styles of contemporary poetry, from Eliot through the left-wingers to the poets of the self-styled Apocalypse. None of them controlled the over-indulgence of feeling or abated the lure of abstractions. Of them all, he takes most easily to the manner of the transient Apocalyptics. Certainly, he was of all his group the least naturally disposed to 'social' poetry. There is no reason, of course, why he should have been more so, no obligation to write that sort of poetry, and no inherent superiority in it. Spender's style is florid, declamatory, his subject his personal response to human greatness, death, the perplexities of life, apprehended in the most general terms. G. S. Fraser gives a much more generous appreciation of his work than, on much the same evidence, is made here. But it does not seem to me that he does as well with his own fashion as Day Lewis in poems like 'The Ecstatic' which are similarly conceived.

Postscript

THEIR later careers make it easy to deride these poets for the ideas they professed in the thirties. Stephen Spender has been resident poet in the Library of Congress. Day Lewis is now Poet Laureate. W. H. Auden has said that if living in England he would be a Conservative. He has disappointed Mr Brian Jones by looking healthy and unsubversive at a public lecture. It is not now as it hath been of yore; and in his *Collected Shorter Poems* Auden has gone to some pains to make out that it never really was: by emendation and censorship and by disturbing the order of composition. The fact that they have changed their minds has no bearing whatsoever on the merit either of their poetry or of their beliefs, then or now. Their lives simply attest the common observation that age, even middle age, often chastens the left-wing ardours of youth. Auden's revisions and suppressions, however, do pose a special case, most impressively expounded by Joseph Warren Beach.

Clearly, as Professor Beach allows, Auden is often withdrawing a poem either so trivial or so faulty that he will not let it appear in a definitive edition. He was prophetic in *Letters from Iceland* when he expressed his distaste for inurning Juvenilia in a Collected Works. Many of his revisions, too, are designed to correct some want of artistry or seemliness. But his motive is as often to detach his poetry from any suspicion of contact with marxist or even humanist ideas. The human justice which in 'In Time of War'— one of Beach's most startling examples—is the prospective handiwork of Man, becomes after revision a Wholly Other divine Justice in which alone human aspiration may find fulfilment.

Even here, Auden is not altogether playing false with the root conception and the feeling that surrounded it: his response to the ageless hope of a world redeemed. He is transferring, from one frame of symbol and imagery to another, ideas of archetypal amplitude that will conform to either.

In carrying out the operation at all, Auden is practising his own principle that 'False beliefs lead in fact to bad poetry', and ridding his poems of ideas he now thinks wrong. It is difficult to believe that he would seriously defend this principle. It sounds more like an impromptu rationalisation. He has been performing a kind of act of contrition. His repudiation of his own works, had he avowed as error what he silently corrected, would have recalled the public confessions in Soviet trials of the thirties. Indeed, a recently authorised re-publication[1] of 'Sir, no man's enemy', 'A Communist To Others', *Spain* and '1 September, 1939' were prefaced by a statement that the poems were 'trash which he is ashamed to have written'. The unregenerate Auden might have said this tongue in cheek, but he has been diligent in enforcing his embargo. One can only hope that recent acts of clemency, like the re-issue of *The Orators*, herald a general absolution. The whole revamping exercise is an absurd one. As a consequence of it, the *Collected Shorter Poems*, for all the fine poetry it contains, gives the most partial impression of Auden's variety, development and total achievement.

Auden's is unquestionably the outstanding poetic talent of his generation. He has suffered at various stages of his career from being cried up, then, in disgruntlement, down. He has never written a work of quite the stature of Eliot's *Quartets* or the best of Yeats, though one could argue a case from *Poems* (1930), *The Orators* and *Look, Stranger!* It would be foolhardy to relegate him to some qualitatively nether category. Apart, however, from the weightiness of his achievement, his example has been salutary. His work re-affirmed the relevance both of traditional forms and of current speech. He restored as a possible subject the stuff of political life, its actors and managers, its daily alarms, rumours, lies, events, and their intellectual and emotional underlay: here was a genuine re-birth of the 'public' verse of the eighteenth century, equally wide-ranging in tone and manner. One might

1. R. Skelton (ed)., *Poetry of the Thirties.*

say that after Eliot had breached a poetic barrier against the modern sensibility, Auden brought through it, as the staple of other myths, the swarming detail of contemporary experience.

In this Auden is typical of the liveliest and most accomplished period in recent English poetry. Its central political event was, of course, the Spanish Civil War. With this, left-wing feeling amongst intellectuals reached its height. But 1938, whose end was marked by the return to England of the British Battalion of the International Brigades, was its zenith: the Spanish sections of *Autumn Journal*, 'The Nabara', 'In Time of War' (Auden's last fully marxist poem, written in 1938). Early in that year Day Lewis began to withdraw from political work. Spender, when he came back from Spain late in 1937, turned away from political subjects. The mood now was rather that of the bleak opening poems of *Overtures to Death*, changed as Republican Spain itself was changing from the fervour of 1936 to the last shifty debacle of Loyalist hopes. It was in this year, then, so far as one can localize it, that the marxist poetry of the nineteen-thirties died.

The poetry of the thirties generation was by no means exclusively social, political, marxist. But it is the fruit of that planting which has best retained its bloom. What Auden and the others did was not, of course, a qualitative advance on, say, the theory and practice of T. S. Eliot. Their achievement was to have done again what had been done before and perpetually remains to be done again. That is, to find forms of poetic expression at once appropriate to and not constricted by their age. Marxism had an imaginative potential and a general relevance unfamiliar now. The poets did not so much seek it out; they involuntarily came upon it. Their success in extracting a working aesthetic from its dogma was considerable. They had, in fact, chanced on a route, difficult but passable, to lead them on from the fresh departures of their predecessors; in their poems the excitement of the journey is still alive.

Select Bibliography

I. AUTHORS

W. H. AUDEN

1. POEMS AND OTHER POETIC WORKS

Poems, privately printed by Stephen Spender 1928.
Poems, London: Faber & Faber 1930, 1933.
The Orators, London: Faber & Faber 1932, 1934; new edition 1966.
The Dance of Death, London: Faber & Faber 1933.
Poems, London: Faber & Faber 1934; New York: Random House 1935.
  [consists of *Poems* (1933), *The Orators* (1932),
  The Dance of Death (1933)]
The Dog Beneath the Skin (with Christopher Isherwood), London:
  Faber & Faber 1935; New York: Random House 1935.
Look, Stranger! London: Faber & Faber 1936; New York: Random
  House 1937 (entitled *On This Island*).
Spain, London: Faber & Faber 1937.
Letters from Iceland (with Louis MacNeice), London: Faber & Faber
  1937; New York: Random House 1937.
On the Frontier (with Christopher Isherwood), London: Faber & Faber
  1938; New York: Random House 1939.
Journey to a War (with Christopher Isherwood), London: Faber &
  Faber 1939; New York: Random House 1939.
New Year Letter, London: Faber & Faber 1941; New York: Random
  House 1941 (entitled *The Double Man*).
For The Time Being, New York: Random House 1944; London:
  Faber & Faber 1945.
The Age of Anxiety, New York: Random House 1947; London:
  Faber & Faber 1948.
The Collected Poetry of W. H. Auden, New York: Random House 1945;
  London: Faber & Faber 1948.
Collected Shorter Poems 1930–1944, London: Faber & Faber 1950.

Bibliography

Poems selected by the author, London: Penguin Books in association with Faber & Faber 1958.

Collected Shorter Poems 1927–1957, New York: Random House 1966; London: Faber & Faber 1966. [References in the text are to the English editions and to *Collected Shorter Poems 1930–1944* except where otherwise stated.]

Note: Poems referred to in the text omitted from or revised in *Collected Poetry* and *Collected Shorter Poems; CP—Collected Poetry; CSP—Collected Shorter Poems*:

(a) *Periodicals, anthologies*

from *New Country*

'A Happy New Year', Part I not reprinted in any collection; Part II reprinted in *Look, Stranger!* (X), *CP* ('Not All the Candidates Pass'), *CSP*, 1950 ('Not All the Candidates Pass'), 'The Watchers' in Penguin Selected Poems and thus in *CSP* 1966; increasingly extensive revisions.

'A Communist to Others', reprinted in *Look, Stranger!* (XIV) with some revisions. Not in *CP, CSP.*

'Poem', reprinted with some revisions in *Look, Stranger!* (XV) and *CSP* ('Two Worlds'). Withdrawn 1966.

'Prologue', reprinted with some revisions in *Look, Stranger!* (I, 'Prologue') and in *CP, CSP* ('Perhaps'). Withdrawn 1966.

from *The Listener*

12 July 1933 'The Witnesses'. The third part of this poem is given to the Leader of Semi-Chorus I in *The Dog Beneath the Skin*.

15 March 1934 'Out on the lawn I lie in bed' reprinted in *Look, Stranger!* (II) and in *CP, CSP* ('A Summer Night 1933') with some revisions.

(b) *Collections of Auden's poetry*

from *The Orators*, Six Odes

II, To Gabriel Carritt, Captain of Sedbergh School XV, Spring 1927; IV, To John Warner, Son of Rex and Frances Warner. Neither Ode is included in *CP, CSP*, nor in the 1966 reprinting of *The Orators*.

from *Poems* (1930)

XVI, ('It was Easter') 16 lines omitted in 1933 ed., and thus in *CP, CSP* ('1929'); XXII, ('Get there if you can'). Not in *CP, CSP*.

Note: The 1933 edition also omits a number of poems included in the 1930 volume and substitutes others. See Chapter IV.

2. MISCELLANEOUS PROSE

Instinct and Intuition. A Study in Mental Duality by G. B. Dibblee [a review of] in *The Criterion* (April 1930), pp. 567–9.
'Life's Old Boy' [a review of], *Lessons from the Varsity of Life* by Lord Baden Powell, *Scrutiny*, March 1934, pp. 405–9.
'Goldsworthy Lowes Dickinson' [a review of] *Goldsworthy Lowes Dickinson* by E. M. Forster, *Scrutiny*, December 1934, pp. 303–6.
The Poet's Tongue (with John Garrett) London: G. Bell & Sons, 1935 (Introduction, pp. v–x).
'Psychology and Art Today', *The Arts Today*, ed. G. Grigson, London: Bodley Head 1935, pp. 1–21.
'The Good Life', *Christianity and the Social Revolution*, ed. John Lewis, Karl Polyanyi, Donald K. Kitchen, London: Gollancz 1935.
'The Bond and the Free' [a review of four books], *Scrutiny*, September 1935, pp. 200–2.
'Impressions of Valencia', *New Statesman and Nation*, 30 January 1937, p. 159.
Illusion and Reality by Christopher Caudwell [a review of], *New Verse*, May 1937, pp. 20–2.
'The Public *vs* the late Mr. William Butler Yeats', *Partisan Review*, VI, Spring 1939, pp. 46–51.
'I Believe', *I Believe* (ed. Clifton Fadiman), New York: Simon & Shuster 1939; London: Allen & Unwin 1940, pp. 17–31.
'Criticism in a Mass Society', in *The Intent of the Critic*, ed. D. A. Stauffer, Princeton, Princeton University Press 1941, pp. 125–47; *The Mint* (ed. G. Grigson), London: Routledge & Sons 1946, pp. 1–13.

3. CRITICAL STUDIES

(a) *Books wholly devoted to W. H. Auden*

Beach, Joseph Warren, *The Making of the Auden Canon*. Minnesota, The University of Minnesota Press 1957.
Blair, John G., *The Poetic Art of W. H. Auden*. Princeton, N.J.: Princeton University Press 1965.
Bloomfield, Barry, *W. H. Auden, a Bibliography: the early years through 1955*, foreword by W. H. Auden. Charlottesville, University of Virginia 1964.
Bogan, Louise, *The Quest of W. H. Auden: Selected Criticism*. New York: Noonday Press 1955.
Everett, Barbara, *Auden*. Edinburgh & London: Oliver & Boyd 1964.

Hoggart, Richard, *Auden: An Introductory Essay*. London: Chatto & Windus 1951.

Spears, Monroe K., *The Poetry of W. H. Auden: The Disenchanted Island*, Oxford 1963.

Spears, Monroe K. (ed.), *Auden: A Collection of Critical Essays*. Englewood Cliffs, N.J., Prentice Hall, 1964.

(b) *Essays*

Daiches, David, 'W. H. Auden: The Search for a Public'. *Poetry*, LIV, 1939, pp. 148–56.

Grigson, Geoffrey, 'Auden as a Monster'. *New Verse*, November 1937, pp. 13–17.

Isherwood, Christopher, 'Some Notes on Auden's Early Poetry'. *New Verse*, November 1937, pp. 4–9.

Jarrell, Randall, 'Freud to Paul: The Stages of Auden's Ideology'. *Partisan Review*, XII, 1945, pp. 437–57.

Muir, Edwin, 'Tribute to Auden'. *New Verse*, November 1937, p. 23.

Replogle, Justin, 'Auden's Marxism'. *PMLA*, LXXX, 1965, pp. 585–95.

Replogle, Justin, 'Social Philosophy in Auden's Early Poetry'. *Criticism* II, Fall 1960, pp. 351–61.

Replogle, Justin, 'The Auden Group'. *Wisconsin Studies in Contemporary Literature*, V, 1964, pp. 133–50.

Rickword, Edgell, 'Auden and Politics'. *New Verse*, November 1937, pp. 21–2.

'Which Side Am I supposed to be On?: The Search for Beliefs in W. H. Auden's Poetry'. *Virginia Quarterly Review*, XXII, 1964, pp. 570–80.

C. DAY LEWIS

I. POEMS AND OTHER POETIC WORKS

Country Comets, London: Martin Hopkinson & Co. 1928.

Transitional Poem, London: Hogarth Press 1929 (Hogarth Living Poets No. 9).

Collected Poems (1929–33), London: Leonard & Virginia Woolf 1935; Hogarth Press 1938.

From Feathers to Iron, London: Hogarth Press 1931.

The Magnetic Mountain, London: Hogarth Press 1933.

A Time to Dance, London: Hogarth Press 1935.

Noah and the Waters, London: Hogarth Press 1936.

Overtures to Death, London: Jonathan Cape 1938.

The Georgics of Virgil, London: Jonathan Cape 1940.

Poems (1943–47), London: Jonathan Cape 1948.

An Italian Visit, London: Jonathan Cape 1953.
Collected Poems, London: Jonathan Cape with Hogarth Press 1954.

Note: Poems referred to in the text not included in *Collected Poems* or other volumes:

(a) *Anthology*
from *New Signatures*
Four *Satirical Poems.* 'The Wife Speaks', 'The Schoolmaster Speaks', 'The Mother Speaks', 'The Observer Speaks', all included in their original form in *The Magnetic Mountain* with the exception of 'The Schoolmaster Speaks', which was almost wholly re-written. See Chapter III.

(b) *Collections of C. Day Lewis's poetry*
A Time to Dance substantial cuts and re-organisation in *Collected Poems*.

(c) *Noah and the Waters*
Prologue and two Choruses included in *Collected Poems*.

2. MISCELLANEOUS PROSE
(a) *Novels*
The Friendly Tree, London: Jonathan Cape 1936.
Starting Point, London: Jonathan Cape 1937.
Child of Misfortune, London: Jonathan Cape 1939.
The Smiler with the Knife ('Nicholas Blake'), London: Collins 1939.

(b) *Criticism*
A Hope for Poetry, Oxford: Basil Blackwell 1934 (with postscript 1936).
Revolution in Writing (Day to Day Pamphlets No. 29), London: Hogarth Press 1935.
The Mind in Chains (ed.), London: Frederick Muller 1937.
Ralph Fox: A Writer in Arms, ed. with T. A. Jackson and John Lehmann, London: Lawrence & Wishart 1937.
Anatomy of Oxford, ed. with Charles Fenby, London: Jonathan Cape 1938.

(c) *The Buried Day* (autobiography), London: Chatto & Windus 1960.

3. CRITICAL STUDIES
(a) *Bibliography*
Hendley-Taylor, G., and D'Arch Smith, T., *Cecil Day Lewis The Poet Laureate*, a bibliography, foreword by W. H. Auden. London: St James Press 1968.

(b) *Articles*

Elton, William, 'Day Lewis, *Rest from Loving and Be Living*'. *Explicator*, VII, Item 25.

Engle, Paul, 'New English Poets'. *English Journal* (College ed.), XXVII, pp. 89–101 (Auden, Lewis, Spender).

Flint, Cudworth F., 'New Leaders in English Poetry'. *Virginia Quarterly Review*, XIV, pp. 502–18 (Auden, Lewis, Spender).

Gierasch, Walter, 'Lewis' *Rest from Loving and Be Living*'. *Explicator*, VI, Item 34.

Glicksberg, C. I., 'Poetry and Social Revolution'. *Dalhousie Review*, XVII, pp. 493–503.

Harris, Henry, 'The Symbols and Imagery of Hawk and Kestrel in the Poetry of Auden and Day Lewis in the Thirties'. *Zeitschrift Fur Anglistik und Amerikanistik* (Berlin Ost), XII, pp. 276–85.

Hazard, Forrest Earl, 'The Auden Group and the Group Theatre: The Dramatic Theories and Practices of Rupert Doone, W. H. Auden, Christopher Isherwood, Louis MacNeice, Stephen Spender and Cecil Day Lewis'. *Dissertation Abstracts*, XXV, pp. 1913–14.

Larkin, Philip, 'C. Day Lewis' *The Buried Day*' (a review of). *Spectator*, 20 May 1960. p. 742.

Nelson, Hugh Alan, 'Individuals of a Group: The 1930's Poetry of W. H. Auden, Stephen Spender, C. Day Lewis.' *Dissertation Abstracts*, XIX, p. 1389.

Povey, John Frederick, 'The Oxford Group: A Study of the Poetry of W. H. Auden, Stephen Spender, C. Day Lewis and Louis Mac-Neice'. *Dissertation Abstracts*, XXV, pp. 6633–34.

Replogle, Justin, 'The Auden Group'. *Wisconsin Studies in Contemporary Literature*, V, pp. 133–150.

Southworth, James G., 'Cecil Day Lewis'. *Sewanee Review*, XLV, pp. 469–83.

Stallman, Robert, 'Lewis' *Come Live with Me and Be My Love*.' *Explicator*, II, Item 6.

Times Literary Supplement, 13 May 1960, pp. 297–8, review of *The Buried Day*.

LOUIS MACNEICE

I. POEMS AND OTHER POETIC WORKS

Blind Fireworks, London: Gollancz 1929.

Poems, London: Faber & Faber 1935.

Letters from Iceland (with W. H. Auden), London: Faber & Faber 1937.

Out of the Picture, London: Faber & Faber 1937.

The Earth Compels, London: Faber & Faber 1938.

Bibliography

I *Crossed the Minch*, London: Longmans & Co. 1938.
Autumn Journal, London: Faber & Faber 1939.
The Last Ditch, Dublin: Cuala Press 1940.
Plant and Phantom, London: Faber & Faber 1941.
Springboard, London: Faber & Faber 1944.
Christopher Columbus, London: Faber & Faber 1944.
The Dark Tower and Other Radio Scripts, London: Faber & Faber 1947.
Holes in the Sky, London: Faber & Faber 1948.
Collected Poems 1925-48, London: Faber & Faber 1949.
Ten Burnt Offerings, London: Faber & Faber 1952.
Autumn Sequel, London: Faber & Faber 1954.
The Other Wing, London: Faber & Faber 1954.
Visitations, London: Faber & Faber 1957.
The Mad Islands and The Administrator, London: Faber & Faber 1964.
Collected Poems (ed. E. R. Dodds), London: Faber & Faber 1967; New York: Oxford 1967.

2. MISCELLANEOUS PROSE

Roundabout Way, London and New York: Putnam 1932.
'Poetry Today' (ed. G. Grigson), *The Arts Today*, pp. 25–67.
The Agamemnon of Aeschylus, London: Faber & Faber 1936.
Zoo, London: Michael Joseph 1938.
Modern Poetry, London: Oxford University Press 1938.
The Poetry of W. B. Yeats, London: Oxford University Press 1941.
'The Tower that Once', *Folios of 'New Writing'*, Spring 1941, pp. 37–41.
Meet the U.S. Army, Prose for Ministry of Information 1943.
Goethe's Faust, London: Faber & Faber 1951.
The Sixpence That Rolled Away, London: Faber & Faber 1956.
Varieties of Parable, Cambridge University Press 1965.
The Strings are False, London: Faber & Faber 1965.

3. CRITICAL STUDIES

Fraser, G. S., 'Evasive Honesty: The Poetry of Louis MacNeice'. *Vision and Rhetoric*. London: Faber & Faber 1959.
Povey, John Frederick, 'The Oxford Group: A Study of the Poetry of W. H. Auden, Stephen Spender, C. Day Lewis and Louis Mac-Neice', *Dissertation Abstracts*, XXV, pp. 6633–4.
Press, John, *Louis MacNeice*. London: Longmans Green, for the British Council (Writers and their Work No. 187) 1965.
Southworth, J., *Sowing the Spring*. Oxford: B. Blackwell 1940 (chapters on Lewis, Spender, MacNeice).
Times Literary Supplement, 'A Poet of Our Time', 28 October 1949.

Wall, S., 'Louis MacNeice and the Line of Least Resistance'. *The Review* (ed. Iain Hamilton), No. 11–12.

STEPHEN SPENDER

1. POEMS AND OTHER POETIC WORKS

Twenty Poems, London: Blackwell 1929.
Poems, London: Faber & Faber 1933.
Vienna, London: Faber & Faber 1934.
Trial of a Judge, London: Faber & Faber 1938.
The Still Centre, London: Faber & Faber 1939.
Ruins and Visions, London: Faber & Faber 1942.
Poems of Dedication, London: Faber & Faber 1947.
The Edge of Being, London: Faber & Faber 1949.
Collected Poems, London: Faber & Faber 1955.

2. MISCELLANEOUS PROSE

'Poetry and Revolution', *New Country*, ed. Michael Roberts, London: Hogarth Press 1933, pp. 62–71.
The Destructive Element, London: Cape 1935.
The Burning Cactus (short stories), London: Faber & Faber 1936.
Forward from Liberalism, London: Gollancz 1937.
'Oxford to Communism', *New Verse*, November 1937, pp. 9–10.
'The Left Wing Orthodoxy', *New Verse*, Autumn 1938.
Preface to *Poems for Spain*, ed. with John Lehmann, London: Hogarth Press 1939.
The New Realism, London: Hogarth Press 1939.
Tisselcote House (a novel), London: Hogarth Press 1940.
Life and the Poet, London: Secker & Warburg 1942.
World Within World, London: Hamish Hamilton 1951.

2. CRITICAL STUDIES

Béra, March-André, 'L'Autobiographie de Stephen Spender'. *Critique*, 122, pp. 593–604.
Blakeslee, Richard C., 'Three Ways Past Edinburgh: Stephen Spender's "The Express" '. *College English*, XXVI, April, pp. 556–8.
Engelborghs, Maurits, 'Stephen Spender over "Modernen".' *Dietsche Warancle en Belfort*, CVIII (1963), pp. 759–61.
Gerstenberger, Donna, 'The Saint and the Circle: The Dramatic Potential of an Image'. *Criticism*, II, pp. 336–41.
Jacobs, Willis D., 'The Moderate Poetical Success of Stephen Spender'. *College English*, XVII, pp. 374–8.

Jacobs, Willis D., 'Spender's "I think continually of those"'. *Modern Language Notes*, LXV, pp. 491–2.

Jarka, Horst, 'Pre-War Austria as Seen by Spender, Isherwood and Lehmann'. *Proceedings of the Pacific Northwest Conference on Foreign Languages* (17), XV, 1964, pp. 231–40.

Kneiger, Bernard, 'Spender's *Awaking*'. *Explicator*, XII, Item 30.

Kulkarni, Hanmant B., 'Stephen Spender: Poet in Crisis'. *Dissertation Abstracts*, XXIII, pp. 2529–30.

Marcus, Mordecai, 'Walden as a Possible Source for Stephen Spender's "The Express"'. *Thoreau Society Bulletin*, No. 75, 1.

Potter, James L., 'The "Destined Pattern" of Spender's "Express"'. *College English*, XXVII, pp. 426–8.

Seif, Morton, 'The Impact of T. S. Eliot on Auden and Spender'. *South Atlantic Quarterly*, LIII, pp. 61–9.

Sellers, W. H., 'Wordsworth and Spender: Some Speculations on the Use of Rhyme'. *Studies in English Literature*, Autumn, V, pp. 641–650.

Southworth, James G., 'Stephen Spender'. *Sewanee Review*, XLV, pp. 272–83.

Walcutt, Charles C., 'Spender's *The Landscape near an Aerodrome*'. *Explicator*, V, Item 37.

Wilson, Angus, 'Mood of the Month—III'. *London Magazine*, V, pp. 40–4.

Wunsch, Ellis Andrews, 'Stephen Spender: Critic of Modern Literature'. *Dissertation Abstracts*, XXV, pp. 3586–7.

CHRISTOPHER CAUDWELL

Poems, London: Bodley Head 1939; London: Lawrence & Wishart 1965.

Illusion and Reality, London: Macmillan & Co. 1937; London: Lawrence & Wishart 1946.

Studies in a Dying Culture, London: Bodley Head 1939.

Further Studies in a Dying Culture, London: Bodley Head 1939.

The Concept of Freedom, London: Lawrence & Wishart 1965.

JOHN CORNFORD

John Cornford: A Memoir, ed. Pat Sloan, London: Cape 1938.

CHARLES MADGE

The Disappearing Castle, London: Faber & Faber 1937.

REX WARNER

Poems and Contradictions, London: Boriswood 1937; revised London: John Lane 1945.

II. BACKGROUND WRITINGS

(a) *Critical, historical and other studies*

Bayley, John, *The Romantic Survival*. Constable 1957.

Brenner, Rica, *Poets of our Time*. New York: Harcourt Brace 1941.

Brooks, Cleanth, *Modern Poetry and the Tradition*. Chapel Hill: University of North Carolina Press 1939, pp. 110–35.

Coombes, B. L., 'Below the Tower', *Folios of New Writing*. Spring 1941, pp. 30–6.

Daiches, David, *Poetry and the Modern World*. Chicago: University of Chicago Press 1940, pp. 214–39.

Deutsch, Babette, *Poetry in Our Time*, 2nd ed., rev. and enl., New York: Doubleday 1963, pp. 378–400.

Eliot, T. S., *The Sacred Wood*. London: Methuen 1920, Fountain Library 1934.

Eliot, T. S., *Selected Essays, 1917–1932*. London: Faber & Faber 1932.

Eliot, T. S., *The Use of Poetry and the Use of Criticism*. London: Faber & Faber 1933.

Eliot, T. S., *On Poetry and Poets*. London: Faber & Faber 1957.

Ford, Hugh D., *A Poet's War*. London: Oxford University Press 1965; Philadelphia: University of Pennsylvania Press 1965.

Forster, E. M., 'Liberty in England' (1935), *Abinger Harvest*. London: E. Arnold & Co. 1936, pp. 62–8.

Forster, E. M., 'Virginia Woolf' (1941), *Two Cheers for Democracy*. London: E. Arnold & Co. 1951, pp. 251–66.

Fraser, G. S., *The Modern Writer and His World*. London: André Deutsch 1955, pp. 230–66; New York: Criterion Books 1955.

Grigson, Geoffrey, *The Harp of Aeolus*. London: Routledge 1948.

Hamilton, George, *The Tell-Tale Article: a Critical Approach to Modern Poetry*, London: Heinemann 1949, pp. 40–50.

Hamilton, Iain, *The Review* No. 11–12: 'The Thirties'—a Special Number.

Lehmann, John, 'A Postscript'. *Folios of New Writing*, Spring 1941, pp. 42–6.

Mander, John, *The Writer and Commitment*. London: Secker & Warburg 1961.

O'Connor, Philip, *The Lower View*. London: Faber & Faber 1960.

Raine, Kathleen, 'Michael Roberts and the Hero Myth'. *Penguin New Writing*. No. 39, Penguin Books 1950.

Roberts, Michael, *Critique of Poetry*. London: Cape 1934.

Upward, Edward, 'The Falling Tower', *Folios of New Writing*. Spring 1941, pp. 24–9.

Wilson, Edmund, 'The Oxford Boys Becalmed' (1937), *The Shores of Light*. London: W. H. Allen & Co. 1952.

Wilson, Edmund, 'The Classics on the Soviet Stage' (1935), *The Shores of Light*. London: W. H. Allen & Co. 1952.

Woolf, Virginia, 'The Leaning Tower', *Folios of New Writing*, Autumn 1940, pp. 11–33.

★   ★   ★

Charques, R. D., *Contemporary Literature and Social Revolution*. London: Secker & Warburg 1933.

Cockburn, Claud, *In Time of Trouble: An Autobiography*. London: Hart-Davis 1956.

Cohn, Norman, *The Pursuit of the Millenium*. London: Secker & Warburg 1957; London: Mercury Books 1962.

Crossman, R. H. S. (ed.), *The God that Failed*. London: Hamish Hamilton 1950; New York: Bantam Books rev. ed. 1954.

Crossman, R. H. S., *Plato Today*. London: Allen & Unwin 1937.

Graves, Robert, and Hodge, Alan, *The Long Week-End: A Social History of Great Britain 1918–1939*. London: Faber & Faber 1940.

Greene, Graham, *The Lost Childhood*. London: Eyre & Spottiswoode 1951.

Grigson, Geoffrey, *The Crest on the Silver*. London: Cresset Press 1950.

Grubb, Frederick, *A Vision of Reality*. London: Chatto & Windus 1965.

Halle, Louis J., 'Marx's Religious Drama'. *Encounter*, XXV, No. 4, October 1965, pp. 29–37.

Isherwood, Christopher, *Lions and Shadows*. London: Hogarth Press 1938.

Kemp, Harry, and Riding, Laura, *The Left Heresy in Literature and Life*. London: Methuen 1939.

Lehmann, John, *The Whispering Gallery*. London: Longmans 1955.

Lewis, John, Polyanyi, Karl, Kitchin, Donald K. (eds.), *Christianity and the Social Revolution*. London: Gollancz 1935.

Marcuse, Herbert, *Eros and Civilization*. New York: Random House 1962.

Marx, K., *Capital*. Chicago: C. H. Kerr & Co. 1906.

Marx, K., and Engels, Friedrich, *The German Ideology*. New York: International Publishers 1947.

Marx, K., *Selected Writings in Sociology and Philosophy*, trans. T. B. Bottomore, ed. T. B. Bottomore and M. Rubel. London: Watts & Co. 1956.

Marx, K., *Selected Correspondence 1846–1895*. New York: International Publishers 1934.

Mirski, Dmitri, *The Intelligentsia of Great Britain*, trans. Alec Brown. London: Gollancz 1935.

Muggeridge, Malcolm, *The Thirties: 1930–1940 in Great Britain*. London: Hamish Hamilton 1940.

O'Neill, John, 'Marxism and Mythology'. *Ethics* LXXVII, No. 1, October 1966, pp. 38–49.

Orwell, George, 'Writers and Leviathan' (1948), *England, Your England*. London: Secker & Warburg 1953, pp. 17–26.

Orwell, George, 'Inside the Whale' (1940), *England, Your England*. London: Secker & Warburg 1953, pp. 93–142.

Orwell, George, *Homage to Catalonia*. London: Secker & Warburg 1938.

Orwell, George, 'Politics *vs* Literature', *Shooting an Elephant*. London: Secker & Warburg 1950, pp. 57–83.

Pelling, Henry, *The British Communist Party: A Historical Profile*. London: Adam and Charles Black 1958.

Rowse, A. L., 'The Theory and Practice of Communism', *The Criterion*. January 1930, pp. 451–69.

Skelton, R. Introduction to his anthology *Poetry of the Thirties*. London: Penguin Books 1964.

Stansky, Peter, and Abrahams, William, *Journey to the Frontier*. London: Constable 1966.

Symons, Julian, *The Thirties: A Dream Revolved*. London: Cresset Press 1960.

Upward, Edward, 'Sketch for a Marxist Interpretation of Literature', *The Mind in Chains*, ed. C. Day Lewis. London: F. Muller Ltd. 1937, pp. 41–55.

Weintraub, Stanley, *The Last Great Cause, The Intellectuals and the Spanish Civil War*. New York: Weybright & Talley 1968; London: W. H. Allen 1968.

Wood, Neal, *Communism and British Intellectuals*. London: Gollancz 1959.

(b) *Fiction*

Ambler, Eric, *Uncommon Danger*. London 1937.

Ambler, Eric, *Cause for Alarm*. London 1938.

Buchan, John, *The Thirty-Nine Steps*. London 1915.

Buchan, John, *The Power-House*. London 1916.

Buchan, John, *Huntingtower*. London 1922.

Buchan, John, *The Three Hostages*. London 1924.

Buchan, John, *Castle Gay*. London 1930.

Greene, Graham, *It's A Battlefield*. London 1934.
Greene, Graham, *England Made Me*. London 1935.
Greene, Graham, *A Gun for Sale*. London 1936.
Greene, Graham, *The Confidential Agent*, 1939.
Hamilton, Patrick, *Mr. Stimpson and Mr. Gorse*. London 1953.
Isherwood, Christopher, *Mr. Norris Changes Trains*. London 1935.
Isherwood, Christopher. *Goodbye to Berlin*. London 1939.
'Sapper,' *Bulldog Drummond. His Four Rounds with Carl Peterson*. London 1929.
Upward, Edward, 'The Colleagues' and 'Sunday' in *New Country* (ed. Michael Roberts).
Upward, Edward, *In the Thirties*. London 1962.

(c) *Anthologies, periodicals*

Bell, Quentin (ed.), *Julian Bell: Essays, Poems and Letters*. London: Hogarth Press 1938.
Davenport, John, Sykes, Hugh, Redgrave, Michael (eds.), *Cambridge Poetry 1930* [Hogarth Living Poets No. 30]. London: Hogarth Press 1930.
Grigson, Geoffrey, *New Verse Anthology*. London: Faber & Faber 1939, Preface, pp. 15–24.
Roberts, Michael (ed.), *New Signatures*. London: Hogarth Press 1932.
Roberts, Michael (ed.), *New Country*, London: Hogarth Press 1933.
Saltmarshe, Christopher, Davenport, John, Wright, Basil (eds.), *Cambridge Poetry 1929* [Hogarth Living Poets No. 8]. London: Hogarth Press 1929.
Wellesley, Dorothy, *A Broadcast Anthology of Modern Verse* [Hogarth Living Poets No. 17]. London: Hogarth Press 1930.

★　　★　　★

The Criterion, ed. T. S. Eliot, 1922–39.
Left Review, ed. Montague Slater, Amabel Williams-Ellis, T. H. Wintringham, Edgell Rickword, Randall Swingler and others, 1934–38.
New Statesman and Nation.
New Verse, ed. Geoffrey Grigson, Nos. 1–32; New Series Vol. 1, Nos. 1–2. 1933–39.
New Writing, ed. John Lehmann Nos. 1–6 (1936–38); New Series Nos. 1–3 (1938–39).
Folios of New Writing, ed. John Lehmann Nos. 1–4 (1940–41).
New Writing and Daylight, ed. John Lehmann Nos. 1–7 (1942–46).
Penguin New Writing, ed. John Lehmann Nos. 1–40 (1940–50).

Index